Keynote

ADVANCED
Student's Book
AND **Workbook**

SPLIT **B** EDITION

Lewis Lansford
Paul Dummett
Helen Stephenson

Contents Split A

PRONUNCIATION	READING	LISTENING	SPEAKING	WRITING
Vowel sounds at word boundaries	Why do we sleep?	Planning a trip	Luxury and necessity Talking about things we need Hedging	A statement of opinion Writing skill: Hedging expressions
Weak *of* Sounding encouraging	Image, identity and clothing	Preparing for a job interview	Evaluating data Talking about image Making suggestions	Giving feedback Writing skill: Being diplomatic
Sentence stress in cleft sentences Stress in expressions of disagreement	How groupthink closed the 'flying bank'	Choosing a logo	Evaluating teamwork Dealing with groupthink Dealing with disagreement and reaching consensus (Choosing a logo)	Emails dealing with disagreement Writing skill: Encouraging cooperation
Approximations Intonation in questions	One man's meat …	Asking how something works	Using approximations Talking about sales potential Asking for clarification and repetition (Giving and receiving instructions)	Information for a house guest Writing skill: Instructions
Softening negative statements	Eureka moments?	Planning a party	Talking about life experience Where my ideas come from Brainstorming and choosing the best ideas	A to-do list Writing skill: Abbreviations
Stress in content and function words	The parable of the stones	Discussing options for solving a problem	Talking about why things are useful Describing a solution Finding solutions	Online advice form Writing skill: Softening advice or recommendations

Communication activities | TED Talk transcripts | Wordlist

Contents Split B

PRONUNCIATION	READING	LISTENING	SPEAKING	WRITING
/ŋ/ sound Contraction with *have*	The power of visualization	Speculating about a mystery	The benefits and drawbacks of daydreaming Talking about visualization Speculating	A news story Writing skill: Neutral reporting
Voicing in final consonants Emphasizing the main focus of the sentence	Bad team building	Reviewing a project	Cause-and-result relationships Work issues Taking part in a meeting	Debriefing questionnaire Writing skill: Linking devices
Stress with intensifying adverbs Polite and assertive intonation	Can stress be good for you?	Dealing with awkward situations	Holiday lessons learned Talking about stress Having difficult conversations	A record of a meeting Writing skill: Reporting verbs
Saying lists	Understanding risk	Assessing risk	A TV news story Facing risks Discussing alternatives (Health and safety issues)	A consumer review Writing skill: Using qualifiers
Intonation in subordinate clauses Sure and unsure tones	Visionaries	Life coaching	Looking after what matters Talking about visionaries Sharing dreams and visions of the future (Talking about a vision of the future)	An endorsement Writing skill: Persuasive language
Sentence stress in explaining outcomes Sentence stress in making arrangements	Is pessimism really so bad?	Arranging to meet	Past views of the present Talking about financial decisions Making arrangements	A group email Writing skill: Impersonal language

Featured TED Talks in Split Editions A and B

Unit 1
Less stuff,
more happiness
Graham Hill

Unit 2
Who am I? Think
again
Hetain Patel and Yuyu Rau

Unit 3
Making peace
is a marathon
May El-Khalil

Unit 4
How I beat
stage fright
Joe Kowan

Unit 5
I'm not your inspiration,
thank you very much
Stella Young

Unit 6
How to make
filthy water
drinkable
Michael Pritchard

Unit 7
Taking imagination seriously
Janet Echelman

Unit 8
Build a tower, build a team
Tom Wujec

Unit 9
All it takes is 10 mindful minutes
Andy Puddicombe

Unit 10
Protecting Twitter users (sometimes from themselves)
Del Harvey

Unit 11
How to build with clay … and community
Diébédo Francis Kéré

Unit 12
Image recognition that triggers augmented reality
Matt Mills and Tamara Roukaerts

7 Imagination

BACKGROUND

1 You are going to watch a TED Talk by Janet Echelman called *Taking imagination seriously.* Read the text about the speaker and the talk, then answer the questions.

  1 The title of the talk is *Taking imagination seriously*. What do you think this means?

  2 Echelman's sculptures are 'huge, flowing objects that respond to environmental forces'. What materials do you think she uses that behave this way?

3 Are there sculptures in public spaces in your city? Why do you think they are there? Do you have a favourite? If so, describe it.

TEDTALKS

JANET ECHELMAN is a North American artist who found her true voice as an artist when her paints went missing — forcing her to find a new medium for her projects. As a result, she turned from painting to sculpture, and now reshapes urban airspace with huge, flowing objects that respond to environmental forces — wind, water and light— and become inviting points of focus for city life. Janet Echelman's idea worth spreading is that by combining traditional art forms with high-tech materials, you can create public art that pays tribute to nature and brings people together.

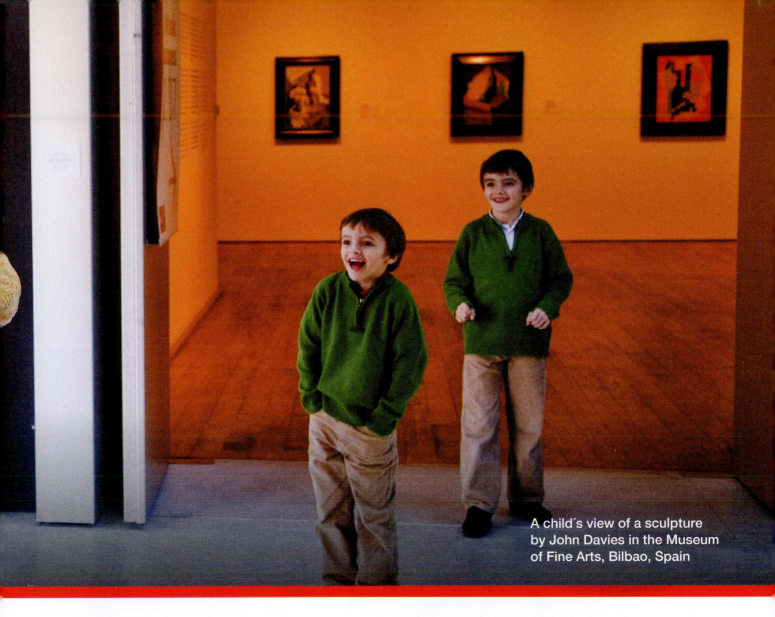

A child's view of a sculpture by John Davies in the Museum of Fine Arts, Bilbao, Spain

KEY WORDS

2 Read the sentences (1–6). The words in bold are used in the TED Talk. First guess the meaning of the words. Then match the words with their definitions (a–f).

1 His work is **idiosyncratic** and striking but can be difficult to understand.

2 The sculptures are **ephemeral** because of the material they're made from.

3 The edges of the cloth were decorated with hand-made **lace**.

4 The ropes are tied together with a tight **knot**.

5 She uses only fabrics that are made from **natural fibres**.

6 Large pieces of fabric were **billowing** from the wires.

a lasting for a very short time

b long, thin pieces of natural material, such as wool or silk

c a fine cloth with patterns of small holes

d filled with air and blowing in the wind

e a fastening made by tying string or rope

f unusual, individual

AUTHENTIC LISTENING SKILLS Inferring meaning from context

When you hear a word you don't know, it can be useful to try to work out what sort of information it carries, to help you understand enough to keep listening. Often you can also gather information from the surrounding words. Sometimes you may also find clues inside words. You may not know the word *intensification*, but if you recognize the adjective *intense* in it, it may help you work out its meaning.

3a 🎧 **37** Look at the Authentic listening skills box. With a partner, try to work out what sort of word is missing. Then listen to the extract from the TED Talk.

1 I painted for ten years when I was offered a [1]_____ to India. Promising to give exhibitions of paintings, I shipped my paints and arrived in [2]_____.

2 This fishing village was famous for sculpture. So, I tried bronze [3]_____. But to make large forms was too heavy and expensive.

3b 🎧 **38** Listen to the next section of the talk. With a partner, use words or gestures to demonstrate what you think the meaning of these three words is.

bundle	mounds	volumetric

7.1 Taking imagination seriously

TEDTALKS

1 ▶ **7.1** Read the statements, then watch the TED Talk. Are these sentences true (T) or false (F)?

1 Janet Echelman became a sculptor by accident.
2 Her first giant net sculpture was made in India and displayed in Madrid.
3 It's impossible to design and make large nets using machines, so all of her sculptures are hand made.
4 Her net sculptures led her to work with other materials, too, including steel and water.
5 A piece that she created in Denver was inspired by scientific data about a natural disaster.
6 Echelman ends with a story about solving legal problems she had with one sculpture.

2 ▶ **7.1** Watch the first part (0.00–5.25) of the talk again. Answer the questions.

1 How did Echelman receive her training as an artist?
2 What two important features of the village of Mahabalipuram led Echelman to produce the work she made there?
3 Who worked with Echelman to make her first satisfying sculpture, and what was it an image of?
4 In addition to fishermen, what craftspeople did Echelman work with?
5 How was the work she was asked to do for the waterfront in Porto, Portugal, different from the work she had done before?
6 Who did Echelman work with to create the sculpture for Porto?

▶ fiber **N AM ENG**
▶ fibre **BR ENG**

▶ college **N AM ENG**
▶ university **BR ENG**

3 ▶ **7.1** Watch the second part (5.26–7.34) of the talk again. Then find and correct six errors in this text.

In Philadelphia, Janet Echelman sculpted with smoke that is shaped by the wind and through interaction with people. It represents the paths of trains that run above the city.

In Denver, Echelman represented the interconnectedness of the 35 nations of the Western hemisphere in a sculpture. She used photographs from NOAA (the National Oceanic and Atmospheric Administration) that showed the 2010 Pacific tsunami. The title '1.26' refers to the number of microseconds that the Earth's day was made longer as a result of the earthquake that started the tsunami.

Echelman couldn't use her usual steel ring to build this sculpture, so instead, she used a mesh fibre that was much more delicate than steel. This allowed the sculpture to be supported by nearby trees.

4 ▶ **7.1** Watch the third part (7.35 to the end) of the talk again. Answer the questions.

1 When she gave her TED Talk, how far along was Janet Echelman's project in New York?
2 What are the two different influences or methods that she combines in her artwork?
3 How did her work affect office workers in Phoenix, Arizona?

VOCABULARY IN CONTEXT

5 ▶ **7.2** Watch the clips from the TED Talk. Choose the correct meaning of the words.

6 Work in pairs. Discuss the questions.

1 Can you think of a time when you've been mesmerized by something?
2 What features do you often find on waterfronts? Can you think of an example you've visited?
3 Are there any places in your town or city that people think are very bland? And what about areas that aren't at all bland?

CRITICAL THINKING Reading between the lines

7 A speaker doesn't always have to say something directly for us to know that it's true. Which of the following can be read 'between the lines' of Janet Echelman's TED Talk? Say why.

1 Echelman is happy to adapt her art to the specifications of the person commissioning it.
2 Echelman is a well-respected artist internationally.
3 Echelman doesn't see firm divisions between art, craft and engineering.

8 Work in pairs. Compare answers. Do you agree?

9 Read these comments* about the TED Talk. Which ones do you think accurately 'read between the lines' of Echelman's talk? Match each comment with the best description (a–c).

a Definitely true b Likely to be true c Unlikely to be true

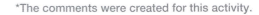

Viewers' comments

P Pierre – Echelman seems to think that her art is somehow more important than the craft of lace-makers or the calculations of engineers.

S Sally – Clearly Echelman loves working closely with other people – both learning from them, and teaching them.

L L8R – I love this work. Echelman obviously feels that art serves an important function in society.

*The comments were created for this activity.

PRESENTATION SKILLS Being authentic

10 What does it mean to be authentic? Tell a partner.

TIPS

There's no magic formula prescribing what a speaker should look like and do. Allow your personality to come through. Being human is an important part of being an excellent speaker.

• Where possible, include yourself in the talk as part of the story. The audience will be interested not only in the topic, but in your relationship to it.
• Use your own natural voice, and speak from the heart. Think of yourself as having a conversation with the audience and talking about something you really care about rather than being a presenter who is passing on information.
• Don't worry too much about being nervous. Even when you feel extremely nervous, the audience often won't even notice. And if they do, they'll usually be on your side because they want you to succeed.
• Stay physically relaxed. Move your body as you normally would. Don't move around so much that it's a distraction, but don't stand completely still, either.

11 ▶ **7.3** Look at the Presentation tips box. Then watch the clips from Janet Echelman's TED Talk. Answer the questions.

1 What examples of Echelman sharing her 'real self' do you notice?
2 How do you think she felt before and during the talk? How does she appear to feel while giving the talk?

12 Think of a something you've done in life that seemed unlikely to you or others at the time. Consider your studies, work, hobbies, or another area of life. Give a short presentation to a partner explaining your accomplishment. Relax and allow your personality to come through.

▶ art school **N AM ENG**
▶ art college **BR ENG**

▶ traffic circle **N AM ENG**
▶ roundabout **BR ENG**

7.2 I was miles away!

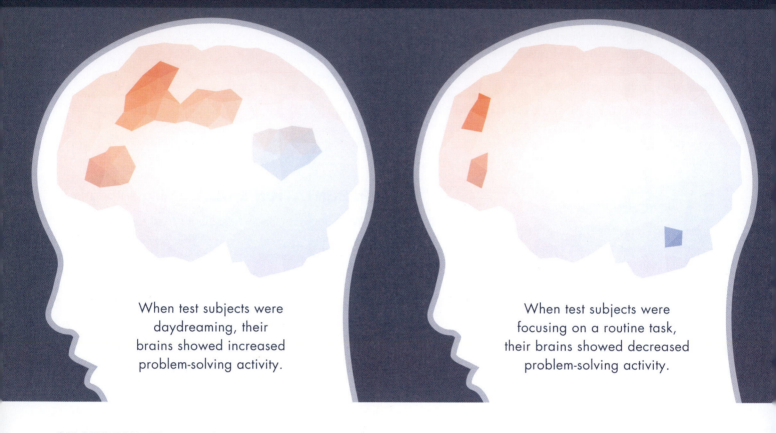

THE DAYDREAMING BRAIN
What does science tell us?

When test subjects were daydreaming, their brains showed increased problem-solving activity.

When test subjects were focusing on a routine task, their brains showed decreased problem-solving activity.

GRAMMAR The continuous aspect

1 Work in pairs. Discuss the questions.

1 When, where and how often do you daydream?
2 Do you find it a waste of time, or useful?

2 Look at the infographic. Answer the questions.

1 What's happening in the 'colourful' parts of the brain?
2 When does it happen?

3 Read the text in the Grammar box. Answer the questions (1–5).

THE CONTINUOUS ASPECT

Scientists in Canada **have been studying** the brain in the hope of understanding more about what happens when we daydream. In one recent experiment, researchers monitored the brain activity of test subjects while they **were performing** a simple routine task – pushing a button when numbers appeared on a screen. After the subjects **had been performing** the task for several minutes, they began daydreaming – and parts of their brain associated with problem-solving began lighting up on the brain scanner. The research **is altering** scientists' perception of daydreaming, because it shows that when we daydream, our brains are more active than when we focus on a routine task. One conclusion of the study is that when people are struggling to solve complex problems, it might be more productive to switch to a simpler task and let their mind wander. Psychologists interested in creativity and imagination **will be watching** developments in this area closely as our understanding of the mind and its workings deepens.

Look at the structures in **bold**. Can you find:

1 a changing situation in the present?
2 an action in progress from a point in the past to now?
3 an action in progress in the past?
4 an action in progress before an earlier point in the past?
5 an action in progress in the future?
Check your answers on page 74 and do Exercises 1–6.

4a Choose the correct forms to complete the text. In some cases, both options may be possible.

The power of daydreaming

When you ¹*suddenly realize / 're suddenly realizing* you've been daydreaming – especially when you ²*work / 're working* on a difficult problem – the usual response is to snap out of it and try to get back to work. But what scientists now ³*understand / are understanding* is that while we ⁴*daydream / 're daydreaming*, we are often solving problems at the same time. So daydreaming is actually one way the mind ⁵*has / is having* of getting work done.

Albert Einstein's story is a famous example. He ⁶*was thinking / had been thinking* about his special theory of relativity for about seven years when he finally had a breakthrough. In 1904, he ⁷*'d been / was* working for months on complex mathematical exercises when he ⁸*decided / was deciding* to take a break. As he rested, he ⁹*began / was beginning* to daydream. His mind ¹⁰*had been / was* wandering for several minutes when the image of a train formed in his brain – a train being struck by lightning. At that moment, it all ¹¹*fell / was falling* into place. Because he ¹²*hasn't / hadn't* been trying to think about it, Einstein ¹³*was / was being* able to produce a completely new description of the universe.

We probably ¹⁴*won't see / won't be seeing* teachers encouraging students to stare out the window instead of doing their lessons anytime soon. But we ¹⁵*'ll certainly see / 'll certainly be seeing* more research into the power and workings of the imagination.

4b Answer the questions. Which action(s):

1 were in progress when Einstein had his breakthrough?
2 had been in progress for the longest time. How long?
3 had been in progress for the shortest. How long?

5 Complete the article with the correct form of the verbs in brackets. In some cases, more than one form is correct.

'I'm not completely sure what went wrong,' says Mark Foyle. 'I ¹ _'ve been commuting_ (commute) by car every day for ten years and nothing like this has ever ² _____ (happen) to me.' On 30th November last year he got quite a shock. 'One minute, I ³ _____ (drive) to work, and the next I realized I ⁴ _____ (crash) into a parked car,' he explained. The police asked Foyle if he'd ⁵ _____ (text) at the time, but he hadn't. When I thought back, he says, 'I realized I ⁶ _____ (not pay attention).' A recent study in France found that of nearly 1,000 drivers injured in car accidents, 52 per cent reported that their mind ⁷ _____ (wander) at the time that it ⁸ _____ (happen). Not surprisingly, the study also confirmed that if you ⁹ _____ (daydream) while driving, you greatly increase the likelihood of being the person responsible for the crash. 'I ¹⁰ _____ (concentrate) on the road a lot more from now on,' said Foyle. 'I'm just glad no one was hurt.'

6 🎧 **39** Listen to Tom describing how his life changed. List the actions Tom talks about, in the order they happen.

7 Compare lists with a partner. Did you agree about the key events?

8 Which two activities mentioned are definitely still going on now?

Pronunciation /ŋ/ sound

9a 🎧 **40** Listen. Notice the /ŋ/ sound in the continuous verbs.

1 I'd been living here for four years when I met Ella for the first time.
2 We'd both been going to the same Spanish class for several weeks.
3 We've been going out together since then, and in about six months, we'll be getting married.

9b Practise saying the sentences in Exercise 9a with the /ŋ/ sound.

SPEAKING The benefits and drawbacks of daydreaming

10 **21st CENTURY OUTCOMES**

Work in small groups. Think of a time in the past when you have daydreamed. Explain what happened.

I was in a maths class at school. I had been paying attention, but then I started daydreaming and when the teacher called on me, I didn't hear my name until the third time he said it. It was really embarrassing.

11 Based on the stories that people shared, can you name any benefits of daydreaming? What about drawbacks of daydreaming?

7.3 In my mind's eye

READING The power of visualization

1 Work in pairs. Discuss the questions.

1 Think of a place you would really love to be right now.
2 Try to imagine the place in as much detail as possible. Also think about what you can hear and smell.
3 Tell a partner some things about your experience. Was it easy or difficult? Were you able to imagine a lot of detail?

2 Read the article. Match the summaries (1–5) with the paragraphs (A–E).

1 Visualizing the process rather than the success is probably the most effective approach.
2 Imagining performing an athletic activity without ever doing it can affect the parts of the body you visualize using.
3 Visualization can't create things that don't exist.
4 For athletes, visualising both the process of competition and a successful outcome improves performance.
5 Some people believe that visualization can be used to improve physical health.

3 Read the article again. Choose the correct options to complete the sentences.

1 Researchers in the USA measured the response of weightlifters' *brains / muscles* to visualization.
2 The research shows that visualization can strengthen your *mind / body*.
3 Dr Shelley Taylor asked one group to focus on *emotions / memories* associated with success.
4 Dr Taylor's more successful subjects visualized themselves *working / feeling* relaxed.
5 Tiger Woods visualizes *the precise movements his hands will make* when *the golf club hits the ball / the path the ball needs to take*.
6 Olympic athletes have found success visualizing themselves *competing / training*.
7 Dr Marcia Angell believes that the mind *can't possibly help / can sometimes be effective in helping* to heal the body.
8 Dr Bernie Siegel says that the mind can *convince / be convinced by* the body that something is happening.

4 Answer the questions.

1 According to the weightlifting research, what is the most effective way to use visualization?
2 What measurable benefit did experimental test subjects gain simply by visualizing themselves exercising?
3 What was Dr Taylor's explanation for the results of her experiment?
4 How does the golfers' use of visualization differ from what successful students do?
5 Whose view is more supported by the information in the other parts of the article: Dr Angell's or Dr Siegel's?

VOCABULARY Expressions with *mind*

5 Complete the expressions from the text with these words.

be   bear   put   see

1 When I visualize something, I try to _____ it in my mind's eye in as much detail as possible.
2 To succeed at anything difficult, you really need to _____ your mind to it.
3 While visualization might be helpful, you have to _____ in mind that there is no substitute for hard work.
4 You seem to _____ in two minds about whether you want to do a master's degree or not.

6 Match the two parts of the sentences.

1 When I try to concentrate for more than a few minutes,
2 Knowing you'll be here to help me gives
3 Sorry, I'm a bit distracted today because
4 I know you're suspicious of these techniques, but try to
5 Thinking about the hugeness of the universe
6 Knowing that my brother is looking after my parents

a I have something on my mind.
b blows my mind.
c my mind wanders.
d me peace of mind.
e keep an open mind.
f eases my mind.

7 Think of:

1 an amazing idea that blows your mind. What is it?
2 a time when you put your mind to something challenging. What was it?
3 a job in which it's important to keep an open mind. What is it? Why is it important to keep an open mind?
4 a tough decision you are or have been in two minds about. What is or was it?
5 something you do to feel better when you're worried or have a lot on your mind. What do you do?

SPEAKING Talking about visualization

8 **21st CENTURY OUTCOMES**

Work in small groups. Discuss the questions.

- Do you believe the scientific claim that muscle mass can be increased by 13.5 per cent simply by thinking of moving your muscles? Why? / Why not?
- The article discusses visualization in sport, academic work and medicine. Can you think (or have you heard) of other areas where it might be useful?
- Do you agree or disagree with the idea that the mind could be used to heal the body? Can you think of examples to support your position?
- Do you think there's any real difference between everyday planning about the future and visualization? Why? / Why not?

9 Present your ideas to another group.

The POWER of
visualization

A Wouldn't it be great if you could lie in your bed and think about exercising and get some of the benefits of an actual workout? It sounds too good to be true, but researchers in the USA have discovered a stronger mind–body link than
5 was previously realized: in experiments, the patterns of brain activity in weightlifters were the same when they lifted weights as when they only imagined lifting weights. According to the journal *Frontiers in Human Neuroscience*, other research shows that, in some cases, mental practice is almost as good
10 for developing skills as physical practice, and that doing both together gives better results than doing either one alone. One experiment compared people who worked out at the gym and people who visualized workouts in their heads and found that people who put their mind to visualizing the
15 repetition of certain muscle actions – without actually doing the physical actions – experienced a 13.5 per cent increase in muscle mass in the areas they'd imagined exercising. Your imagination may be more powerful than you thought.

B Psychologist Shelley Taylor, Ph.D., of the University of
20 California conducted an experiment on a class of students who were preparing for an exam. She divided the group into two and got one group to use visualization to concentrate on the great feeling of getting a high mark on a test. The second group, by contrast, were instructed to picture themselves in
25 the library, reviewing their notes and studying their textbooks to prepare for the test, keeping their minds focused on the process rather than on the eventual feelings of success. Who performed better? The second group, the one that imagined themselves doing the work necessary to succeed. Taylor's
30 view is that visualization works as a 'mental rehearsal' of the actions needed to perform well when the time comes. (If you're a student, you should definitely bear this technique in mind!)

C This idea is supported by the typical use of visualization by athletes. Tiger Woods, one of the world's greatest golfers, has
35 been using mental images to help him since he was a boy. He says that before each shot, he sees in his mind's eye exactly where he wants the ball to go. And judging by his game, the technique is highly effective. A generation before Woods, top golfer Jack Nicklaus used the same process to anticipate
40 exactly how the shot would be played – also to great success. And it isn't just golf; more and more Olympic athletes from all over the world use the power of imagination in this way – often visualizing their competitions in great detail. 'The more an athlete can image the entire package, the better it's going to
45 be', says sports psychologist Nicole Detling.

D Though many people have claimed to have cured themselves of serious diseases through the power of visualization and positive thinking, the medical profession appears to be in two minds about it. Dr Marcia Angell, a senior
50 lecturer in social medicine at Harvard Medical School and a visualization sceptic says, 'There's tremendous arrogance to imagine that your mind is all that powerful.' On the other hand, Dr Bernie Siegel, a retired clinical assistant professor of surgery at Yale Medical School and author of a book called *Love,
55 Medicine & Miracles* believes that visualization can improve the function of the human body in the same way that it has been shown to improve athletic performance. Siegel says, 'When you imagine something, your body really feels like it's happening.'

E Visualization is powerful, but it has its limits. As the comic
60 actor Jim Carrey is supposed to have said, visualizing eating a sandwich when you're hungry isn't going to satisfy you. Our imagination may be an extremely useful tool, but it is most useful when used alongside genuine ability and actual effort and sometimes there's no substitute for the real thing.
65

7.4 That doesn't seem possible!

LISTENING Speculating about a mystery

1 Look at the photo. What do you think happened?

2 🎧 **41** Listen to this conversation about the photo. Tick which things are definitely true and which things are maybe true.

		Definitely true	Maybe true
1	The cars in the photo are in a forest in Belgium.		
2	There was a forest fire.		
3	There was an earthquake.		
4	The cars were abandoned suddenly.		
5	They were in the forest for about 70 years.		
6	The people were taken from their cars suddenly.		
7	The cars were added one by one.		
8	The cars were removed from the forest.		

3 🎧 **41** Listen again. Complete the sentences.

1 There _____ some natural disaster – a forest fire, maybe?
2 I _____ the cars were just abandoned.
3 And they _____ able to go back for them, right?
4 I _____ whatever happened, the cars couldn't be moved afterwards.
5 Or it _____ practical to move them.
6 That _____ why they could never go back!

Pronunciation Contraction with *have*

4a 🎧 **42** Listen. Underline *have* or *had* when it's contracted. Circle it when it isn't contracted.

1 Have you seen this picture?
2 There might have been some natural disaster.
3 It looks as though people had to run away quickly for some reason.
4 And they can't have been able to go back for them, right?
5 Or it mightn't have been practical to move them.
6 They'd been there for about 70 years when this picture was taken.

4b Practise saying the sentences, using contractions where possible.

SPEAKING Speculating

5 Look at the illustration and read the text. Speculate about what the book might be about, who may have written it, and what it might show.

I imagine it was some kind of code.

THE WORLD'S MOST MYSTERIOUS MANUSCRIPT

Named after the bookseller Wilfrid M. Voynich, who acquired it in 1912, The Voynich Manuscript is a 240-page book written in a completely unknown language. It contains colourful drawings of unknown plants and strange diagrams. The original author is unknown, but it is estimated to have been written between 1404 and 1438. It has been called 'the world's most mysterious manuscript'.

SPECULATION

Speculating

I imagine
I expect   something happened suddenly.
I guess

They/He/She/It

… must/may/might/can't be right.
… must have / may have / can't have just disappeared.
… is / are likely to have left quickly.
… probably left quickly.

Could/Might there have been a fire?
What if there was an earthquake?
It/There was bound to have been some kind of sudden event.
Is it possible that the cars were put there?
It seems highly probable that there's a logical explanation.

Agreeing

That seems a likely explanation.
It certainly looks that way.
I think you're on to something there.

Disagreeing

That can't be right.
That doesn't seem at all that likely to me.
I'm not entirely convinced.
That doesn't seem possible.

WRITING A news story

6 Read the article. Answer the questions.

  1 What object has been found?
  2 What does the person who found it believe it is?
  3 What other explanation has been offered?

Writing skill Neutral reporting

7a The article carefully avoids commenting directly on whether or not McCoy's find is really an alien artefact. Underline the expressions that are used to say what is believed / has been said rather than to state what actually happened.

7b Rewrite the sentences using the expressions in brackets.

  1 Mr Price's car was stolen from in front of his house. (reportedly)
  2 My neighbour saw strange lights in the sky. (claim)
  3 The new metal sculpture in the park made strange noises. (is said to have)
  4 Local children avoided playing near the old tree. (apparently)
  5 Some people says the stones are magnetic. (speculation)
  6 The guitar made music even when no one was touching it. (allegedly)
  7 Hundreds of visitors have heard laughter coming from the empty room. (supposedly)
  8 The rocks move without being touched. (seemingly)
  9 A local police officer said it was a joke. (was quoted as saying)
  10 Pieter isn't the sort of person to make up stories. (by all accounts)

8 **21st CENTURY OUTCOMES**

Think of an object someone might find or an occurrence they might witness that would lead them to imagine that something very strange is going on. Write a news story about it similar to the one in Exercise 6. Use neutral reporting expressions.

9 Exchange stories with your partner. Read your partner's account. Did your partner use neutral reporting language?

Hiker claims to have found evidence of alien technology

Hill walker James McCoy has reportedly found what he believes may be evidence of past alien visits to planet Earth. While stopped for lunch on a riverbank, McCoy claims to have spotted a small piece of rusted metal in the soil. When he picked it up, he apparently realized that it was firmly attached to a rock weighing roughly five kilograms. On closer inspection, McCoy is said to have discovered that the metal ring appeared to be part of the stone itself, and that it was unlike anything he'd ever seen before.

Several locals I spoke to have claimed that McCoy told them about the find and its possible links to alien activity, but that he has reportedly refused to show them the rock itself. Despite our repeated attempts to contact him, McCoy couldn't be reached for comment and has allegedly returned to the area of the original find. There's speculation that he may try digging in the area in hopes of finding more supposedly alien artefacts. By all accounts McCoy has shown no previous interest in UFOs or unexplained mysteries but is seemingly obsessed with his find, the exact location of which he has reportedly refused to reveal.

Local geologist Horst Lehman was quoted as saying that he believes the more likely explanation is that it's related to one of the many disused mines in the area, which were abandoned in the late 1800s.

8 Working together

BACKGROUND

1 You are going to watch a TED Talk by Tom Wujec called *Build a tower, build a team.* Read the text about the speaker and the talks. Then work in pairs and discuss the questions.

   1 Wujec studies how we communicate. What are your preferred ways to share and absorb information?

2 Wujec helps businesses present information visually – in a way that's easy to understand and apply. What types of business information might benefit from a visual treatment?

3 What's the connection between the photo above and Wujec's work?

TEDTALKS

TOM WUJEC, a North American writer, designer and business consultant, studies how we share and absorb information. He's an innovative practitioner of business visualization – using design and technology to help groups solve problems and understand ideas. Wujec is also interested in the individual qualities and team-working styles that lead to successful cooperation. In his talk, he describes how a simple design challenge using marshmallows can reveal surprising things about the ways we work together. Tom Wujec's idea worth spreading is that successful teamwork and problem-solving require not only specialized experience but also skillful facilitation.

Fishermen pulling a boat out of the sea in Kerala, India.

KEY WORDS

2 Read the sentences (1–6). The words in bold are used in the TED Talk. First guess the meaning of the words. Then match the words with their definitions (a–f).

1 I never work alone. **Collaboration** is important in my job.
2 The team leader doesn't tell us exactly what to do, but she provides **facilitation** and makes her own suggestions.
3 When I saw that her name was Giovanna Abbiati, I made the **assumption** that she was Italian.
4 The **executive admin** took detailed notes in the meeting.
5 We don't develop our finished product all at once. Instead, we follow an **iterative** process.
6 Joe is a **kindergartener**, but he's already a good reader.

a the process of making a task happen more easily, for example by helping assign roles or select priorities
b a person who works as an assistant to a top manager in a company
c a child in the first year of school
d the process of working together with other people
e an idea or belief that people have or a thing we imagine to be true without actually having seen any proof
f a way of developing an idea or products where things are continually changed and developed, and improved each time

AUTHENTIC LISTENING SKILLS
Understanding contrastive stress

Speakers often stress pairs of words when they are trying to emphasize the difference between them. The stress helps listeners focus on the contrast. For example, *I thought I was **late**, but actually I was **early**.*

3a 🎧 **43** Look at the Authentic listening box. Then listen to the extracts from the TED Talk. Underline the words that are stressed. Which pairs of words are stressed to emphasize contrast between two things?

1 And though it seems really simple, it's actually pretty hard.
2 So CEOs: a little bit better than average, but here's where it gets interesting. If you put an executive admin on the team, they get significantly better.
3 So the same team went from being the very worst to being among the very best.

3b 🎧 **44** Listen to extracts 4 and 5.
Extract 4: which two ideas are being contrasted?
Extract 5: which two groups of people are being contrasted?

8.1 Build a tower, build a team

TEDTALKS

1 ▶ **8.1** Watch the TED Talk. Are these sentences true (T) or false (F)?

1 Most teams build a successful tower on their first try.
2 Business people and kindergarteners approach the project similarly.
3 Teams that use prototypes and iterative processes are the most successful.
4 The addition of executive admins makes the CEO teams more successful.
5 When a cash prize is offered, teams perform very well.
6 The marshmallow challenge can help to identify hidden assumptions about tasks and teamwork.

2 ▶ **8.1** Watch the first part (0.00–1.00) of the talk again and complete these sentences.

1 The _____ has to be on top.
2 It's pretty hard because it forces people to _____ very quickly.
3 It reveals deep lessons about _____.

3 ▶ **8.1** Number the steps in order. Then watch the second part (1.01–1.43) of the talk again and check your answers.

a They plan, organize, sketch, then lay out the spaghetti.
b They say ta-da and admire their work.
c Participants orient themselves to the task, talk about it, and jockey for power.
d Ta-da turns into uh-oh as the structure collapses.
e Someone carefully puts the marshmallow on the top.
f They assemble the structure.

4 ▶ **8.1** Watch the third part (1.44–3.11) of the talk again. Choose the correct word to complete each sentence.

1 *Business school graduates / Engineers* are the worst at completing that challenge successfully.
2 *CEOs / Kindergarteners* are the most successful.
3 Teams often *fail / succeed* because they make one plan and try to implement it.
4 Trial and error and 'playing in prototype' *waste time / are keys to success*.

▶ executive admin (executive administrative assistant) **N AM ENG**
▶ PA (personal assistant) **BR ENG**
▶ kindergarten **N AM ENG**
▶ reception (the first year of formal education) **BR ENG**

5 ▶ **8.1** Watch the fourth part (3.12 to the end) of the talk again and complete the summary with these words.

engineers and architects	executive admins
hidden assumptions	prototyping
questions	skills

Wujec says a winning team needs people with specialized skills – for example [1]_____ – and people with facilitation skills such as [2]_____.
When Wujec first offered a prize of $10,000 for the tallest structure, no one even built a standing structure, because they didn't have the right [3]_____ on the team. However, when the same group tried a second time, they succeeded, because they had learned the importance of [4]_____. Wujec says every project has its own marshmallow, by which he means [5]_____. In the case of the marshmallow challenge, everyone seems to assume that the marshmallow should go on last, for example. It seems so obvious that no one [6]_____ it.

VOCABULARY IN CONTEXT

6 ▶ **8.2** Watch the clips from the TED Talk. Choose the correct meaning of the words.

7 Work in pairs. Complete the sentences in your own words. Then discuss with a partner.

1 The last time I had a 'ta-da' moment was when I …
2 I saw people jockeying for power when …
3 A high-stakes decision you can make in life is …

CRITICAL THINKING Supporting the main idea

8 A talk usually has a main idea supported by other ideas. In a sentence of your own words, what would you say is the main idea of Tom Wujec's TED Talk?

9 Read these comments* about the TED Talk. Answer the questions.

1 Which of the ideas described in the comments does Tom Wujec present in his TED Talk?
2 Which comment describes the *main* idea of Wujec's talk?
3 Overall, do you think Wujec presents and supports his main idea well? Why? / Why not?

Viewers' comments

D **Dom** – Training and team-building exercises are essential and without training such as the marshmallow challenge, most companies will never reach their full potential.

A **Alicia** – Dom, it isn't just training. I think Wujec's idea is that teams need to have people with both specialized and facilitation skills – because it isn't only about what the team does, but how the team works together.

I **Ian** – You're right, Alicia. And business schools are producing graduates who don't understand 1) teamwork and 2) iterative processes.

B **Bert** – Right. What Wujec is saying is that identifying our hidden assumptions about team-work may help us avoid failure.

E **Elise** – I think it's so cool that kindergarteners perform well on the marshmallow challenge when they're just playing. We should make our work more like play!

* The comments were created for this activity

PRESENTATION SKILLS Using visuals

TIPS

Slides can be an extremely useful tool for presenters, but be careful: they also can be a distraction. Remember, slides should:

• present data clearly and simply.
• offer a few, powerful examples or illustrations of the main points.
• reinforce or amplify the speaker's words.
• not distract the audience or compete with the speaker.
• not require the audience to read a lot.

10 Work in pairs. List three slides you remember from Tom Wujec's TED Talk. Then answer the questions for each slide.

1 What type of image did it contain (graphic, photo, etc.)?
2 What information did it present?
3 How did it contribute to the presentation?
4 What made this slide especially memorable, in your opinion? What would have been a less memorable way to present it?

11 ▶ **8.3** Watch the clips from Wujec's talk. Match the clips (1–3) with the types of slide (a–c).

a a funny slide that surprises the audience
b a slide that helps clarify the significance of data
c a slide that repeats and reinforces the speaker's words

12 Work in pairs. Imagine you want to give a presentation about your English class.

1 Choose three pieces of information to present as graphics.
2 Choose three things to show photographs of.
3 Choose an image to support your main idea and also make people laugh.

13 Work with another partner. Take turns to give your presentation. Did you come up with similar ideas?

8.2 Having an off day?

THE REASONS WE MISS WORK

81%

10%

6%

1%

2%

MINOR ILLNESS (for example, colds/flu, stomach upsets, headaches and migraines)

INJURIES (for example, neck strains, repetitive strain injury, back pain)

STRESS AND MENTAL ILL-HEALTH (for example, clinical depression and anxiety)

HOME/FAMILY RESPONSIBILITY (for example, caring for sick children)

OTHER (for example, acute or recurring medical conditions, pulling a 'sickie')

GRAMMAR Cause and result

1 Work in pairs. Discuss the questions.

   1 What do you think is a valid reason to miss work?
   2 How would you solve the problem faced by some companies of employees regularly calling in 'sick'?

2 Look at the pie chart. Answer the questions.

   1 What are the two main causes of missed work days?
   2 What percentage of absences result from injuries?

3 Read the text in the Grammar box. Answer the questions (1–3).

CAUSE AND RESULT

Research carried out by a UK-based organization to find the common causes of absenteeism in the workplace shows that over three quarters of working days missed **are the result of** minor illness. Unscheduled days off by some members of a team can force their already busy colleagues to take on more work, which can, in turn, **kill** motivation or **lead to** delays and missed deadlines.

The research found that another ten percent of missed days in manual jobs **result from** injury (but only three per cent in non-manual jobs which is presumably **due to** the lower physical risks at work). Stress and mental ill-health **cause** another six percent of missed work days; one per cent **arise from** home and family responsibilities such as caring for a sick relative; and 'other' causes, including 'pulling a sickie' account for another two percent. Poor employee attendance sometimes **stems from** low morale. Many companies have found that a flexible working schedule can **foster** good will and **bring about** improved employee attendance.

1 In each sentence, say which part is the cause and which is the result.
2 Which of the cause verbs clearly implies a negative result?
3 Which clearly implies a positive result?
Check your answers on page 76 and do Exercises 1–7.

4 Complete the text with these words.

bring	contributes	fosters	from	gives
kills	lead	make	produce	result

Dos and don'ts of successful teamwork

An effective team divides work and multiplies success. However, serious problems are often the ¹_____ of the failure to apply some basic principles to teamwork. Here are three team-working dos and three don'ts that should ²_____ about success and reduce the possibility of failure.

DO

- have clear goals. They ³_____ work meaningful and ⁴_____ to efficient use of time and energy.
- have well-defined roles and responsibilities. Good cooperation results ⁵_____ this.
- recognize contributions and strengths. This ⁶_____ collaboration.

DON'T

- force the group to agree. This ⁷_____ creativity.
- let small conflicts grow. This ⁸_____ rise to bigger conflicts for the whole team.
- assume everyone thinks like you. This ⁹_____ to misunderstanding and a failure to really listen.
- Following these simple rules will ¹⁰_____ results – fast.

5 Look at the causes and results. For each pair, make a cause–result sentence using the phrase in brackets.

1 good reports about the local schools → more families moved into the area (because of)

   More families moved into the area because of good reports about the local schools.

2 moving to a new house → people thinking about how many possessions they have (causes)

3 replacing our heating system → a reduction in our home energy costs (resulted from)

4 the failure to back up regularly → lost data (a consequence of)

5 effective driver education → safer roads (brings about)

6 being rude to customers → a local shop's popularity (kills)

6 Choose the most natural sentence (a or b) in each pair.

1 a Illness is often the consequence of bad diet.
  b Bad diet often fosters illness.

2 a The audience's lack of enthusiasm arose from the stormy weather.
  b Stormy weather killed the audience's enthusiasm for the outdoor theatre production.

3 a The success of the project was largely thanks to her hard work.
  b The failure of the project was largely thanks to her laziness.

Pronunciation Voicing in final consonants

7a 🎧 45 Listen. Is the bold final consonant sound in these words voiced or unvoiced?

1 foster**s**   4 produ**ce**
2 brought abou**t**   5 goo**d** will
3 cau**se**   6 ari**se** from

7b The vowel sound before a voiced consonant tends to be longer than before an unvoiced consonant. Try saying the words in Exercise 7a with a longer vowel sound before the voiced consonants.

SPEAKING Cause-and-result relationships

8 *21st* **CENTURY OUTCOMES**

Look at the photos. Think of as many cause-and-result relationships as you can for each. Use expressions from the Grammar box.

Example (Photo 1)

Conflict at work kills creativity.
Poor organization gives rise to conflict at work.
Arguments are often the result of misunderstandings.
Overwork contributes to conflict in the office.
Office fighting often results in a negative atmosphere.

8.3 How *not* to motivate people

READING Bad team building

1 Work in pairs. Discuss the questions.

1 What teams are you in? At work? In sports? Clubs? Choirs?
2 What team-building activities have you heard about or participated in at work or elsewhere?
3 Were they effective? Why? / Why not?

2 Read the article. Which team-building activity:

1 wasn't taken seriously by the participants?
2 was an opportunity for revenge?
3 forced employees to perform in a way they didn't like?

3 Complete each sentence with the correct company name: A, B or C.

1 _____'s management chose a team-building exercise that forced people to perform.
2 _____'s team didn't have a lot of disagreement in the office before the training.
3 _____'s employees were happy about the team-building exercise for the 'wrong' reasons.
4 The main lesson from _____ is that for training to be effective, it needs to be suitable for the particular people it's being used with.
5 _____'s team-building exercise made angry people even angrier.
6 _____'s training was painful for one employee because of bad childhood memories.
7 When _____ announced plans for a team-building exercise, employees felt very negative about the idea.
8 _____'s employees treated the training as a joke and laughed about it together.

4 How would you feel about each of the team-building activities?

VOCABULARY Teams and teamwork

5 Complete the teamwork expressions with these verbs.

be bond do feel go have pull share

1 It's good when new employees _____ as a group.
2 If you don't _____ a part of things, it can be hard to contribute to the team effort.
3 You have to _____ your weight if you expect to be promoted.
4 You always _____ your fair share of the work.
5 I think it's important to _____ a team player if you want to succeed in business.
6 I like to _____ a sense of belonging, because it motivates me to work.
7 I hope my boss has noticed that I try to _____ the extra mile when she asks me to do something.
8 If you and your colleagues can _____ the load, everyone can work more productively.

6 Use the expressions from Exercise 5 to describe each of these situations (1–8).

1 I asked her to write some notes about the meeting by the end of the week. In fact, she wrote a full report by the end of the day. She _____.
2 Three of us seemed to be doing all the work, but one guy hardly contributed at all. That man _____.
3 There were 400 phone calls to make, so each of the three of us made about 130 calls. We _____.
4 She's very good at anticipating what her co-workers need. She's _____.
5 He feels that he has an important role in the office, and that other people appreciate and value his work. He has _____.
6 He had Friday off work because he was ill, but he came in on Saturday. He wanted to _____.
7 They didn't know each other when they started working together, but after several weeks of facing some big challenges, they learned to rely on each other. They _____ a team.
8 At first Jo's new job was difficult because she didn't know what to do. But after she got to know people and figured out her role, she _____.

SPEAKING Work issues

7 Complete the guidelines with these words.

conflict cooperation employees motivation
promote tasks team

EFFECTIVE ACTIVITIES FOR TEAM BUILDING:

- guide trainees to accomplish [1]_____ that are in some way similar to tasks they do at work.
- provide [2]_____ for participants and engage [3]_____ members.
- enhance [4]_____ rather than encouraging too much competition.
- motivate [5]_____ to work well together when they return to work.
- [6]_____ harmony and give participants tools to resolve [7]_____.

8 **21st CENTURY OUTCOMES**

Work in small groups. What kind of work issues can be resolved by team building? Choose one and recommend some activities to help make the team stronger. Plan a team-building day following the guidelines in Exercise 7.

9 Explain your team-building day and how it follows the guidelines to another group.

BAD TEAM BUILDING

A good manager understands the benefit of teamwork and of making every employee feel a part of things in the workplace.

As a result, an industry has grown up around the provision of team-building exercises and events for businesses. However, talking to businesspeople in my network lately, I've come across many stories of team-building exercises that didn't have the effect that the organizers intended. So, managers, rather than my usual tips and advice on what works in management, this week I'm offering three case studies of situations that you should avoid at all costs. The stories are based on interviews with people who participated in the activities.

COMPANY A **Paintball 'Fun'** There were definitely problems with teamwork and cooperation in Company A. A number of people reported feeling anger and resentment about two junior colleagues who had been promoted over the heads of the rest of the team, and the negative feelings were affecting work badly. So when the manager announced a full day out of the office for a team-building activity, so that everyone could learn to cooperate better and maybe even bond as a group, motivation was low and most people didn't feel good about it. But then the team found out what the training day was: paintballing. The mood lightened, because many of the workers saw it as a great opportunity. But it wasn't the prospect of improving teamwork that was appealing, it was rather that they were looking forward to having the chance to shoot paintballs at the colleagues they were angry with.

The exercise apparently didn't result in any immediate improvements at work – it just made most of the team members feel angrier. My advice to managers? Think carefully when planning a team-building exercise. Ask yourself: will it help employees to resolve conflict and have a sense of belonging, or could it possibly make things worse?

COMPANY B **Office Sing-Along** The Company B employee I interviewed told me that she is a team player and doesn't object to the idea of team-building exercises in principle. She also said that though she loves music, she can't sing. So when her company announced an awayday to enhance teamwork through singing, it brought up some very negative feelings for her – mostly childhood memories of being forced to sing at school. She participated in the training because she had to, but from start to finish, all she could think about was how to get out of there.

Many participants found the day somewhat stressful and in their reviews of the session, said that it didn't accomplish anything. Hey, managers: If you're planning a team-building day, choose an activity that people won't hate. If a team-building activity makes people feel bad, chances are it's not going to work.

COMPANY C **Group Therapy** The marketing team at Company C already knew how to cooperate pretty well. They were sharing the load with almost no conflict, and when there was work to be done, everyone was always willing to go the extra mile. So when the management announced a half-day of team-building exercises, no one thought too much about it and simply got on with their work. But on the day of the course, the 'corporate motivation specialist' in charge soon had everyone's attention. The first activity? Make a list of things you *don't* like about your colleagues. The second activity? Tell them. The Company C employee I spoke with said that, not surprisingly, the session was not at all effective.

Fortunately, the team that was being worked with get along well and many of them are friends outside of work. They all immediately understood that doing the exercise as instructed could only lead to problems. So they all just made up answers in order to complete the task, but many had difficulty keeping a straight face. After the session, the team were given a kind of computerized personality test to discover their 'teamwork style'. Lessons learnt? If you ever have to arrange any corporate team-building activities or teamwork training, try to choose something that's actually relevant to the team it's designed for. It seems kind of obvious, doesn't it?

8.4 If you'll just let me finish ...

LISTENING Reviewing a project

1 An advertising agency is working for a small smoothie maker to promote and sell their product in parks using small carts. Look at the photo. Answer the questions.

1 What team roles would be necessary to promote and sell smoothies in this way? Think about getting the carts, decorating them, getting permission to sell from them, supplying the product itself, and so on.

2 Who would need to work together closely to produce an effective product promotion?

3 Think of three ways the project could go wrong.

2 🎧 **46** Listen to some people talking about a similar project. Choose the correct options to complete the sentences.

1 This meeting takes place at the *beginning / end* of a project.

2 There was no *administrator / project manager* on the team.

3 The team lacked *leadership / teamwork*.

4 Rudy thinks there should be better communication during *product analysis / development*.

5 Helen agrees that *shorter / longer* meetings encourage communication.

6 At the end of the meeting, everyone feels that the main points *have / haven't* been covered.

Pronunciation Emphasizing the main focus of the sentence

3a 🎧 **47** Listen to four different versions of a sentence. Underline the main stress in each version.

1 I'd be interested in hearing your views.

2 I'd be interested in hearing your views.

3 I'd be interested in hearing your views.

4 I'd be interested in hearing your views.

3b Match each version 1–4 from Exercise 3a with the sense given by the stress (a–d).

a You may think I don't want to hear them but I would be interested in hearing your views.

b I've heard about your experience, now I want to hear about your views.

c I've heard about everyone else's views, now I want to hear yours.

d The others heard your views, but I haven't heard them yet.

SPEAKING Taking part in a meeting

4 Which expression in each pair is more polite? In each, what makes it polite?

1 Let's begin.   Shall we begin?

2 If you'll allow me to finish ... .   Be quiet. I'm talking.

3 What do you think?   I'd be interested in hearing your views.

4 Sorry for interrupting, but ... .   I think …

5 That's all.   I think we can finish there.

5 Work in groups of three. Roleplay a meeting. Use structures from the Useful expressions box and the information below. Remember to be polite rather than abrupt.

> Your team has recently hosted a conference for about 200 people. It wasn't seen as a big success because it wasn't very well organized.

> A: Introduce meeting topic: talking about issues with teamwork on the recent conference – coordination, administration, leadership. Invite views.

> B: Mention the conference organizer's role.

> C: Try to interrupt, to say that you think next time, the conference organizer needs to be a more active leader.

> A: Stop C's interruption.

> B: Suggest analysis of planning process – not enough time was allowed to plan the details.

> A: Invite C's views.

> C: Agree with B and add that people complained that the food was bad and it should be better next time.

> A: Close meeting.

TAKING PART IN A MEETING

Opening a discussion

Shall I go ahead / get us started / start the discussion?
I'd like to start the discussion by …

Stopping interruption

If you'll let me / allow me to finish …
I know you're dying to jump in, but …
Could I just finish what I was saying?

Inviting participation

I'd be interested in hearing your views.
Can you give me your thoughts?
What's your take on … ?
Any thoughts on … ?

Interrupting

Before you continue, can I just say … ?
Can I just say something here?
I hate to interrupt, but ...
Sorry for interrupting, but ...

Wrapping up

If no one has anything else, I think we can stop there.
I think we can finish there.
I guess we've covered everything.
All right, I think that's everything.

WRITING Debriefing questionnaire

6 Use these words to complete the questionnaire.

delivered	designed	featured	finished	led
looked	lost	started	took	went

Writing skill Linking devices

7a The writer uses linking words and phrases to connect ideas. In the debriefing questionnaire, find the following.

1 four cause-and-result expressions
2 two adverbials of time, one referring to the past and one referring to the future
3 an adverb that signals additional information
4 an adverb that contrasts two pieces of information
5 an adverb that signals summary

7b Complete the sentences with the expressions from Exercise 7a.

1 The project was delivered on time; _____, we were way over budget.
2 We didn't spend the entire budget _____ that the materials were cheaper than expected.
3 _____ finished the project, everyone was ready for a break.

PROJECT DEBRIEFING
QUESTIONNAIRE

1 Briefly (up to 60 words) summarise the project.

We had six weeks from start to finish to create a mobile product-promotion cart for a small organic drinks company. We [1] _____ and built the cart which [2] _____ the name of the company, an attractive logo, and a cooler to store the drinks. It also included a sunshade for hot, sunny weather.

2 What went well and why?

The design phase [3] _____ very well owing to the fact that we [4] _____ the time to have several meetings with the drinks company owners and to develop a look and feel for the cart that they were completely happy with. As a result, we had a very clear vision for the project before we [5] _____ building it.

3 What was the project's biggest challenge?

Because of the lack of coordination, we [6] _____ the cart about ten days late. This wasn't a huge problem; however, it [7] _____ bad – and we [8] _____ some money as a consequence.

4 What was the project's biggest success?

When we finally [9] _____, the cart looked great and the company is getting a lot of business from it.

5 What would you do differently next time and why?

In future, we need to make sure that the team is coordinated. Everyone was very focused on their own contribution, but this [10] _____ to problems when the elements came together. Overall, we think having shorter meetings more often will improve communication among team members.

4 _____ his design expertise, George's contributions were particularly helpful.
5 The client cancelled the order at the last minute. _____, they lost their deposit.
6 _____, we plan to build extra time into the schedule for possible delays.
7 Our communication wasn't clear at times, and there was some confusion _____.
8 _____, we think the project was a success, but some aspects could have been improved.

8 **21st CENTURY OUTCOMES**

Write a similar debriefing of a project you have worked on using the questionnaire in Exercise 6 as a model. You can choose something serious from your job or school or something less serious, such as preparing a family meal.

9 Exchange debriefing documents with your partner. Read the debriefing document. Has each section been explained clearly?

Review 4 | UNITS 7 AND 8

LISTENING

1 🎧 **48** Read the introduction and listen to the extracts from a radio programme about how three companies deal with waste. Then say if each sentence below is true (T) or false (F).

1 Boxcycle doesn't allow people to buy or sell anything using their website.
2 Boxcycle manages a facility that recycles all kinds of paper and cardboard, mostly for boxes that are no longer usable.
3 Hipcycle features art and functional items that are made from junk.
4 Hipcycle takes bicycles that no one wants and repairs them so that they can be ridden again.
5 Marriott Construction builds buildings entirely from waste materials.
6 Marriott's innovation resulted in reduced traffic, noise and pollution on their construction site.

2 Read the definitions. Which word could be used to describe the activities of all three companies? Which company does each of the other two words describe?

1 **Downcycling** is turning waste material into something that is of lower quality than the original material.
2 **Upcycling** is turning waste material into something that is of higher quality or value than the original material.
3 **Recycling** is using a product or material again after it has already been used at least once.

Boxcycle, Hipcycle and Marriott Construction

BOXCYCLE is devoted exclusively to matching up people who need cardboard boxes with people or companies who have spare ones.

HIPCYCLE is a marketplace for art and household items created from materials that were otherwise going to have been thrown away.

MARRIOTT CONSTRUCTION is a builder that immediately reuses waste products on building sites to create materials that in the past had to be bought and delivered.

GRAMMAR

3 Complete the text with six of these eight expressions.

arose from	because	contributes to	make
fosters	killed	the result of	results in

Architect Marcio Kogan's decision to build a shop out of discarded shipping containers ¹ _____ his client's request for a low-budget furniture showroom that could be built quickly. ² _____ they didn't want to damage palm trees on the site, the design needed to be narrow – making the 2.5-metre-wide containers the perfect choice. It's part of a new wave of shops and homes made from used containers, which is ³ _____ a growing desire worldwide to recycle and to minimize carbon footprint. The six containers, stacked two high, are each painted a different bright colour, which greatly ⁴ _____ the overall eye-catching look of the place and ⁵ _____ the shipping containers themselves being more noticeable. Glass windows at either end of the containers ⁶ _____ the inside of the shop light and airy rather than cramped.

4 Complete the text with the correct simple or continuous form of the verbs. In some cases, more than one form is correct.

I ¹ _____ (collect) sculpture made from junk metal for about ten years, and my collection ² _____ (grow) bigger all the time. I ³ _____ (buy) my first piece in Barcelona. I ⁴ _____ (study) the Catalan language there one summer and ⁵ _____ (get) to know some local artists because I ⁶ _____ (hang out) in local art galleries a lot. I ⁷ _____ (not look) for artwork to buy – especially not steel sculpture, because it ⁸ _____ (be) very heavy – but I ended up buying one and paying a lot to ship it home. The pieces I ⁹ _____ (like) the most are animals, because they ¹⁰ _____ (look) so real. Next month, I ¹¹ _____ (go) to a major art show in Croatia.

Right now, I ¹² _____ (research) the artists whose work will be shown there. I ¹³ _____ (want) to find something special for my collection, but here in Croatia, I ¹⁴ _____ (look) for smaller items that are cheaper to ship!

VOCABULARY

5 Complete the interview with the correct verbs.

A: As a site manager of a construction team, how do you make sure your team works effectively and safely?

B: One of the most important things a building site manager can do is to help a construction team ¹ _____ as a group.

A: How do you do that?

B: By example. If you're in charge of a building site, make sure everyone can see that you ² _____ your weight. This will establish your authority, but it will also show that you ³ _____ a team player.

A: So you join in on some tasks?

B: Right. When I ask a group of workers to do something, I need to be willing to ⁴ _____ the load sometimes.

A: How important is it that workers ⁵ _____ a sense of belonging in the workplace?

B: It's incredibly important. When people ⁶ _____ a part of things, it creates a culture where people feel proud to ⁷ _____ their fair share of the work and to ⁸ _____ the extra mile to help others when necessary.

6 Complete the expressions with mind in the text.

I ¹ _____ something ² _____ mind that I'd like to share. I read recently that 500 billion plastic bags are used globally each year. That number ³ _____ my mind! And picture this in your mind's ⁴ _____: there's a patch of plastic rubbish in the middle of the Pacific Ocean that's the size of France! We're drowning in plastic! And the fact that we recycle doesn't really ⁵ _____ my mind because it takes most plastic 500 to 1,000 years to degrade. Having said all that, I think it's important for us to ⁶ _____ our minds to reducing the amount of plastic we use. If, every day, you ⁷ _____ in mind the ever-growing plastic problem and stop using plastic, one bag and one bottle at a time, we may be able to solve the problem. Of course with so much plastic packaging, you'll have to keep ⁸ _____ mind about what products you choose or accept the inconvenience of buying loose, unpackaged goods. If you're in a shop and you're ⁹ _____ minds about whether you need a plastic bag, just say no. Once you get used to it, knowing that you're doing something good for the world will give you ¹⁰ _____ mind.

DISCUSSION

7 Work in pairs. Discuss the questions.

1 Are there examples in your area of recycling, upcycling or downcycling? If not, can you think of any opportunities that exist for these activities?

2 Can you think of a building that is especially suited to its immediate environment – the size or shape of the site, the local climate, or the use of the building? What features make the building special?

3 In many places around the world, paper, cardboard and plastic are collected and recycled. What products are created from these recycled materials? Do you use any?

SPEAKING

8 Tom, Jo and Lena are discussing one of the two locations of the art gallery they run, which sells work by local artists. Put the phrases and sentences (a–h) in the correct order. Then use them to complete the conversation below.

a me / to / likely / seem / doesn't / That / that / all

_____

b I / Could / finish / just / I / what / saying / was

_____

c the / start / like / I'd / to / discussion / sales / talking / by / about

_____

d It / seems / highly / probable / that

_____

e you / say / continue, / Before / just / I / can

_____

f be / in / I'd / interested / views, / your / hearing / Tom

_____

g a / explanation / likely / seems / That

_____

h imagine / I / because / it's / of

_____

Jo: ¹ _____. Why have they dropped off in our Dean Street location in the past few months?

Tom: ² _____ the increased parking charges. People are really upset about them.

Lena: ³ _____. I think there's a more obvious explanation. We really need to consider whether …

Jo: ⁴ _____ that I've met with a group of other shop owners in the area, and everyone agrees that customers are staying away because of the parking charges. So what we need …

Lena: ⁵ _____? I think we really need to consider whether Dean Street is still the best area for us. ⁶ _____ the area has lost its artistic edge. In the past two years, several national chain shops and expensive coffee shops have opened, and it feels like any high street.

Jo: ⁷ _____.

Lena: So as I said, I think we need …

Jo: Sorry for interrupting, Lena. ⁸ _____.

9 Stress and relaxation

Alexandra Kosteniuk, Russian chess Grandmaster, competing at the 2015 Women's World Chess Championship in Sochi, Russia.

TEDTALKS

ANDY PUDDICOMBE wants you to take a break – not just from work, but from your own mind, which is so full of anxieties about the world and anxieties about its own anxieties. To help you do that, Puddicombe, a former Buddhist monk, co-founded Headspace, a project to make meditation more accessible to more people in their everyday lives. Andy Puddicombe's idea worth spreading is that if we meditate for just 10 minutes a day, we can feel more focused and experience the world with more calm and clarity.

BACKGROUND

1 You are going to watch a TED Talk by Andy Puddicombe called *All it takes is 10 mindful minutes.* Read the text about the speaker and the talk. Then work in pairs and answer the questions.

    1 What types of things typically cause people anxiety?

    2 What do people do to try to cope with stress and anxiety?

    3 What comes to mind when you hear the word 'meditation'?

KEY WORDS

2 Read the sentences (1–6). The words in bold are used in the TED Talk. First guess the meaning of the words. Then match the words with their definitions (a–f).

    1 If we learn to be **mindful**, it's easier to deal with life's challenges.

    2 My pace of life is **frantic** and my mind is always busy.

    3 Our lives can become so busy that we rarely do anything **spontaneous** anymore.

    4 You can avoid getting so stressed by taking some simple **preventative** measures.

    5 I wish I felt less **restless** and more relaxed at the weekends.

    6 We sometimes feel **inundated** by work and other people's demands.

    a faced with more than we can easily deal with

    b intended to stop something from happening

    c unable to be still

    d very hurried and using a lot of energy

    e aware of the state and activity of our own thoughts

    f able to act without a plan

AUTHENTIC LISTENING SKILLS
Understanding mid-sentence changes in direction

Sometimes we begin a sentence, but part-way through it, we go off in a different direction. This often happens because, as we're speaking, we think of a better way of making the point and sometimes the change in direction might be used for a particular effect. But it can mean that the second part of the sentence doesn't always match the first part. If you can focus on the ideas contained in the sentence as a whole and not worry about 'the missing part of the sentence' (grammatically), it can help you to understand the speaker's message.

3a 🎧 **49** Look at the Authentic listening skills box. Listen to this sentence. What do you notice about the speaker's way of constructing this sentence?

3b 🎧 **50** Listen to another sentence. What did you expect to hear the speaker say after 'than we'?

3c 🎧 **51** Read two more extracts from the talk. How do you think the sentences might end? Now listen to find out.

    1 But when you sit down and you watch the mind in this way, you might see many different patterns. You might find a mind that's really, sort of, restless and –
    _____ .

    2 You might find a mind that's very, sort of, dull and boring, and it's just, almost mechanical, it just, sort of, seems it's as if you're getting up, going to work,
    _____ .

9.1 All it takes is 10 mindful minutes

TED TALKS

1 ▶ 9.1 How much do you know about meditation? Decide whether you think each statement is true or false. Then watch the TED Talk and say whether Andy Puddicombe sees them as true (T) or false (F).

1 Meditation involves basically doing nothing.
2 Meditation is a way of caring for the mind.
3 The purpose of meditation is to stop thoughts, get rid of emotion and control the mind.
4 Meditators try to watch their thoughts come and go without getting too involved in them.
5 Meditation needs to be done while sitting on the floor.

2 ▶ 9.1 Watch the first part (0.00–3.38) of the talk again. Answer the questions.

1 Puddicombe lists a series of things that we rely on our mind for. Note down as many as you can.
2 What does Puddicombe say happens when we fail to care for our mind properly?
3 Puddicombe talks about his past view of meditation as an Aspirin (headache tablet) for the mind. What does he mean by this?
4 In his twenties, when Puddicombe's life became very stressful, where did he go and what did he do?

▶ round and round **BR ENG**
▶ around and around **N AM ENG**

▶ mum **BR ENG**
▶ mom **N AM ENG**

3 ▶ **9.1** Watch the second part (3.39–6.49) of the talk again. Choose the best options to complete the sentences.

1 When he became a monk, Puddicombe learned to be very aware of the workings of his *mind / emotions*.

2 Research shows that we spend nearly half of our lives thinking about *how to find happiness / something other than what we're actually doing*.

3 Puddicombe says that meditation is basically a way of getting to know *ourselves / the present moment*.

4 Puddicombe uses the balls to illustrate the way *physical activity / focus* affects our mind.

5 According to Puddicombe, the key to successful meditation is *balance / total relaxation*.

4 ▶ **9.1** Watch the third part (6.50 to the end) of the talk again. Which statement (a–c) best gives the main idea of Puddicombe's TED Talk?

a Meditation doesn't give you a different perspective, but it does give you some control over your thoughts and emotions.

b Meditation won't change what happens to us in life, but it can help us respond to life in a different way.

c Meditation is a good way to stop feeling bored by the cycle of waking up, going to work, eating, and sleeping.

5 If you've tried meditation, has it been effective for you? If you haven't, would you like to try it?

VOCABULARY IN CONTEXT

6 ▶ **9.2** Watch the clips from the TED Talk. Choose the correct meaning of the words.

7 Complete the sentences in your own words. Then discuss with a partner.

1 I like to reminisce about …

2 When I want to take my foot off the gas, I usually …

3 I would like to feel more clarity in my life about …

CRITICAL THINKING Understanding the speaker's technique

8 Speakers use different techniques to engage us with their ideas. Match each sentence (1–4) from Andy Puddicombe's TED Talk with the best description of the technique it demonstrates (a–d).

1 'We spend more time looking after our cars, our clothes and our hair than [our minds].'

2 'There was a research paper that came out of Harvard, just recently, that said on average our minds are lost in thought almost 47 per cent of the time.'

3 'It just kind of seems tragic, actually, especially when there's something we can do about it.'

4 'If you think about the last time, I dunno, you had a wobbly tooth.'

a referring to scientific studies

b using everyday images that the audience can relate to

c appealing to emotions

d appealing to common sense

9 Which technique do you think is the most effective in Puddicombe's talk?

10 Read these comments* about the TED Talk. Which part of the talk are they referring to? Find it in the transcript on pages 94 and 95.

Viewers' comments

N **Nell** – Andy's description near the beginning of the talk, about the stressed mind and all the confusion of thoughts going round, really hit home for me. It makes the human condition seem hopeless!

U **Uwe** – Yes, but that's if you choose to focus on the negative! Remember, he says it doesn't have to be that way!

S **Seb** – I agree with Uwe. What I'm taking away from this is that we have the power to change things.

*The comments were created for this activity.

11 Do you agree with the viewers' comments? Why? / Why not? What techniques did you notice him using in the section they describe?

PRESENTATION SKILLS Thinking about your audience

> **TIPS**
> Consider your audience and imagine the talk from their perspective. Ask yourself the following.
> - What will they already know, or what assumptions will they have about the topic?
> - What will get them excited?
> - What jargon or technical language should I avoid because the audience won't know it?

12 ▶ **9.3** Look at the Presentation tips box. Then watch the clips from Andy Puddicombe's TED Talk and answer the questions.

1 What does Puddicombe assume the audience believes about meditation?

2 What idea(s) does Puddicombe think the audience may get excited about?

3 Did you notice any words that might be considered technical language and jargon?

13 Think of a practical way of dealing with stress. Prepare a short presentation about it. Remember to think about the points in the Presentation tips box.

14 Work in pairs. Take turns to give your presentation.

▶ quit my degree **BR ENG**
▶ dropped out of school **N AM ENG**

▶ wobbly tooth **BR ENG**
▶ loose tooth **N AM ENG**

9.2 Even holidays are stressful

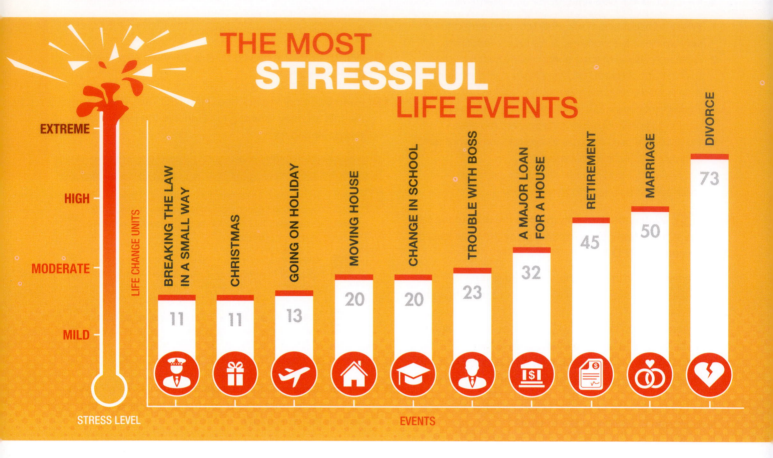

THE MOST STRESSFUL LIFE EVENTS

STRESS LEVEL									
EXTREME									
HIGH									
MODERATE									
MILD									
LIFE CHANGE UNITS	BREAKING THE LAW IN A SMALL WAY	CHRISTMAS	GOING ON HOLIDAY	MOVING HOUSE	CHANGE IN SCHOOL	TROUBLE WITH BOSS	A MAJOR LOAN FOR A HOUSE	RETIREMENT	MARRIAGE	DIVORCE
	11	11	13	20	20	23	32	45	50	73

EVENTS

GRAMMAR Intensifying adverbs

1 Work in pairs. In a typical week, what are the three most stressful situations you have to deal with?

2 Look at the table. What do 'life change units' measure?

3 Read the text in the Grammar box. Answer the questions (1–7) about the bold words in the text.

INTENSIFYING ADVERBS

Stress can make you ill. In extreme cases, severe stress can **utterly destroy** a person's health, confidence and well-being. Early research in this area was begun in the late 1960s by psychologists Thomas Holmes and Richard Rahe, who were **quite** certain that there was a link between stress and health and **really wanted** to get to the bottom of it. They asked 5,000 North Americans to rank the degree of stress caused by certain events in life, then assigned 'life change units' to each one. Then they added up the units in each person's life for a total stress score.

The results of their research made the connection **absolutely undeniable**: people who had more life change units for the previous year also had more health problems. One **extremely interesting** finding was that even supposedly relaxing activities like going on holiday were never completely stress-free. This shouldn't be **in the least bit surprising** if we think what is involved in getting away. It can also be **quite difficult** to relax if we've been very busy beforehand. But don't worry. Apparently we start to relax by the end of the third day!

1 Which adverb modifies a gradable* adjective?

2 Which adverb modifies an ungradable** adjective?

3 Which adverb modifies another adverb?

4 Which adverb can modify gradable and ungradable adjectives and verbs?

5 Which adverb is generally used with negative verbs and adjectives?

6 Which negative adverbial construction modifies a verb?

7 Which of the two uses of *quite* is an intensifying adverb? Is the adjective gradable or ungradable?

Check your answers on page 78 and do Exercises 1–6.

* gradable adjectives can be measured on a scale
** ungradable adjectives express extreme or absolute qualities

4 Complete the sentences with the expressions. Some words may fit in more than one sentence.

| not at all   quite literally   so   totally   utterly   whatsoever |

1 A: We had a scary taxi ride from the airport.
  B: Scary? It was _____ terrifying!
2 A: The weather was a bit rainy.
  B: A bit rainy? It _____ rained the whole time.
3 A: The first hotel wasn't cheap.
  B: Not cheap? It was _____ expensive!
4 A: It's a bit silly to get lost if you have a map.
  B: Silly? In a complex city like Tokyo, I think it's _____ understandable!
5 A: The hotel's staff weren't very helpful.
  B: Weren't very helpful? They were _____ interested in their guests.
6 A: The tour guides didn't give us much information about travel arrangements.
  B: Not much? They gave us no information _____!

5 Complete the three texts with the correct options.

Text 1

My first holiday abroad was to Singapore. I felt ¹*extremely / utterly* nervous about using the local public transport and getting around, but once I discovered the ²*so / absolutely* amazing food in the markets, I began to feel ³*really / entirely* happy with my choice of destination.

Text 2

My holiday in Australia was of no benefit ⁴*in the least / whatsoever* for reducing stress. I'd bought cheap plane tickets several months before I went, but I didn't make a hotel reservation before leaving. The first night, I ended up in a business hotel that was ⁵*not at all / completely* pleasant – the room smelled of cigarette smoke – and I spent the whole next day trying to find a nicer place to stay. Rather than make last-minute arrangements, it would have been more relaxing to cancel the trip ⁶*extremely / entirely*.

Text 3

I had a ⁷*totally / so* boring holiday! That was definitely my first and last 'staycation' – you know, going on holiday near home rather than going abroad. I had a reasonably relaxing time, but it wasn't ⁸*not at all / the least bit* exotic, so it didn't feel ⁹*at all like / entirely* a proper vacation. Next summer, I definitely want to go further from home!

6 Complete the conversation with appropriate intensifying adverbs. There is more than one right answer for most gaps. Don't use the same word twice.

A: How was your long weekend?
B: It was ¹_____ stressful.
A: Oh, no! It was a music festival, right? When you told me about it, your plans sounded ²_____ brilliant!
B: Right. I mean, we ³_____ expected it to be a brilliant weekend, but it … got off to a very bad start.
A: So can I ask what went wrong?
B: Well, first, I have to say, I accept the blame ⁴_____. But basically, what happened is we went to the wrong place … or I booked the hotel in the wrong place.
A: The wrong place … you mean the wrong part of town?
B: No, I ⁵_____ literally booked a hotel in the wrong city – in a city far away.
A: Oh, no! But it was Spain, right? Girona?
B: Well, that's where we flew to. But the hotel I booked was a thousand kilometres away – in Gerena, near Seville.
A: Gerena … Girona …
B: I know … it's ⁶_____ embarrassing! There's no excuse ⁷_____!

Pronunciation Stress with intensifying adverbs

7a Look at the sentences with intensifying adverbs. Underline the words you think will be stressed.

1 The weather was incredibly stormy.
2 The flights were so expensive.
3 I'm quite certain that was the worst holiday ever.
4 The hotel rooms were absolutely lovely.
5 The guidebook was of no help whatsoever.
6 Our host was really kind.

7b 🎧 **52** Listen and check your answers. Then practise saying the sentences with natural stress.

SPEAKING Holiday lessons learned

8 Think of the most relaxing holiday you've ever had. Work in small groups and discuss the questions. Then do the same with the least relaxing holiday you've ever had.

- Where did you go?
- Who were you with?
- What did you do?
- Why was it relaxing/unrelaxing?

9 21st **CENTURY OUTCOMES**

Use the group's responses to the questions in Exercise 8 to create a list of tips and hints for how to have a really relaxing holiday. Think about the following.

- planning
- where to go
- how to get the details right

10 Share your tips and hints and your holiday with another group.

9.3 Alert and alive

READING Can stress be good for you?

1 Look at the photo. Work in pairs. Discuss the questions.

1 Why do you think people do activities like this?
2 What do you think the woman is thinking or feeling at this moment?
3 Have you ever done anything that made you feel that way? Or would you like to?

2 Work in pairs. Look at the title of the article. Do you think stress can be good for you?

3 Read the introduction. Does the writer think stress can be good for us?

4 Read the article and answer the questions.

1 In what ways does the article say that stress can be good for us?
2 As very few people in the world are ever actually chased by wild animals, why does Elizabeth Kirby compares a burst of stress to being chased by a bear?
3 In what ways could moderate stress make people more effective in a job?

5 Match the words (1–7) and (8–10) with their definitions (a–g) and (h–j).

Nouns

1 adrenaline
2 awareness
3 burst
4 exposure
5 immune system
6 thrill
7 vaccination

Adjectives

8 alert
9 chronic
10 clinical

a the state of knowing about something
b the state of having no protection from something
c the parts and processes of the body that fight illness
d a chemical produced by the body when we feel excited or frightened
e a short period of emotion or energy
f a medicine given to prevent disease
g a sudden feeling of excitement or pleasure

h lasting for a long time
i relating to the treatment of patients
j very awake and aware

6 Do you think it would be possible to have too little stress in your life? If so, what problems could it cause? If not, what would be the benefits of having a totally stress-free life?

VOCABULARY Idioms related to parts of the body

7 Complete these three expressions with parts of the body in the text. What does each mean?

1 on your _____ (line 14)
2 a shot in the _____ (line 41)
3 in over your _____ (line 48)

8 Look at the expressions in bold and discuss what each one means.

1 **I'm up to my eyeballs** in work. I really need a break!
2 **Keep your chin up** – things will look better in the morning.
3 It really **makes my blood boil** when people drive slowly in the fast lane on the motorway.
4 It's good to go out with colleagues and **let your hair down** a bit.
5 Handing in that report will **be a** big **weight off your shoulders**, I imagine.
6 You look nervous. Are you **getting cold feet** about asking for a pay increase?
7 Can we talk? I'm having problems and I need to **get some things off my chest**.
8 All of this unnecessary paperwork I'm supposed to complete **is a pain in the neck**.

9 Use six of the expressions in Exercises 7 and 8 to make six sentences about your own life.

SPEAKING Talking about stress

10 *21st* **CENTURY OUTCOMES**

Work in small groups. Discuss the questions.

1 What can people do to avoid getting into a situation where they have constant stress?
2 If people are in a situation where they are stressed too often, what techniques can they use to cope with it? Diet and nutrition tips? Exercise? Relationships? Using mobile phones and other devices more thoughtfully?
3 What ways other than stress do you use to stimulate your brain?

CAN STRESS BE GOOD FOR YOU?

Google 'stress' and the search results paint a very negative picture: stress is a problem with symptoms, causes and treatments – something that needs to be defeated, like an illness. And
5 indeed, chronic stress is a proven cause of many major health problems such as heart disease and cancer. But did you know that a degree of stress can be good for you? Recent research by Dr Staci
10 Bilbo, an associate professor of psychology and neuroscience at Duke University in the USA, and others, indicates that the effects of stress are more complicated than we think.

KEEPING US ON OUR TOES?

15 Our bodies and minds naturally respond to our environment, to the things going on in the world around us. What's interesting is that whether our experience is negative or positive, the body's reaction is the same. It doesn't distinguish between the feelings we experience when we're under
20 pressure at work – the boss asks us as the last minute to give a complex presentation – or the ones associated with a thrill such as parachuting out of an aeroplane; it just releases a chemical called adrenaline. This is called the 'fight or flight' response; adrenaline gives us a burst of energy either to face
25 a challenge (fight) or run away from it (flight). In moderate amounts, adrenaline makes us feel alert and alive, though a big burst of adrenalin can be unpleasantly overwhelming. Dr. Pamela Peeke, an internationally recognized expert, physician,
30 scientist and author says, 'What stress does is it keeps us on our toes, it keeps us energetic, it keeps us engaged', adding that of course, too much stress can lead to real problems.

STIMULATING THE BRAIN?

Adrenaline and the 'fight or flight' response are only the
35 beginning, though. Clinical research shows that short periods of stress may help the brain work better. When we're stressed, the brain releases cortisol, a chemical that calms the mind. According to brain researcher Elizabeth Kirby, the moderate amount of cortisol produced during a brief burst of stress –

what she compares to being chased by a bear – provides an
40 energizing shot in the arm and motivates a quick response. In these amounts, cortisol improves the brain's ability to learn and remember. The key difference between good stress and bad stress is how long it lasts, according to Kirby. 'If a bear chases you all day, every day', she says, then the system will
45 be activated constantly, giving us a high and steady dose of the body's stress chemicals, which in the long run is harmful rather than helpful. So constantly feeling that you're in over your head at work may make you ill. And that can lead to serious health issues.
50

HELPING US LEARN TO DEAL WITH ANXIETY?

The mind isn't the only part of us that responds when the going gets tough. Our bodies also react in a variety of ways: a stiff neck, a tight stomach, tense shoulders. These symptoms are unpleasant because they cause discomfort, but they can also
55 be helpful, as we can use them to increase our awareness of the sources of anxiety – and therefore become more able to identify and deal with them. If we're mindful of how it affects us, we can practise improving our response and thereby slowly reduce the negative effects stress can have on us. But
60 there's more. Research has also shown that if, as children, we experience moderate stress – for example separation from our parents as part of the weekly routine – we grow into healthier, more relaxed adults. Practice dealing with low-level childhood anxiety can make it much easier to deal with more intense
65 grown-up pressures.

BOOSTING THE IMMUNE SYSTEM?

There's one more clear physical benefit of stress. We know that strong exercise 'stresses' the body and causes the release of adrenaline in much the same way that a sudden shock or
70 thrill does. Researchers have discovered that strong physical activity before certain medical procedures can improve their effectiveness. For example, when cancer patients have a fast workout just before receiving a dose of cancer treatment, it
75 improves the effectiveness of the drugs. Similarly, recipients of a vaccination can increase the body's ability to fight disease by doing a short but intense run just beforehand.

Stress can unarguably cause serious problems, but if we understand how it works, we can learn to use it
80 advantageously. So next time your boss gives you two hours to come up with the best presentation of your life and you're feeling seriously stressed, remember: it may be good for you!

9.4 Have you got a minute?

LISTENING Dealing with awkward situations

1 Work in pairs. Tell you partner what you would do in each of the following situations.

1 In the company car park, you accidentally scratch your boss's car while parking. No one sees it happen.
2 You left your company smartphone on the table in a restaurant. When you went back to look for it, it was gone and no one had turned it in. It holds sensitive information, including details of clients.
3 You are scheduled to work next Saturday, but you want the day off to go to a concert. The only person who might cover for you on that day is a relatively new employee who you don't know very well.

2 🎧 **53** Listen to five conversations. Answer the questions.

Conversation 1

1 What does the woman want?
2 What does the man say?

Conversation 2

3 What does the woman tell the man?
4 What is the man's reaction?

Conversation 3

5 What did the man do?
6 How does the woman react?

Conversation 4

7 What does the woman want the man to do?
8 How does the man react?

Conversation 5

9 What does the man want?
10 How does the woman respond?

3 🎧 **53** Listen again. Tick the sentences you hear in the Useful expressions box.

HAVING DIFFICULT CONVERSATIONS

Starting a conversation

Could I have a word?
Have you got a minute?
Sorry, but if you have a moment …

Accepting a request to speak

What's on your mind?
What's up?
What can I do for you?

Raising an awkward topic

There's something I wanted to ask you / talk with you about.
I've got a confession to make.
I have to apologize.
I have a favour to ask.

Explaining the situation

The thing is …
There's a slight / a bit of a problem with …

Asking a favour

I don't suppose … ?
You couldn't … could you?
Is there any way … ?

Responses

That's a shame, but I understand.
Actually, that's a bit tricky / awkward.
Don't worry. It doesn't matter / It's not important.
Unfortunately, …
I'm sorry, but …

Pronunciation Polite and assertive intonation

4a 🎧 **54** Listen. Which version of the sentence is polite (write P)? Which is more assertive (write A)?

1 I'm really sorry, but I'm going to have to ask you to pay for the damage.
2 I'm really sorry, but I'm going to have to ask you to pay for the damage.
3 Could you possibly help me out?
4 Could you possibly help me out?
5 That's an awkward situation, isn't it?
6 That's an awkward situation, isn't it?

4b Practise saying the sentences both politely and assertively.

SPEAKING Having difficult conversations

5 Work in pairs. Have conversations imagining you are in these situations. Use the language in the Useful expressions box. Deal with the situation in a way that feels natural to you.

Student A	Student B
You were trying to unjam the only office photocopier, and instead of fixing it, you caused it to spark and start smoking. Tell your boss (Student B).	You are Student A's boss. Have a conversation, then propose a solution.
You are Student B's colleague. Have a conversation, then propose a solution.	You want to go out after work. You have two-year-old son, and you need a babysitter. Ask your friend (Student A), who you know has a very busy life, to babysit for you.
You were supposed to give some extremely important research results to your colleague (Student B) yesterday, but you noted the date incorrectly in your diary. You will need another day to complete the work. Tell your colleague about the situation.	You are Student A's colleague. Have a conversation, then propose a solution.
You are Student B's friend. Have a conversation, then propose a solution.	You borrowed your friend's (Student A's) leather jacket to wear to a party. Unfortunately, someone at the party spilled food on the jacket and there's a big stain on it now. Tell your friend.

WRITING A record of a meeting

6 Read the report. Answer the questions.

1 Why did David Peters believe he wasn't given a pay increase?
2 What is probably the real reason he wasn't given a pay increase?
3 What will happen next?

RECORD OF MEETING: DAVID PETERS

Today at 10:45, I met with David Peters regarding his pay. During the meeting, Mr Peters claimed that his pay had not increased as quickly as he had expected it to. He alleged that he was being treated unfairly and even accused me personally of not liking him and therefore not recommending a pay increase.

In response to that, I acknowledged that his request for a pay increase hadn't yet been approved, but denied that this had any connection with my personal feelings about him. I urged him to consider the fact that he had arrived late for work more than 50 per cent of the time in the previous six months. He admitted that he had indeed been late to work frequently, but insisted that he still performed his job as well as anyone and refused to admit that being on time is a basic part of doing acceptable work.

In order to assist Mr Peters in improving his performance, I proposed that he start arriving at work on time or a few minutes early every day and suggested that we have a follow-up meeting after one month. He agreed with this suggestion.

Signed: _M. Davis_   Date: _06 / 15 / 15_

Print name: _Melanie Davis_

Writing skill Reporting verbs

7a Find twelve verbs in the report that paraphrase something that was said.

7b Match each statement (1–6) with the correct reported version (a–f).

1 It was my fault.
2 I'm sorry, I should have been more careful.
3 The data was left without password protection.
4 That's not quite right, actually.
5 You really should consider apologizing.
6 I absolutely didn't do it.

a He confirmed what had happened.
b I urged him to say he was sorry.
c He accepted responsibility for the mistake.
d He apologized for what had happened.
e He refused to admit he'd done it. / He denied doing it.
f He contradicted Ms. Fung's version of the story.

8 **21st CENTURY OUTCOMES**

Choose one of the conversations you had in Exercise 5 or imagine a similar conversation. Write a record of it using reporting verbs to summarize the conversation.

9 Exchange reports with the partner you worked with in Exercise 5. Were your reports similar?

---

10 Risk

Workers erect scaffolding at a construction site near the financial district in Panama City, Panama.

TEDTALKS

DEL HARVEY works at Twitter to ensure user safety and security, balancing the need for free and open communication on the social network with the need to protect users from online abuse. The security expert spends her days thinking about how to prevent bad things from happening while giving voice to people around the globe. Del Harvey's idea worth spreading is that companies have the responsibility to keep every user safe, by imagining the worst and designing products to avoid it happening.

BACKGROUND

1 You are going to watch a TED Talk by Del Harvey called *Protecting Twitter users (sometimes from themselves)*. Read the text about the talk and the speaker, then answer the questions.

1 Harvey believes it's important for Twitter to give a voice to people around the globe. What kinds of stories or news do you think are spread by Twitter and other social media users?

2 What do you think is meant by the term *online abuse*? How do some people use social media to hurt others?

3 What do you think it means to protect Twitter users from themselves?

KEY WORDS

2 Read the sentences (1–6). The words in bold are used in the TED Talk. First guess the meaning of the words. Then match the words with their definitions (a–f).

1 We need to **root out** possible abuse and stop it.

2 If users' personal information were stolen, it would be a real **calamity**.

3 At first the tweet looked threatening, but it turned out to be **innocuous**.

4 The situation wasn't **cut and dried** because the tweet was genuinely intended as a joke.

5 With product safety, the **stakes** are high because people can get seriously hurt.

6 The couple's **prenuptial agreement** helped prevent a legal battle when they split up.

a risks, potential losses

b find and indentify

c clear and already decided

d disaster

e a legal contract made before a wedding stating how the couple will divide their money and possessions in a divorce

f not likely to hurt anyone

AUTHENTIC LISTENING SKILLS Avoiding frustration

When you listen to authentic English speech, it's easy to feel frustrated, because it can be difficult to understand. However, regular exposure to natural speech will help you develop your English. Try these tips.

- Before you listen, try focusing your thoughts on the topic. What do you already know about it? What do you think the speaker might say?
- When you listen, don't try to translate every word and don't worry if you don't understand everything. Relax and do your best to get a general sense of the message from the words you do understand.
- Keep practising. Regular listening related to topics you're interested in will help train your ear.

3a 🎧 **55** Look at the Authentic listening skills box. Then listen to the opening sentences from the TED Talk. Focus on the general sense. In what order (1–2) does Del Harvey do these things?

a She explains Twitter's growth.

b She talks about her obligations to Twitter's customers.

3b 🎧 **56** Listen to the next few sentences from the TED Talk. Try to get the general sense. Which of these things (1–4) does Del Harvey do?

1 She explains that Twitter is generally very safe.

2 She gives specific examples of risky behaviour.

3 She continues to explain the idea of 'scale'.

4 She mentions how Twitter protects users' private data.

3c Work in pairs. Tell your partner what you understood.

10.1 Protecting Twitter users (sometimes from themselves)

TEDTALKS

1 ▶ 10.1 Watch the TED Talk. Take notes on the following topics:

The size of Twitter:
The size of risk:
Examples of users' behaviour:
Examples of risk:

2 ▶ 10.1 Watch the first part (0.00–2.21) of the talk again. What do these numbers refer to?

1	two million	**5**	500
2	500 million	**6**	99.999
3	six	**7**	150,000
4	24,900		

3 ▶ 10.1 Watch the second part (2.21–4.44) of the talk again and answer the questions.

1 What does Del Harvey say makes her job especially challenging?

2 What example does Del Harvey give of each of the following?

   a Possible spam (sending the same message to a lot of people)

   b Possible phishing (trying to steal people's personal information)

▶ 2009 = two thousand nine **N AM ENG**
▶ 2009 = two thousand and nine **BR ENG**

▶ behavior **N AM ENG**
▶ behaviour **BR ENG**

4 **10.1** Watch the third part (4.45 to the end) of the talk again. Answer the questions.

1 Harvey says she could imagine a situation where tweeting a picture of her cat could lead to her death. How could that possibly happen?
2 'Odds' are numbers used to express how likely something is to happen. For example, the odds of being born in January are 1 in 12 because there are twelve months. Harvey finishes her talk by saying that for Twitter, 'a one-in-a-million chance is pretty good odds'. What does she mean by this?

VOCABULARY IN CONTEXT

5 **10.2** Watch the clips from the TED Talk. Choose the correct meaning of the words.

6 Complete the sentences in your own words. Then discuss with a partner.

1 My country's most famous landmarks are …
2 A lot of bystanders usually gather when …
3 When I feel gloomy, I try to cheer myself up by …

CRITICAL THINKING Analogies

7 In her TED Talk, Del Harvey says her job is like writing your wedding vows and your prenuptial agreement at the same time. Why does she make this comparison? Choose the best explanation (a–d).

a To put forward the argument that the work she's doing is as important as thinking carefully when getting married.
b To give an explanation of the very different considerations involved in her job.
c To argue that people must think very carefully before sending out tweets.
d To explain that the level of risk in using Twitter is very low.

8 Read the comments* about the TED Talk. Do you think the analogies are effective or not? Which one do you agree with the most?

Viewers' comments

K Kumiko – Harvey's job seems very interesting. She's a kind of psychologist – trying to understand what people are thinking.

J Jack – I think it's more like being a police officer. But I don't think any of the 'crimes' she's fighting are so serious. I can't really see why her job is necessary.

T Theodora – To me, Harvey is like a lifeguard in a swimming pool. There isn't usually any problem, but she's got to watch carefully to keep everyone safe. That's why it seems to me like a really important job. She is keeping Twitter users safe.

A Arturo – Harvey's main point is that even a small percentage of 500 million tweets is a lot. Think of it this way: 0.5% of the world's population (7 billion) seems tiny, but it's still an incredible 35 million people!

*The comments were created for this activity.

PRESENTATION SKILLS Pace and emphasis

TIPS

Pay attention to the pacing of your words. Pause for emphasis at the most essential points of your talk.

- In general, speaking clearly and not rushing through your points will help you relax and make it easier for the audience to follow your talk.
- You can speed up slightly for asides – short statements that may be interesting but aren't part of the main message.
- Pauses can help emphasize essential points and grab the audience's attention – but don't overuse this.

9 **10.3** Look at the Presentation tips box. Then watch the clips to see how Del Harvey varies the pace of her TED Talk. Answer the questions.

1 What information does Harvey slow down for and say in a very clear way?
2 When she says 'People do weird things', what effect does the emphasis have?
3 When talking about phishing, what does Harvey slow down for? Why do you think she chooses to emphasize these words?
4 What question that she always asks herself does Harvey emphasize? What answer does she give that describes a big part of her job?

10 You are going to give a short presentation on a risk you took at work or outside work. Make some notes about what happened.

- What was the risk?
- When did it happen?
- Why was it dangerous?
- What were the possible consequences?
- How did you avoid them?

11 Work in pairs. Take turns to give your presentation. Vary your pace. Slow down to emphasize key information.

 visualize **N AM ENG** / **BR ENG**
▶ visualise **BR ENG**

▶ we'll start off easy **N AM ENG**
▶ we'll start with an easy example **BR ENG**

10.2 Not as risky as it sounds

THE MOST DANGEROUS SPORTS

Every year, there are ten million sports injuries in the USA. So what are the ten most dangerous sports? When we think of dangerous sports, we think of rock climbing and skydiving, but those aren't even on the list. The top ten are ...

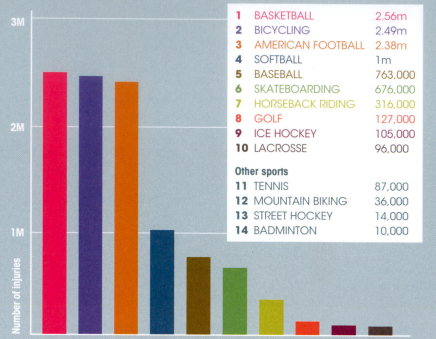

1	BASKETBALL	2.56m
2	BICYCLING	2.49m
3	AMERICAN FOOTBALL	2.38m
4	SOFTBALL	1m
5	BASEBALL	763,000
6	SKATEBOARDING	676,000
7	HORSEBACK RIDING	316,000
8	GOLF	127,000
9	ICE HOCKEY	105,000
10	LACROSSE	96,000
Other sports		
11	TENNIS	87,000
12	MOUNTAIN BIKING	36,000
13	STREET HOCKEY	14,000
14	BADMINTON	10,000

DIFFERENT WAYS TO MEASURE INJURIES

 IF YOU TAKE INTO ACCOUNT THE **NUMBER OF PEOPLE** WHO PARTICIPATE IN A SPORT, **AMERICAN FOOTBALL IS THE MOST DANGEROUS**

IF YOU CALCULATE THE NUMBER OF INJURIES PER 1,000 HOURS*:

	RUGBY:	91
	COMPETITIVE SURFING:	13
	INDOOR WALL CLIMBING:	0.02

*ACCORDING TO A GERMAN SURVEY

GRAMMAR Passive reporting verbs

1 Work in pairs. Have you ever tried a sport that is seen as risky? Would you like to? Why? / Why not?

2 Look at the infographic. Answer the questions.

 1 Which sport is the most dangerous?
 2 Which sport is the safest?
 3 Which sport would you never want to try?

3 Read the text in the Grammar box. Answer the questions (1–3).

4 Rewrite the sentences using the passive form of the reporting verbs.

 1 People say that skateboarding causes 676,000 injuries a year.
 Skateboarding _____ .
 2 Studies have shown that cycling is more dangerous than football.
 Cycling _____ .
 3 The newspaper reported that horseriding is the seventh most dangerous sport.
 Horseriding _____ .

PASSIVE REPORTING VERBS 1

As safe as ice hockey?
Ice hockey **has** long **been considered** to be one of the most dangerous North American sports, because the puck – the hard rubber piece that the players hit and score with – can travel at 170 kilometres per hour, causing painful injuries when it hits a player. However, according to recent research, basketball **has been shown** to be America's most dangerous sport. Why? One reason may be that ice hockey players wear equipment to protect them from injury, while basketball players have none. Basketball **is estimated** to cause about 2.5 million injuries each year, compared with ice hockey, which **is reported** to cause only about 100,000.

1 What grammatical form follows the bold passive reporting verbs?
2 Do we know who the agent of each passive reporting verb is?
3 Why is a passive verb used, rather than an active verb?

Check your answers on page 80 and do Exercises 1 and 2.

4 Records show that golf is more dangerous than ice hockey.
Golf _____ .

5 Hospitals expect to see a million baseball injuries this year.
A million baseball injuries _____ .

6 Doctors understand that softball can cause serious injuries.
Softball _____ .

5 Read the text in the Grammar box. Answer the questions (1 and 2).

Climbing: Not as risky as you thought
When the first indoor climbing gym was opened in Seattle in 1987, **it was thought** that it would provide a relatively safe indoor training alternative for serious climbers. Now **it's been shown** that indoor climbing is less risky than both surfing and rugby. A study in Germany discovered that indoor wall climbers have an average of 0.02 injuries per 1,000 hours spent climbing, while **it's estimated** that competitive surfers have on average 13 per 1,000 hours, and rugby players 91. **It's expected** that the publication of this data will boost Germany's already popular indoor-climbing business.

1 What grammatical form follows the passive reporting verbs in bold?
2 Which of the sentences refers to something that will occur in the future?

Check your answers on page 80 and do Exercises 3 and 4.

6 Complete the text with passive reporting structures with *it*, using the words in brackets.

These days ¹_____ (expect) in any given year that hundreds of climbers will reach the top of Mount Everest. But after climbers George Mallory and Sandy Irvine failed to return alive from the peak in 1924, ²_____ (widely believe) that the great mountain would never be climbed. This was especially true after the failure of ten more expeditions in the next 30 years. Then in 1952, ³_____ (report) that an attempt would be made the following year by a British team. The group, consisting of about 400 people, arrived on the slopes of the mountain early in 1953. ⁴_____ (estimate) that their baggage, containing food, camping gear and scientific equipment, weighed more than 4,500 kg. As spring came, they waited for a safe weather conditions for climbing. Finally, on May 26, ⁵_____ (reveal) that Edmund Hillary and Sherpa Tenzing Norgay would attempt the summit. However, because of terrible weather conditions at the top, ⁶_____ (announce) that there would be a delay. Finally, on May 28, 1953, ⁷_____ (prove) that Everest could be climbed when Hillary and Norgay reached the summit

and returned to tell the story. Though Everest is the highest mountain in the world, ⁸_____ (think) today that several other mountains are more dangerous, including Annapurna, the world's tenth highest mountain.

7 Rewrite the following statements as they might appear in a news article, using passive reporting verbs.

1 We know that BASE jumping is very risky. (It)
It's known that BASE jumping is very risky.

2 We think there are a few thousand cave divers in the world.
There are _____ .

3 A medical study reported that head injuries were the most common white-water rafting injuries.
It was _____ .

4 We expect injuries in big-wave surfing to increase as more people try the sport.
Big-wave surfing injuries _____ .

5 We hope that BMX teams will set a good example by always wearing head protection.
It _____ .

SPEAKING A TV news story

8 **21st CENTURY OUTCOMES**

Work in pairs. You're going to create a short TV news story about the following situation using passive reporting verbs.

An unknown person climbed to the top of a university building and hung a banner from the roof.

The news story should answer the following questions:
• Who was the person?
• What did they do?
• Where did it happen?
• When did it happen?
• Why did they to it?
• How did they do it?

The person was believed to be …

The message banner which read 'Just say no' is thought to refer to …

9 Present your news story to another pair. Were your stories similar?

10.3 Follow your gut instinct

READING Understanding risk

1 Look at the risks. Number them in order of what you think is most likely (1) to least likely (5) to happen.

a ____ Being killed by a bee sting
b ____ Being injured by a toilet this year
c ____ Being killed by an asteroid impact
d ____ Being attacked by a shark
e ____ Being struck by lightning in your lifetime

2 Check the answers to Exercise 1 on page 99. Then answer the questions.

1 Which possible event seems the scariest to you? Why?
2 Has anything ever happened to you that seemed extremely unlikely or an amazing coincidence?
3 What is your attitude to risk? Do you avoid it as much as possible, or can some risk make life exciting?

3 Read the article. Put the four headings (1–4) in the correct place (A–D).

1 Look critically at statistics.
2 Be sceptical of expert advice.
3 Follow your gut instinct.
4 You probably know more than you realize.

4 Read the article again. Answer the questions.

1 Why might choosing to drive make things worse?
2 What sort of evidence do you think supports the claim about transport safety?
3 What is the usual result of visiting the doctor frequently, and why does Gigerenzer think they are problems?
4 How did Gigerenzer choose good investments?
5 What are two signs that a person is likely to make good choices based on feelings?
6 In 2011, what did the news media incorrectly report as having increased?
7 What factors work together in our minds to calculate risk – even if we aren't aware that we're doing it?

5 Find these words and expressions in the text and explain their meanings in your own words.

1 (line 4) make matters worse
2 (line 8) get behind the wheel of a car
3 (line 9) statistically
4 (line 29) medication
5 (line 45) intuition
6 (line 45) gut instinct
7 (line 59) following your heart
8 (line 64) antidepressant

6 Which statements are supported by the article?

1 I'm safe driving a car because I'm in control, and I'm a good driver.
2 I visit the doctor when I know I'm ill, but not before.
3 I don't have a good enough understanding of business to be a good investor.

4 I've been in this business a long time and I just had a bad feeling about the company, which turned out to be right!
5 If the newspaper says that something is based on statistics, it's very likely to be true.
6 We aren't always completely aware of our thinking process when we solve problems and make decisions.

7 Would you use Gigerenzer's method for choosing companies to invest in? Why? / Why not?

VOCABULARY Risk and probability

8 Complete the sentences with these verbs.

| are   increases   is   poses   reduces   run |

1 Increasing sugar consumption _____ a threat to public health.
2 Regular exercise _____ the odds of developing heart disease.
3 There _____ a one-in-11.5 million chance of being attacked by a shark in the USA.
4 Regularly eating fresh produce _____ the likelihood of a long and healthy life.
5 The chances of recovering from many types of cancer _____ high.
6 People who collect honey _____ the risk of bee stings.

9 Complete the sentences with the correct form of the expressions from Exercise 8.

1 What do you think are the best ways to _____ of becoming ill later in life?
2 What's something unexpected that has happened to you that felt like it was _____ ?
3 What do you think _____ to global public health?
4 What medical developments have made the _____ from many diseases high?
5 Do you ever break the rules and _____ of getting caught or do you prefer be careful and stay safe?
6 What's the best way to _____ of success in your work or studies?

10 Work in pairs. Discuss the questions in Exercise 9.

SPEAKING Facing risks

11 **21st CENTURY OUTCOMES**

Work in pairs. Each think of a country and the possible risks of travelling there. Write advice to a visitor, using the Internet if it is available. Think about food, accommodation, health, climate, transport, customs, etc. Take turns to tell your advice to your partner but don't mention the country. Your partner should guess which country you are talking about.

understanding
RISK

Risk expert, Gerd Gigerenzer, believes that we talk a lot about risk, but that we don't really understand it very well. In particular, Gigerenzer believes that in trying to avoid risk, sometimes we make matters
5 worse rather than better.

For example, when we hear a news story about a frightening incident involving an aeroplane, many of us will choose to avoid air travel and instead get behind the wheel of a car. But statistically, there is
10 clear evidence that even though scary things happen in aeroplanes, driving clearly poses a greater threat to personal safety than flying does. According to the World Health Organization, 1.24 million deaths occurred on the world's roads in 2010 while the per-
15 year average for deaths while travelling in an airliner is 720 people globally.

Here are three lessons we can draw from Gigerenzer's research.

A _____
20 According to Gigerenzer, we're all aware of the risk of various common diseases – cancer, heart disease and so on – and many people choose to go for regular medical checkups to try to avoid these. They believe expert advice will help them reduce the odds
25 of developing a serious illness. But Gigerenzer isn't convinced. 'I follow the evidence', he says, pointing out that there are not fewer cases of disease among those who visit the doctor regularly. 'They just get more treatment, take more medication, and worry more
30 often', he says, adding that this is another example of creating problems by trying too hard to avoid them.

Gigerenzer once did an experiment. He stopped people in the street at random, gave them a list of companies, and asked them a single question: Which
35 ones have you heard of? He then invested in those companies, and also in companies recommended by financial experts. Which investments performed better? Perhaps surprisingly, the ones named by people in the street. And it turns out that this isn't just random
40 luck. There's actually a correlation between how well companies perform and how well known they are – though Gigerenzer admits that of course there are many exceptions.

B _____
In politics and business, feelings and intuition – gut 45
instincts – are not openly considered a good guide for assessing risk and making important decisions. People often feel that if they rely on their heart rather than their head, they run the risk of making serious mistakes. However, Gigerenzer points out that people with a 50
lot of experience who have shown good judgement in the past are very likely to be able to assess situations unconsciously, and will often have a better understanding of a situation than can be expressed by complex data or statistical predictions. One reason 55
that gut instinct is important is that many systems – the global financial system, for example – behave in ways that are ultimately unpredictable. So when the evidence is unclear or extremely complex, following your heart can be a good solution. 60

C _____
In 2011, England's National Health Service reported that the number of individual prescriptions for antidepressants in the country had increased. The news media immediately interpreted this to mean that 65
more people were depressed, and ran headlines about the 'depression crisis'. But statistics expert Dr Ben Goldacre points out that while you might think the only reason for more antidepressants would be more depression, it could easily be the case 70
that doctors are writing more frequent prescriptions for smaller amounts to reduce the risk of patients taking too many pills. Goldacre cautions strongly against assuming relationships between the statistical information available and possible underlying causes. 75

D _____
In all areas of life, people regularly need to make quick decisions in situations where there is uncertainty or a lack of complete information. The mind can be seen as a set of tools: your ability to learn, your memory and your 80
ability to reason. Whether you're aware of it or not, they work together whenever you have to make a choice or decision or calculate a risk. That doesn't mean you'll always get it right, but it does mean your mind may have a natural capacity to calculate risk – one that maybe you 85
didn't even know about.

10.4 All things considered ...

LISTENING Assessing risk

1 Look at the photo. Work in pairs. Discuss the questions.

1 What kind of seat do you use for your work or studies?
2 Do you know about any non-traditional office chairs such as the one in the photo?
3 What are the risks of sitting for long periods of time in an unsuitable chair?
4 Does your country have strict rules about workplace safety, including safe seating?

2 🎧 **57** Listen to three people who are deciding which chairs to buy for their new office. Number the chair options (A–E) in the order they are discussed.

3 🎧 **57** Listen again. Complete the sentences.

1 The most obvious one is _____.
2 In light of the research, ball chairs probably aren't _____.
3 On the plus side, the high stool isn't _____.
4 One downside of standing desks is _____.
5 A final option that might do the job is _____.

4 Work in pairs. Discuss the questions.

1 What are the pros and cons of each chair?
2 What type of chair do you think they choose?
3 Is it the same chair you would choose?

Pronunciation Saying lists

5a 🎧 **58** Listen to two people saying lists of options for sports activities they'd like to take part in during the work day. Which list sounds complete? Which list does the speaker leave open for more suggestions?

5b Name your top three favourite foods as a 'closed' list. Then make another list, describing ways you try to stay fit, leaving the list 'open'.

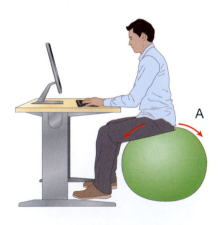

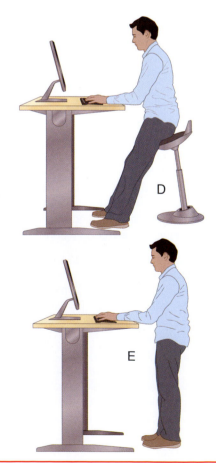

SPEAKING Health and safety issues

6 Work in groups of three. Read the new health and safety measures. Discuss options and decide the best way to implement them.

MEMO

RE: Health and Safety Measure Enforcement

From next week, all offices must enforce the following health and safety measures:

- All workers must have access to outdoor space in which to play sport.
- Equipment for at least three different ball sports must be supplied.
- At least three healthy options must be included in all food or drinks machines.
- All employees must have access to at least one organized indoor physical fitness session per day: a basic exercise class, yoga, martial arts, etc.

DISCUSSING ALTERNATIVES

Presenting options

There are some pretty interesting options to choose from.
Possibly the most obvious one is … as long as …
A third alternative that might do the job is …
… is another option to consider.

Discussing pros and cons

One downside/drawback of this option is …
What's not so great about this choice is …
On the plus side, …
On the minus side …
… makes this a very attractive possibility.

Considering options

Considering the price, I'm not sure this is the best option.
In light of the research, ball chairs probably aren't the best option.
All things considered, it makes sense to go with …
Ultimately, the best choice seems to be …

WRITING A consumer review

7 Read the online reviews of a ball chair. Match each star-rating/summary (1–3) with the correct review (A–C).

1 ★ ★ ★ ★ ★ I love it
2 ★ ★ ★ Pretty good
3 ★ ★ Not worth it

A I purchased this chair in an effort to address my lower-back problems – I work all day at a fairly demanding desk job. I can sit on this chair reasonably comfortably for periods of about twenty minutes, but after that I need to get up for a stretch. But maybe that's the point? My back pain hasn't gone away, but after two weeks with the chair, it is slightly better, so I'll continue using it.

B Considering it's sold as an office chair, I was a bit surprised to find that it's lower than a conventional office chair and therefore too low for my desk. I feel like a ten-year-old kid sitting at a grown-up's desk! If I use the chair at my desk, I'm sure it will mess up my back. So overall, the ball chair has been rather disappointing. On the plus side, I quite like using it when I'm not at my desk, but what I really need is a desk chair I can use.

C When I ordered this, I was a little concerned that it would be of poor quality, considering the fairly low price. As turns out, this chair is actually rather a good deal! I find that a standard desk chair gets uncomfortable for me pretty quickly – a matter of twenty minutes or half an hour. But with this one, I'm able to sit for long periods of time, and my back problems, which have always been a bit of an annoyance, are now non-existent.

Writing skill Using qualifiers

8a Look at these words from the reviews. Answer the questions.

fairly	reasonably	slightly	a bit
rather	quite	a little	pretty
rather a	a bit of		

1 What kind of word is being qualified in each case?
2 What effect does the qualifier have on this word?

See page 80 for more information about qualifiers, and do Exercises 5–7.

8b Add the qualifiers to the sentences.

1 You've been working hard recently so you deserve a holiday. (quite)
2 I'm afraid we were late arriving at the meal last night. (a little).
3 They had a quiet day at the office because most of the staff were on a course. (rather)
4 I'm having a problem with my computer crashing all the time. (a bit of)
5 They finished the work quickly. (reasonably)

9 **21st CENTURY OUTCOMES**

Think of something you have bought recently that you would give a three-out-of-five (3/5) star rating. Write an online review of it. Use qualifiers.

10 Exchange your review with your partner.

LISTENING TRIODOS BANK

1 🎧 **59** Read the introduction and listen to the podcast about Triodos Bank. Then answer the questions.

1 What were some of the results of the global financial crisis of 2007 mentioned in the podcast?
2 What types of business does Triodos support with investment?
3 What sector of business is each of the three named examples engaged in?

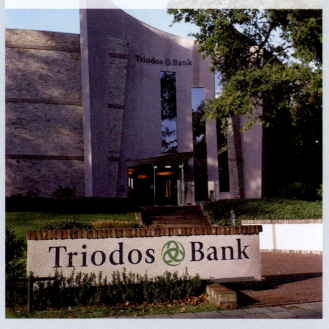

Triodos Bank, with its headquarters in Zeist, in the Netherlands, offers sustainable banking services to nearly 100,000 savers and provides finance for hundreds of organizations such as social enterprises, fair trade businesses, organic farms and renewable energy generators.

2 🎧 **59** Listen again. Choose the correct word or phrase (a, b or c) to complete these sentences.

1 Many customers moved to sustainable banking because they _____ .
 a didn't like increased regulation
 b no longer trusted mainstream banking
 c wanted to earn more from their savings

2 Triodos would not invest its customers' money in a company that was involved in _____ .
 a making weapons
 b food production
 c social work

3 Triodos's philosophy is that a bank
 a shouldn't make a profit
 b can't be both ethical and competitive
 c can be ethical and offer good returns

4 In addition to growing food, Belle Vue Farm _____ .
 a hosts music festivals
 b offers accommodation
 c manufactures camping gear

5 Key Driving Competences _____ .
 a makes in-car electronics
 b trains people to drive electric cars
 c has developed an alternative fuel source

6 Escuela del Actor has students _____ .
 a from the national government
 b who work in factories
 c of all ages

3 Would you like to do business with an ethical bank such as Triodos? Why or why not?

GRAMMAR

4 Complete the text with the correct form of the reporting verbs.

¹_____ (It / believe) that the concept of money, as we know it today, didn't appear in one place all at once, rather it emerged gradually in many different cultures around the world. The first 'cash' ²_____ (say / be) commodities: grain and cattle, used like money to buy and sell other things, as long ago as 11,000 years. And seashells ³_____ (know / use) as currency on every continent as a type of coin. The first true cash – metal coins as we know them today – ⁴_____ (think / make) independently in Greece, India, Turkey and China around 2,700 years ago. Until just a few years ago, ⁵_____ (it / not thought) that the world would ever be without notes and coins. However, despite its long history, cash ⁶_____ (report / be) under threat as more forms of electronic payment, including contactless cards and mobile phone payments, become more common.

5 Choose the correct options to complete these sentences.

A: I heard something ¹*really / the least bit* surprising today.
B: What was that?
A: City buses are going to stop taking cash ²*incredibly / entirely*. You have to pay either by contactless credit or debit card, or with a transport card.
B: You mean they'll take no cash ³*whatsoever / totally*?
A: Right. It will be ⁴*absolutely / very* impossible to travel without a card of some kind. It's going to be ⁵*completely / extremely* cashless.
B: That won't be ⁶*utterly / at all* convenient for out-of-town visitors who don't have a card, will it?

VOCABULARY

6 Complete the texts with words related to the body.

It makes my [1]_____ boil when I read about cyber criminals stealing people's bank details – and their money – over the Internet, so I don't use the Internet for banking. Sometimes it is a pain in the [2]_____ going out to the bank, but I'm sure it's safer.

When I borrowed a lot of money for university, I worried that I was getting in over my [3]_____ financially, but I'm glad I got my education. When I finally finished paying off the loans, it was a big weight off my [4]_____. I was very lucky to get a job quickly. Sometimes I complain when I'm up to my [5]_____ in work and feel too busy, but a little stress keeps you on your [6]_____, doesn't it? It's certainly better than being unemployed.

Last year, I almost borrowed a large sum of money for a new car, but at the last minute, I got cold [7]_____ and didn't take the loan. I decided instead to carry on cycling and using public transport. When the opportunity came up for me to leave my 9–5 office job in England and work for a year on an organic farm in Australia, I was able to do it, because I had some savings. Arriving in a hot country was a real shot in the [8]_____. I loved working outdoors and was finally able to let my [9]_____ down.

7 Match the two parts of the sentence.

1 Some say that too much regulation in banking is
2 Regular saving reduces
3 There is much less than
4 Careful financial planning increases
5 The chances are
6 If you aren't careful with your credit card details, you run

a a one-in-a-million chance of a big win in the lottery.
b high that there will be another global economic crisis.
c a threat to economic growth.
d the risk of being a fraud victim.
e the odds of ending up with no money in retirement.
f the likelihood of reaching your financial goals.

DISCUSSION

8 Work in pairs. Discuss the questions.

1 In addition to banking, what other ethical or sustainable businesses are you aware of? What features make them ethical or sustainable?
2 What features do you look for in a bank? Good interest rates? Good customer service? Something else?
3 What are the pros and cons of a cashless society?

SPEAKING

9 Two friends are discussing which tablet to buy. Put the phrases (a–l) in the correct order. Then use them to complete the conversation below.

a are / choose / from / interesting / options / pretty / some / There / to
_____

b a / got / Have / minute / you
_____

c On / side / the / plus
_____

d can / do / for / I / What / you
_____

e an / attractive / it / makes / possibility
_____

f minus / on / side / the
_____

g a / ask / favour / have / I / to
_____

h any / could / I / Is / there / way
_____

i All / considered / things
_____

j doesn't / Don't / it / matter / worry,
_____

k a / Actually, / awkward / bit / that's
_____

l is / The / thing
_____

A: [1]_____ ?
B: Sure. [2]_____ ?
A: I want to buy a new tablet, and I know you just bought one. Which one do you think is the best?
B: [3]_____. The first thing to think about is size. Do you want a 175 millimetre one, or a 250?
A: Which size did you buy?
B: I went for a 175. [4]_____, it's very small and light to carry, but [5]_____, the screen is pretty small and can be hard to read, sometimes. Of course the lower price [6]_____.
A: You're right about that! [7]_____, I'll probably go for the smaller size. But …
   [8]_____.
B: Yes?
A: [9]_____, I've just started my new job, but I have to wait a couple of weeks for my first pay cheque. [10]_____ borrow some money from you?
B: [11]_____.
A: [12]_____.

11 Vision

Cliff-hanging walkway on Tianmen Mountain in Hunan Province, China.

TEDTALKS

DIÉBÉDO FRANCIS KÉRÉ grew up in Gando, a small village in the African nation of Burkina Faso. After completing his education and starting work as an architect, he decided to give back to the community that raised him. He does that through the power of architecture. In this talk, Kéré shows off some of the beautiful structures he's helped to build in his small village. Diébédo Francis Kéré's idea worth spreading is that we all benefit from and can give back to our communities, and that those contributions can have profound effects.

BACKGROUND

1 You are going to watch a TED Talk by Diébédo Francis Kéré called *How to build with clay … and community*. Read the text about the speaker and the talk. Then work in pairs and answer the questions.

1 What do you know about Burkina Faso? What do you think life is like there?

2 In Burkina Faso, Kéré builds with clay. What do you think might be the advantages of building with clay? What about the disadvantages?

3 What building materials are the most common in the place where you live?

KEY WORDS

2 Read the sentences (1–6). The words in bold are used in the TED Talk. First guess the meaning of the words. Then match the words with their definitions (a–f).

1 When glass was first put in windows, it was considered a major architectural **innovation**.

2 We tested the **prototype** and discovered several ways we could improve it.

3 We need to improve the **ventilation** because the building gets far too hot in the summer.

4 Very thin clay walls are beautiful but can be **fragile**.

5 The builders **cast** concrete to make the walls of the building.

6 The dirt on the road was **compressed** by the traffic and became very hard.

a easily broken
b flattened, pressed down
c a new method or idea
d a system of providing fresh air to a room or building
e pour liquid into a pre-made shape, so it hardens and makes something solid
f the first version of something

AUTHENTIC LISTENING SKILLS Dealing with accents: different stress patterns

Sometimes, non-native English speakers such as Diébédo Francis Kéré stress different syllables in a word or words in a sentence from those that a native English speaker would stress.

For example, he says *rainy **seas**on* rather than the standard English ***rain**y season* .

Being aware of this and listening to a variety of accents will help you be able to pick out familiar words and phrases even when they are not pronounced as a native English speaker would say them.

3a 🎧 **60** Look at the Authentic listening skills box. Listen to this sentence pronounced first by Kéré in his TED Talk and then by a native British English speaker. Compare the pronunciation of the underlined word.

I would like to show you how <u>architecture</u> has helped to change the life of my community.

3b 🎧 **61** Listen to this sentence pronounced by Kéré and then by a native British English speaker. Underline the word that is stressed by the speaker in each version of the sentence.

1 What does it look like to grow up in a place like that?
2 What does it look like to grow up in a place like that?

3c 🎧 **62** Listen to another extract. Complete the text.

I am an [1] _____ of that. I was born in a little [2] _____ called Gando. In Gando, there was no electricity, no access to clean [3] _____, and no school. But my father wanted me to learn how to read and write. For this reason, I had to leave my [4] _____ when I was seven and to stay in a city far away from my village with no contact with my family. In this place I sat in a class like that with more than 150 other [5] _____, and for six years.

11.1 How to build with clay and community

TEDTALKS

1 ▶ **11.1** Watch the TED Talk. Note down details about Diébédo Francis Kéré's life.

Hometown and early life:
School days:
University:
Return to Gando:
Challenges of the first project in Gando:
Other projects in Gando:
Other challenges in Gando:
A final story from his childhood:

2 ▶ **11.1** Watch the first part (0.00–6.07) of the talk again. Are the statements true (T) or false (F)?

1 Today, Gando is much more modern than when Kéré was a child.
2 When he was an architecture student, Kéré raised US $50,000 to build a school.
3 At first the people of Gando didn't like Kéré's plans for building the school.
4 Clay is never used as a construction material in Burkina Faso.
5 The main design considerations for the building were to make it large enough and cheap to build.

3 ▶ **11.1** Complete the notes on the second part of the talk. Then watch the second part (6.08–9.18) of the talk again and check your answers.

cast mud	clay pots	clay walls	extension
high school	library	prototype	rain

- The school [1] _____ : built a(n) [2] _____ to test whether the construction was strong enough
- The [3] _____ : used [4] _____ in the roof structure to allow heat out and light in
- The [5] _____ : used [6] _____ – very similar to concrete
- The fragile [7] _____ : had to be protected from the [8] _____ during construction

4 ▶ **11.1** Watch the third part (9:19 to the end) of the talk again. Answer the questions.

1 In addition to the buildings, what benefit has Kéré's work brought to his community?
2 What is Kéré's main motivation for doing his work?
3 Why, according to Kéré's mother, did the women of his community give him money?

VOCABULARY IN CONTEXT

5 ▶ **11.2** Watch the clips from the TED Talk. Choose the correct meaning of the words.

6 Complete the sentences in your own words. Then discuss with a partner.

1 For me, it would be a privilege to …
2 I would be happy to participate in fundraising for …
3 When … , I was over the moon.

CRITICAL THINKING Relevance

7 Kéré says he hopes he was able to prove the power of community and show that architecture can inspire communities to shape their own future. Why was each of the following relevant to the talk?

1 He tells us about the poverty in Gando.

This is relevant because it helps us understand the community he comes from.

2 He talks about fundraising while an architecture student in Germany.
3 He explains the traditional process of making a hard clay floor.
4 He talks about Burkina Faso's climate.
5 He explains that usually, young men from Gando have to leave the village and work far away.

8 For both speakers and commenters, it's important to focus on ideas that are relevant. Read the comments* about the TED Talk. Which two are relevant to Kéré's talk? Which one is not?

Viewers' comments

J JJ312 – I love this talk. We so often think of buildings as places in a community, but Kéré shows that the process of building is just as important as the result and that working together can make a community stronger. That's a very valuable lesson that we all should learn.

C Cowboy – As Kéré points out, the rains are definitely a big feature of life in Burkina Faso. They're necessary for farmers or for anyone who is trying to grow food for the community or raise animals. When the rains don't come, it can create serious problems for the community.

C ClarkKent – It's wonderful to see that Kéré's designs work with nature. He doesn't try to find a way to generate electricity in Gando to run air conditioning – he instead designs a building that will be naturally cool and light. Great work!

*The comments were created for this activity.

PRESENTATION SKILLS Varying your tone of voice

Your tone of voice is the overall quality of your voice, including pitch and volume. When you're nervous, you may sound more hesitant or speak in a monotone, without raising or lowering your voice. Try to vary your tone of voice. Doing so can:

- help keep your audience interested
- emphasize key ideas
- convey your enthusiasm for what you're saying

For example, when you briefly lower your voice and speak quietly, for emphasis, it can grab the audience's attention more than raising it. However, it's important not to change your voice so much that it's artificial.

9 ▶ **11.3** Look at the Presentation tips box. Then watch the clip from the TED Talk and notice how Kéré varies his tone. Answer the questions.

1 At the start, is Kéré's voice more excited and passionate or calm and quiet?
2 What's his tone of voice when he describes the finished floor, saying 'And then you have this result, very fine'? What do you feel this tone communicates?
3 What's his general tone as he says 'It can be 45 degrees in Burkina Faso', and then describes his design?
4 What tone does he end on?

10 Think of a time when something exciting happened to you, for example, you won something, accomplished a difficult task, or had a nice surprise. Prepare how you will describe it to a partner. Think of the tone of voice you will use at each stage.

11 Work in pairs. Take turns to give a presentation in which you tell your story.

WHAT IS GEOTOURISM?

ECOTOURISM
visiting unspoiled places, supporting conservation

CULTURAL TOURISM
discovering the lifestyle and customs of different people

INDIGENOUS TOURISM
visiting native lands, often to buy arts and crafts

HERITAGE TOURISM
learning about the history and art of different places

FOOD TOURISM
sampling local dishes and going to food festivals

AGRITOURISM
going to vineyards, farms and ranches

SIGHTSEEING
looking around places of cultural importance and natural beauty

LOCAL PRODUCE

GRAMMAR Subordinate clauses

1 Work in pairs. Discuss the questions.

1 Is your country popular with tourists? Why? / Why not?
2 Where have you travelled / would you like to travel?
3 What benefits / problems can tourism bring to a country?

2 Look at the infographic. Answer the questions.

1 What kinds of places are ecotourists most interested in seeing?
2 Which type of tourism is concerned with native people? history? farming?

3 Read the text in the Grammar box. Answer the questions (1–5).

SUBORDINATE CLAUSES

Considering that global tourism is often blamed for ruining popular holiday destinations, the notion that tourism could save the world might seem surprising. But that's what geotourism's supporters claim, **in spite of the fact that** this is an apparent contradiction. **In case** you are unfamiliar with the idea of geotourism, the most popular definition of this very 21st century concept is leisure travel that enhances the environment, culture, and the well-being of tourist destinations.

Compared to mainstream tourism, which often comes at the expense of unwanted change to local communities, geotourism:

- unites communities and encourages local people and businesses to work together to provide visitors with a real experience.
- informs both visitors and hosts. Residents discover their own history **when** they learn what is interesting to visitors.
- brings economic benefits to the hosts **provided that** businesses use local workers, services and supplies.

While geotourism's vision can't solve all of the world's problems, perhaps it can nonetheless make the world a better place.

Which expression in bold means that:

1 something will happen at the same time as something else? (time)
2 you are referring to a factor that is already known? (cause)

Check your answers on page 82 and do Exercises 1–6.

3 something will happen only if something else happens? (condition)
4 something will happen even though something else seems in conflict with this idea? (contrast)
5 something might or might not be a factor? (precaution)

4 Complete the text with these conjunctions.

> although   by the time   given that   in spite of   in view of

¹_____ many people think of tourism as a jet-age pastime, some would argue that it's actually been around since ancient times. ²_____ the fact that travel was difficult and dangerous, we have several accounts including Pausanias's *Description of Greece* written in the second century, and the journals of fourteenth-century Arab traveller Ibn Batutta to prove that tourism has been popular for many hundreds of years. ³_____ Batutta returned home for the last time, he had been all over Africa, Asia, Eastern Europe and the Middle East – keeping a journal throughout. He's still considered one of the greatest travellers of all time. However, ⁴_____ the fact that all of this travel was such hard work, is it really right to call it tourism? Some people have described Petrarch's climbing of Mont Ventoux – also in the fourteenth century – as the first instance of 'modern' tourism, ⁵_____ his purpose in climbing the mountain was simply to enjoy the view.

5 Join the two sentences using the conjunction in brackets. There may be more than one position in the sentence you can place the conjunction. Use appropriate punctuation.

1 The country has beautiful beaches. Tourists hardly ever visit them. (although)
2 Upper-middle-class people are generally comfortable financially. They frequently travel abroad. (since)
3 Students often spend a few months abroad before starting university. They can save enough money for their travels. (providing that)
4 The weather is terrible. Visitors stay in the hotel rather than going out on a tour. (in the event that)
5 Visitors first arrive in the jungle camp. They're amazed at how beautiful it is. (every time)
6 One study found that single working people prefer to take holidays abroad. Families with young children often like to holiday closer to home. (whereas)

6 Look at the statements about travel. Expand them with your own ideas to write eight sentences with subordinate clauses. Try to use each of the six types of conjunction (cause/reason, condition, contrast, time, precaution, other).

1 Tourism can be great for a local economy.
Given that tourists usually pay for hotels, food and entertainment, **tourism can be great for a local economy.** (cause/reason)
2 Extensive tourism may mean that most of the well-paid jobs in popular destinations are tourism-related.
3 Geotourism makes people feel good about international travel.
4 International travel contributes to the world's environmental problems.
5 The widespread use of English makes communication easy.
6 Some environmentalists feel that some parts of the world should be completely closed to tourism because any visitors to remote areas can cause problems for wildlife.
7 Local people such as the Masai in Kenya become a tourist attraction themselves.
8 Many Masai give up farming or other traditional activities because being photographed earns more money.

Pronunciation Intonation in subordinate clauses

7a Read the sentences. In each one, would you expect the intonation to rise or fall at the end of the subordinate clause?

1 Although geotourism brings benefits to both the visitors and the hosts, some environmentalists feel that some parts of the world should be completely closed to tourism.
2 Considering that the local Masai people in Kenya have become a tourist attraction themselves, it may be worth re-thinking ecotourism.
3 By the time thousands of divers have visited a popular diving spot, damage has been done that can never be repaired.

7b 🎧 63 Listen and check your answers. Then practise saying them.

SPEAKING Looking after what matters

8 **21st CENTURY OUTCOMES**
Work in small groups. Discuss the questions.

- Geotourism is seen by many as being environmentally friendly. Can you think of other activities or products that are described as 'green', when in reality, the greenest thing might be to avoid them altogether?
- It's predicted that in the foreseeable future, 639 known languages will no longer be spoken by anyone. 457 languages (9.2 per cent of the world's total) already have fewer than ten speakers. Is this inevitable, or should something be done to stop it? If so, what?

11.3 A personal calling

READING Visionaries

1 Read the short definition of *visionary*. Then discuss the questions.

visionary (n) a person with original ideas about what the future will or could be like; a person who sees ways to solve problems that no one has thought of, or takes action that no one else is taking.

1 Can you think of anyone who is or was a visionary in …
  a business?   b science?   c politics?
2 What qualities do visionaries often have?
3 Can you think of examples of how some visionaries have been treated by society?

2 Read the article about four visionaries. What is each person's vision for?

1 Peace Pilgrim: a vision for *world peace*
2 Jiro Ono: a vision for …
3 Georges Bwelle: a vision for …
4 Albina Ruiz: a vision for …

3 Read the article again. Are these sentences true (T) or false (F)?

1 Peace Pilgrim's main activity was to raise money for people in countries at war.
2 Peace Pilgrim relied on people to offer her life's basic necessities.
3 Despite the success of his restaurant, Jiro Ono doesn't feel that he has completely mastered the art of making sushi.
4 Ono has tried several different occupations but always returned to making sushi.
5 Georges Bwelle became a doctor so that he could better care for his own father, who was ill.
6 Bwelle now spends all of his time in a rural hospital giving free medical treatment.
7 Albina Ruiz found a way to turn an activity that people were already doing into a business.
8 Ruiz's vision wasn't to end poverty, but to slightly improve the lives of people living in difficult circumstances.

4 Work in groups of four. Make notes on the following. Then share your answers with the group.

Student A: The qualities the four people in the text have in common

Student B: The qualities that some, but not all, of them have

Student C: Anything we know about the specific motivation of the speakers – the thing that started them on their path

Student D: How each person's vision has affected other people's lives

5 In your groups, decide where each visionary is on this scale.

a personal,   ----|-----|----|----|----|---   a practical vision
inward vision   for a better world

6 Work in pairs. Discuss the questions.

1 Which visionary would you most like to join for one day? Why?
2 If you had unlimited time and money, what vision – personal, or for the world – would you like to pursue?

VOCABULARY Expressions with *look* and *see*

7 Choose the correct options to complete the sentences.

1 Jiro *overlooks* / *oversees* a team of people who make sushi.
2 People don't always *look* / *see* eye to eye about what constitutes an ethical life.
3 As far as I can *look* / *see*, the only thing to do is to keep trying.
4 Let's make some changes, then wait and *look* / *see* what happens.
5 Can you *look and see* / *see and look* what time tomorrow's meeting is?
6 I *looked* / *saw* him in the eye and told him that I really admire his work.
7 I'm on the *lookout* / *see out* for an opportunity to try something new.
8 We need to *look* / *see* into why the delivery was late.
9 I'm going to *look* / *see* about volunteering for a charity.
10 I *look* / *see* up to my mother because she followed her artistic vision.

8 Make sentences that are true for you using five expressions from Exercise 7.

I'm on the lookout for a good second-hand car.

SPEAKING Talking about visionaries

9 **21st CENTURY OUTCOMES**

Work in pairs. Discuss the questions.

1 Think of a well-known visionary. What vision did/do they pursue?
2 How do they communicate their vision to others?
3 How are they generally portrayed in the media? Does the media support them? Question them? Some of both?

VISIONARIES

How four people have made the world a better place

We all look at ourselves and our world and imagine how things – and we – could be better. Visionaries, however, devote themselves to following their vision and to bringing reality closer
5 to the ideal that sometimes only they can see.

Peace Pilgrim

On January 1, 1953, 44-year-old Mildred Lisette Norman
10 left her home in California with just the clothes on her back. She didn't stop walking until her death in 1981. The reason? To promote peace. She adopted the name Peace Pilgrim, and by 1964, she had
15 walked 40,000 kilometres. Peace Pilgrim found freedom in living simply. She had no possessions other than her clothes, carried no money, and never asked for food or shelter. She
20 vowed to 'remain a wanderer until mankind has learned the way of peace, walking until given shelter and fasting until given food'. Her message? 'One little person, giving all of her time to peace, makes news. Many people, giving some of their time, can make history.'

25 Jiro Ono

Jiro Ono's story shows that an intensely personal vision can be as powerful as the desire to save the world
30 – and can touch people's lives. Ono was born in 1925 and has been making sushi since he left home at the age of nine. At 85, he said 'All I
35 want to do is make better sushi.' 'Once you decide on your occupation', says Ono, 'you must immerse yourself in your work. You have to fall in love with your work. Never complain about your job. You must dedicate your life to
40 mastering your skill. That's the secret of success.' Although he's been working at it for most of his life, Jiro remains constantly on the lookout for ways to improve. Years ago, he learned to massage an octopus for 30 minutes before preparing it. Then he realized that a 45-minute massage
45 improved the texture of octopus, so he added fifteen minutes to the process. The deep admiration that Jiro's food inspires, and the respect his customers have for his art make his restaurant in Tokyo one of the hardest in the world to get a reservation for.

Georges Bwelle
50

'To make people laugh, to reduce the pain, that's why I'm doing this', says Dr Georges Bwelle. You might not think
55 Bwelle has much to laugh about, having experienced, from both sides, the sadly underresourced medical care in his home country of Cameroon, Central Africa.
60 For 21 years, Bwelle cared for his father through a long illness. What started as a broken arm turned into an infection that eventually spread to the brain. Whenever the situation became worse, he'd take his father to hospital only to find that the necessary medical equipment
65 and experience simply didn't exist in his country. Eventually, his father lost the battle and died. As a direct result of these experiences, Bwelle decided to pursue a career as a doctor. In 2008, he started a nonprofit organization offering free medical assistance to people in need of a doctor. Now, every Friday,
70 he and 30 other volunteers, including medical students, drive long distances over difficult roads to visit rural villages that need medical help. They've treated tens of thousands of patients. 'I am so happy when I am doing this work', Bwelle said. 'And I think about my father. I hope he sees what I am doing.'
75

Albina Ruiz

When Albina Ruiz left her rural village in Peru in the 1990s to study in Lima, she was shocked to find 'waste
80 pickers' crawling over piles of garbage, trying to make a living out of what they found there. Most of them had bare feet and hands and
85 were frequently ill. As far as she could see, there was no reason for this situation to continue. Upon completing her university studies, Albina devoted herself to helping the waste pickers, setting up a business providing uniforms, masks and
90 gloves so that the refuse collectors could work safely. She also supplied them with carts so they could deliver waste to recycling stations in return for payment. In addition, she gave the workers a management system that included training, affordable equipment and clothing, and a reliable source of pay.
95 Perhaps most importantly, she gave them a voice. Her group – Ciudad Saludable (Healthy City) – has, in addition, trained waste-management business professionals from other countries in how to create effective waste-handling systems and created employment for workers in countries as far away as India.
100

11.4 A dream come true

LISTENING Life coaching

1 Work in pairs. Discuss the questions.

  1 When you were a child, what did you want to be when you grew up?

  2 Do you know of anyone who from a very young age had a vision for themselves that they followed into adulthood?

2 Read the definition. Would you like to work with a life coach? Why? / Why not?

> **life coach (n)** a person who helps others develop a vision for the future and to make and meet personal and professional goals. A life coach's main aim is to help others become happier and more satisfied in all areas of life.

3 🎧 **64** Listen to a life coach talking to her client. Choose the correct options to complete the sentences.

  1 Carly asks Mike to talk about things he *hopes to do / he dreams of doing*.

  2 Mike talks about *making / designing* furniture.

  3 Mike talks about things that seem *very difficult to him / exciting to him*.

  4 Mike *has already spent some time / likes the idea of* living and studying abroad.

  5 Carly suggests one way that Mike could *use Spanish / learn Chinese*.

4 🎧 **64** Listen again. What does Mike say? Complete the sentences.

  1 I've always fancied …

  2 I could see myself …

  3 If money were no object, I'd …

  4 I'd love to …

  5 Wouldn't it be great …

Pronunciation Sure and unsure tones

5a 🎧 **65** Listen. Mark each sentence S (sure) or U (unsure).

  1 I could see myself writing a novel.

  2 I've always fancied learning an African language.

  3 I can envisage really enjoying a year's travel.

  4 I'd like to spend some time studying business.

  5 Wouldn't it be great to get a job on a cruise ship?

  6 I can't see myself spending all day just relaxing.

  7 I can see myself working in a restaurant.

  8 If money were no object, I'd stop working.

5b Practise saying the sentences with both sure and unsure tones.

SPEAKING Talking about a vision of the future

6

Roleplay being a life coach and a client. Take turns being Student A and Student B.

Student A – The life coach

Tell Student B you'd just like to hear a bit about some things that really excite Student B, or things Student B could envisage doing in the future. Be encouraging and ask questions for more information where appropriate.

Student B – The client

Respond to Student A. Use the expressions in the Useful expressions box and your own ideas. Use appropriate intonation to show whether you're sure or unsure.

SHARING DREAMS AND VISIONS OF THE FUTURE

I've always fancied learning a new language.
I could/can see myself studying medicine.
If money were no object, I'd buy my own plane.
I can envisage opening my own restaurant.
I'd love to see Antarctica.
Wouldn't it be great to work as a volunteer?

WRITING An endorsement

7 Read the online endorsements (1–3). What do you think the relationship of each endorsement writer was to the person being described? How can you tell?

Writing skill Persuasive language

8a Look at the positive, persuasive words and expressions in bold in the first recommendation. Then underline the positive, persuasive words and expressions used in the other two recommendations.

8b Choose the best options to complete the sentences.

1 Working with Beatta was a real *privilege / asset*.
2 I was very *honoured / pleased* with Heitor's computer programming skills.
3 Shelagh is extremely *real / good* at managing multiple tasks.
4 Joe was *an inspiration / confident* to the whole team, especially when times were tough.
5 Melinda is *impressed / proactive* and doesn't need to be told what to do.
6 Bernard has *a strong sense / an ambition* of personal responsibility.

1

I had the **privilege** of working alongside Tomas Burak for six months. He **worked hard** to fulfil his ambition of improving our team's sales performance, and was **a great example** for the rest of us. He's **proactive**, **focused** and **hard-working**. He's **extremely good** at setting goals and reaching them. I **feel confident** that Tomas would be a **real asset** to any team he joins.

2

Melody Wong joined my team as an intern three years ago. From her first day working with us, we were all impressed by her ability to understand our project's vision and to work toward helping us achieve it. I was extremely pleased when she agreed to stay on working part-time when her internship ended and even more pleased when she joined us full time after completing her degree. Melody is a great team player with a strong sense of personal responsibility.

3

Jorge Benevades is an inspiration for his whole staff. When I started working on his team, I didn't have much of a sense of professional direction. However, Jorge had vision and recommended training and project work that helped me develop skills I didn't even know I had. Rather than telling his team what to do, he leads the way and shows us what's possible. I felt very honoured to work under him. Any company he joins will be lucky to have such an inspiring leader.

9 Write an endorsement for the person you worked with in Exercise 6. You may write as their colleague, or imagine that you are their boss or their employee. Remember to focus on the positives.

10 Share your endorsement with the person you wrote about. Do they think it was a fair an honest assessment of their strengths and abilities? Was it persuasive?

12 The future

BACKGROUND

1 You are going to watch a TED Talk by Matt Mills and Tamara Roukaerts called *Image recognition that triggers augmented reality.* Read the text about the speakers and the talk. Then work in pairs and answer the questions.

   1 What types of Internet content are you the most likely to share with friends, and how do you share it?

2 What do you think augmented reality is, and what do you think it could be used for?

3 Have you heard of or used an app like Aurasma? If so, describe it. If not, would you like to try one? Why? / Why not?

TEDTALKS

MATT MILLS and **TAMARA ROUKAERTS** demonstrate Aurasma, an app that places animated images on top of a user's view of the world using a smartphone. Point your phone at a building, and on your phone's screen you'll see an interactive map. Point it at a film poster, and you'll see a clip of the film. Mills's and Rouakerts's idea worth spreading is that cutting-edge augmented reality tools will allow our devices to see and understand the world more like the human brain does – and enable us to blend virtual and physical realities in amazing ways.

The past meets the future in Medellín, Colombia

KEY WORDS

2 Read the sentences (1–6). The words in bold are used in the TED Talk. First guess the meaning of the words. Then match the words with their definitions (a–f).

1 Image **recognition** software allows computers to 'remember' and identify items and people in pictures.

2 When you point your phone at a certain image, it will **trigger** a video in the phone's memory.

3 **Augmented reality** will change how we see the world.

4 When I point my camera at the Eiffel Tower, an **aura** appears on my phone giving lots of information.

5 The software can **overlay** the background image with maps and other information.

6 We can **tag up** textbooks so that a video clip plays when the smartphone camera is pointed at it.

a digital content that is placed on top of reality on a smartphone screen

b mark or label something

c cause something to happen

d put one thing on top of another

e technology that allows digital information to be viewed 'on top of' something real

f the action of knowing and identifying something or someone

AUTHENTIC LISTENING SKILLS Listening for grammatical chunks

It isn't necessary to hear and process everything a native speaker says in order to understand their message. A lot of natural spoken English is delivered in 'chunks' – small groups of words that function as grammatical units, for example *in order to*, and *A lot of* in the sentences above. Grammatical chunks are often spoken quickly and are unstressed because they don't carry the key meaning. Listeners can learn to ignore the unstressed chunks and focus on the main, stressed content words – usually nouns, adjectives and main verbs.

3a 🎧 66 Look at the Authentic listening skills box. Then listen to the start of the TED Talk and write the main words you hear. Work in pairs. Try to reconstruct the extract.

3b 🎧 67 Now listen to the same extract slowed down. What words did you hear this time that you didn't hear last time?

3c 🎧 66 Listen to the extract at normal speed again. Did you notice more content words within the grammatical chunks?

12.1 Image recognition that triggers augmented reality

TEDTALKS

1 ▶ **12.1** Watch the TED Talk. Choose the correct words to complete the sentences.

1 Mills and Roukaerts are demonstrating their app using a *normal / specially adapted* mobile phone.
2 The picture that Mills holds up is a *modifed 'digitally readable' / traditionally painted* image.
3 Mills's phone *records / recognizes* the newspaper and the router (an electronic device for connecting computers together).
4 The dinosaur is an example of *a tag / an aura*.
5 After Mills and Roukaerts take a video of the audience doing a 'stadium wave', Mills describes *how people have used Aurasma / how simple Aurasma is to use*.
6 Pointing the camera at Mills's conference badge *triggers / records* the content that is overlaid on the badge.

2 Throughout the presentation, what real-life objects do Mills and Roukaerts either use or describe using as triggers for auras?

3 ▶ **12.1** Watch the first part (0.00–3.19) of the talk again. What exactly do the words in bold refer to in the following statements by Matt Mills?

1 'There's nothing done to **this image**.'
2 'All the processing to do that was actually done on **the device** itself.'
3 'And that linking of **the digital content** to **something that's physical** is what we call an aura …'

4 ▶ **12.1** Watch the second part (3.20–6.20) of the talk again. Answer the questions.

1 Who is not very animated (doesn't show much emotion)?
2 What has increased a lot in the past year?
3 What does Mills say that teachers have tagged up?
4 How do their students react?

▶ cell phone **N AM ENG**
▶ mobile phone **BR ENG**

▶ router /ˈraʊtər/ **N AM ENG**
▶ router /ˈruːtə(r)/ **BR ENG**

5 ▶ **12.1** Watch the third part (6.21 to the end) of the talk again. Discuss the questions in small groups.

1 Mills says that with Aurasma, 'we can literally take the content that we share, we discover, and that we enjoy and make it a part of the world around us.' Having seen his demonstration, can you explain how the app works?
2 Do you like the idea of auras? Would you use them?
3 What do you think they would be useful for?
4 What kind of information would you share using Aurasma?

VOCABULARY IN CONTEXT

6 ▶ **12.2** Watch the clips from the TED Talk. Choose the correct meaning of the words.

7 Work in pairs. Discuss the questions.

1 What sort of trickery do people use to deceive other people on the Internet?
2 What technical advancements have taken place during your lifetime that you now feel you can't do without? Which ones do you wish had never happened?
3 A paradigm shift occurred when people realized that the world wasn't flat. Can you think of another example?

CRITICAL THINKING Thinking about the speaker's motivation

8 Look at some of the phrases Matt Mills uses in his TED Talk. What do they all have in common?

Wouldn't it be amazing …
The thing that's incredible about this …
What's great about this …
It's completely free to download …
This process is very, very quick …

9 What does Mills's use of language suggest about his motivation for speaking about Aurasma? That he's trying to teach us how to use the technology? 'Sell' a product to us? Share his enthusiasm for a new idea?

10 Read these comments* about the TED Talk. Which do you think most accurately describes Mills's main motivation for speaking? Why?

Viewers' comments
R	**Rick** – Truly amazing! I really want to try Aurasma. Mills obviously wants to help the public understand the benefits of augmented reality.
D	**DLM** – What an incredible educational tool! Mills clearly shows how augmented reality will soon become part of every child's education.
J	**Jolly89** – Mills does a wonderful job of showing off Aurasma. He promotes the product brilliantly – I'm definitely going to download it!

*The comments were created for this activity.

PRESENTATION SKILLS Being concise

TIPS

Being concise is saying what you want to say using a limited but effective number of words. It compels you to concentrate on your main message and edit out any 'filler'. Try to:

• prepare a talk that isn't lightweight, but also isn't overly repetitive or too dense
• be very clear in your own mind about what you want the audience to take away
• keep sentences relatively short and straightforward
• avoid unnecessary words. Words such as *kind of*, *sort of* and *actually* can be useful, but they can also be overused
• practise and revise your talk a lot. When you practise, you'll usually find that you're able to communicate your message with fewer words.

11 ▶ **12.3** Look at the Presentation tips box. Then watch the clips from Matt Mills's TED Talk. Answer the questions.

1 How would you rate the content of the TED Talk?

|----------------|----------------|----------------|----------------|
too lightweight   just right   too dense

2 How would you rate the presentation of the talk?

|----------------|----------------|----------------|----------------|
not enough   just right   overly
explanation   repetitive

12 Think of a product or service that you use. You are going to explain how it works and why it's useful, and give several reasons why you think others should use it, too.

13 Work in pairs. Take turns to give your presentation. Follow the suggestions below and remember the advice from the Presentation tips box.

• Introduce the product or service.
• Explain how it works.
• Explain why it's useful, and therefore why you think people should use it.
• Summarize.

14 Rate your partner's explanation using the two questions in Exercise 11.

▶ world /wɜrld/ **N AM ENG**
▶ world /wɜː(r)ld/ **BR ENG**
▶ processing /ˈprɑsesɪŋ/ **N AM ENG**
▶ processing /ˈprəʊsesɪŋ/ **BR ENG**
65

12.2 They saw it coming

*Predictions made in 1900 ...
when 2000 was the*

DISTANT FUTURE

GRAMMAR Future in the past

1 Work in pairs. Discuss the questions.

1 How do you think the world will be different ten years from now?
2 How about 100 years from now?

3 Can you think of any technological developments of the last ten years that your grandparents' generation probably never even dreamed of?

2 Look at the infographic. What predictions does it make? Which ones have come true?

FUTURE IN THE PAST

When centuries turn, people invariably look to the future, and the year 1900 was no exception. Following the great inventions of the 1800s, the twentieth century **was bound to** be a time of further technological achievement. In 1900 the Wright Brothers **were about to** make the first powered aeroplane flight, and the horse **was unlikely to** rule the roads for much longer because Henry Ford **was going to** turn the automobile into a mass-market product. 1900 was the year that engineer John Elfreth Watkins **was to** write an article entitled 'What May Happen in the Next Hundred Years'. The article predicted that in the year 2000, people **would** send colour photographs and moving images using electrical signals (digital photography and television) and that trains **were likely to** travel 240 kilometres per hour. It also said that, given the increasing use of electrical power, farmers in the year 2000 were going to grow fruit and vegetables under electric lights. Amazingly, all of those came true. His predictions weren't perfect, though. Watkins also said that the letters C, X and Q were bound to be dropped from the alphabet because they were unnecessary, and that in cities, bridges and underground tunnels would separate all vehicle traffic from pedestrians.. Neither of these turned out to be correct.

Check your answers on page 84 and do Exercises 1–6.

3 Read the text in the Grammar box on page 66. Which expression in bold means:

1 *were at the point of*?
2 *was planning to*?
3 *was almost certain to*?
4 *was/were going* to to describe something in the past as if seen as a future prediction? *(×2)*
5 *probably would*?
6 *probably wouldn't*?

4 Choose the correct options to complete the text.

From 1965 to 2003, the television show *Tomorrow's World* tried to predict how the world ¹ *would / was bound to* change in the near future. Here are some things they got mostly right:

In 1967, the show featured a 'home computer terminal' capable of organizing a diary, updating the user with banking information, and sending and receiving messages. According to the show, the home computer ² *was going to be / was* so convenient and easy to operate that it ³ *was bound to be / was about to be* standard in every home by 1987 – and as cheap to rent as a telephone.

A 1968 episode asserted that gardeners everywhere were ⁴ *about to / unlikely to* replace their plants with artificial ones because they were much easier to care for. While this didn't happen, by the 1980s top football clubs began installing fake grass on their grounds.

In 1994, unknown inventor Trevor Bayliss said that his battery-less radio ⁵ *was going to / was about to* revolutionize communications in poorer countries if he could find funding to produce it. As a result of his going on the show, the Freeplay radio ⁶ *would / was going to* become a huge success.

And one they didn't get right:

In 1981, *Tomorrow's World* featured a robot that played the game snooker*. The programme suggested that robotic snooker players ⁷ *wouldn't / were going to* become commonplace – which we now know was never ⁸ *going to / about to* happen.

---

*__snooker__ (n) a British table game played with sticks and balls

5 Complete the sentences. Use these words. Some have more than one possible answer. Have you or has anyone you know had similar experiences to those described?

bound	going	just about	never going	unlikely

1 For years, I thought I was _____ to get a job in computing, but I ended up in something completely different.
2 I really loved being near my friends and family, so I was _____ to move abroad.
3 I reckoned that if I kept studying and doing my school work, I was _____ to find a subject I really loved eventually.
4 I was _____ ever to have a career as a singer, so I decided I'd better get an education and find a steady job.
5 I was _____ to catch up on some work when my friend phoned and asked me to go out.

Pronunciation Sentence stress in explaining outcomes

6a 🎧 **68** Listen. Underline the word that's stressed in the two versions of the sentence. Which one emphasizes that an intention was changed? Which one emphasizes that an intention was followed through?

1 I wanted to study biology.
2 I wanted to study biology.

6b 🎧 **69** Practise saying these sentences with natural stress. Then listen and check your answers.

1 I always thought I was going to be a teacher (and I was right).
2 I always thought I was going to be a teacher (but I became a mechanic).

SPEAKING Past views of the present

7 **21st CENTURY OUTCOMES**

Work in small groups. Discuss the questions. Try to include future in the past expressions.

1 When you were a child, what did you think you would do when you grew up? Think about work, where you'd live, family, children, travel, and so on. Did any of your ideas come true?
2 And what did you think the world would be like when you grew up? Consider technology, the environment, transport, homes, space travel, cities, communication and so on.
3 Which of the things you discussed in question 2 have come true?
4 Which have not come true? Do you think any of them will come true in the future?

12.3 Half full or half empty?

READING Is pessimism really so bad?

1 Work in pairs. Discuss the questions.

 1 Do you feel generally positive about the future, generally negative, or neither?
 2 Do you ever feel annoyed by people who are very positive or very negative? Why? / Why not?

2 Complete the sentences with *optimist, pessimist* or *realist*.

 1 'The _____ sees difficulty in every opportunity. The _____ sees the opportunity in every difficulty.' – Sir Winston Churchill
 2 'The point of living, and of being a/an _____, is to be foolish enough to believe that the best is yet to come.' – Sir Peter Ustinov
 3 'Optimism means better than reality; pessimism means worse than reality. I'm a/an _____.' – Margaret Atwood
 4 'It's a good idea to borrow money from a/an _____ because they don't expect to get it back.' – Anonymous
 5 A man interviewing for a job said, 'I'm a/an _____.' The interviewers said, 'Can you give me an example?' The man said, 'When do I start?'

3 Read the article. Then choose the best options to complete the sentences.

 1 _____ people in the world are realists.
  a The vast majority of   b Relatively few
 2 Some psychologists now believe that our _____ may change and adapt, depending on circumstances.
  a attitude   b personality
 3 Pessimism leads to a positive outcome _____ .
  a in no situations   b in some situations
 4 Realism _____ pessimism and optimism.
  a offers more benefits   b doesn't offer the same
    than   benefits as
 5 The greatest emotional benefit is likely to come from _____ mindset.
  a an appropriate   b a realistic

4 Read the article again. Which of the following statements are supported by the article?

 1 There's a time to give up and to say you've been beaten.
 2 If you expect great things, great things will come to you.
 3 If you believe enough, you will get what you want.
 4 Optimists rarely get a pleasant surprise.
 5 With the power of positive thinking, there's no limit to what you can achieve.
 6 You're more likely to get what you want if you don't think too much about what's standing in your way.
 7 Taking a pessimistic view of a situation may make a positive outcome feel even more positive.

5 Work in pairs. Discuss the questions.

 1 The article talks about the benefits of optimism and pessimism. Can you think of a time when thinking realistically about a situation is the best approach?
 2 Can you think of a time when you had a pessimistic outlook and were pleasantly surprised?
 3 What kinds of things do you think we can feel optimistic about when we look at the future of the world?

VOCABULARY Optimism and pessimism

6 Expressions relating to optimism often use light or brightness as a metaphor and expressions of pessimism often use darkness as a metaphor. Complete these expressions from the article.

 1 The optimist sees the world through _____.
 2 The pessimist always sees _____ on the horizon.

7 Match the two parts of the expressions.

The optimist says:	The pessimist says:
1 The glass is	5 The glass is
2 There's light	6 There's no hope
3 Every cloud has	7 If something
4 Look on the	
a a silver lining	e at the end of the tunnel.
b in sight.	f half full.
c bad can happen, it will.	g bright side.
d half empty.	

8 Which expressions from Exercises 6 and 7 could describe the following situations? Sometimes there's more than one possibility.

 1 I've lost my job, but it was time for me to make a change anyway.
 2 We had a flat tyre on the way to the airport – of course.
 3 This project has been incredibly difficult, but I'm really looking forward to handing it over next week.
 4 My job is going great, but you just never know when things are going to change for the worse.
 5 I don't like my job, and the promotion I've been offered only means that it will get a lot harder.
 6 There's absolutely nothing bad about my life.

SPEAKING Talking about financial decisions

9 **21st** **CENTURY OUTCOMES**

Work in pairs. Student A turn to page 92. Student B turn to page 99.

Is pessimism really so bad?

There's a simple test to determine whether you're generally an optimist, or a generally a pessimist. When you see this glass of water, if you describe it as half full, you're an optimist, but if you describe it as half empty, you're a pessimist.

And there's a third option: the realist, who sees the water as taking up 50 per cent of the volume of the glass. The truth about realism, though, is that people are rarely completely neutral.

5 Optimists are often seen as the happy, healthy people who cheerfully overcome hardship and always see light at the end of the tunnel. The glass-half-empty crowd, by contrast, are usually thought of as bringing everyone down and maybe even making themselves ill in the process. When
10 you're trying to get a job, no expert would advise that you think negatively. And no one would ever suggest that you'd be better off always looking out for the next dark cloud on the horizon. In fact it's quite the opposite in many cultures, where there can be huge pressure to be optimistic, and to avoid pessimism at all costs.

15 But have we got it wrong? Are there times when a little less optimism and little more pessimism could be helpful?

For decades, psychologists have told us that optimism and pessimism were largely matters of disposition – that
20 most people tended one way or the other, while the self-help industry has been built on helping people work to overcome negativity and train themselves to be more optimistic. However, recent research by Edward Chang, a professor of psychology at the University of Michigan,
25 seems to indicate that the situation is actually far more complex than that. His view is that rather than being a pure optimist or pure pessimist, there are many contexts in which people choose to adopt one or the other mindset depending on the individual situation they're facing, and
30 further, that people often choose the attitude that will lead to the best outcome. It's important to note that the research found that people rarely approach situations as realists, they usually choose to see things either as slightly better than they actually are, or slightly worse. A
35 key conclusion is that pessimism isn't 'bad' and optimism 'good', but rather that they're both functional. Current psychology supports the following example of strategic use of optimism and pessimism.

A woman starting a new business knows it won't be easy,
40 though she doesn't know exactly what the challenges will be. If she chooses to be pessimistic and imagine that the business venture will be more difficult than she can handle, she might decide it's too much trouble and quit without even trying. However, if she decides to be optimistic, she will accept that she will face obstacles, but will also feel 45 confident that she'll find ways to overcome them. Optimism, in this case, would motivate her to start and very likely carry her through the difficulties to success.

After a few successful years, as a result of an economic downturn, the woman is facing the almost certain collapse 50 of her business and needs to decide what to do. If she adopts an optimistic mindset – looking through her rose-coloured glasses – she may imagine that somehow the business will survive, even though all evidence indicates otherwise. She might waste months or even years hoping 55 for the best, only to eventually fail. However, if she takes a pessimistic view and sees the business as already doomed, she will then do what she needs to do to close the business quickly and move on to the next thing. This is as close to success as she could hope to come.

60 It's important to point out that we aren't simply talking about realism, which has no emotional power. In both starting and finishing the business, the realist would look at the future and say that it's largely unknown, but would have no strong emotional motivation in either direction. 65 However, both optimism and pessimism enhance the view of reality with feelings that can lead us to action in a way that simple realism cannot.

Another way that optimism and pessimism can both serve us well, depending on the circumstances, is in the 70 management of emotions. It easy to see that optimism can help us see the silver lining to the dark cloud and help us overcome worry and anxiety in difficult situations. What's less often appreciated is the way pessimism can protect us from disappointment by keeping our expectations low. For 75 example, if you were pessimistic about applying for a job you know you might not get, then the blow of not getting the job would be less painful. At the same time, if you got the job, your joy would be even more powerful because of your pessimistic outlook. So in this case, pessimism leads 80 to a more positive outcome, whether you get the job or not.

So next time someone tells you to cheer up, you can make an informed choice about whether optimism or pessimism really is the best way forward.

12.4 Is Friday good for you?

LISTENING Arranging to meet

1 Work in pairs. Discuss the questions.

   1 How do you usually make arrangements? Email? Face-to-face conversation? By telephone? By text message?

   2 What are the pros and cons of making arrangements with each type of communication?

2 🎧 **70** Listen to the three conversations. Note down the arrangements as you listen. Then answer the questions.

   1 What are Phil, Linda and Mr Dean meeting about?

   2 Where and when have they decided to meet?

   3 What two things does Phil need to do next?

   4 How is Phil's speech different when he speaks with Mr Dean?

3 🎧 **70** Listen to the conversations again. Complete the sentences.

Conversation 1

   1 I _____ make a meeting next week?

   2 I _____ have a work trip then, but it has been cancelled.

Conversation 2

   3 I'm afraid Wednesday _____ me.

   4 Friday's _____ for me.

Conversation 3

   5 I _____ pick up some things in town.

   6 Nine _____ place.

Pronunciation Sentence stress in making arrangements.

4a 🎧 **71** Listen. Which words are the most strongly stressed?

   A: Is Monday any good for a meeting?

   B: I'm afraid not. I'm away till Wednesday. How about Thursday?

   A: I was supposed to have a work trip then, but it's been cancelled. Thursday at ten?

   B: Ten would be perfect.

4b Practise the conversation using natural stress.

SPEAKING Making arrangements

5 Work in groups of three or four. Imagine that you need to meet outside of class time to plan a class party. Use your own diary. Find a time and place that you can meet.

MAKING ARRANGEMENTS

Asking about availability

I was wondering if you could make a meeting next week?
Does/Will/Would next Wednesday at eight work for you?
Is Thursday any good for you?
How about Monday?

Saying yes

Sure, yeah, I'm around.
That should be OK.
That would be good.
Yeah, I can make that.
That's not ideal, to be honest, but if we make it nine instead of eight, I can manage that.

Talking about changing plans already in place

I was going to have a team meeting at that time, but maybe I can reschedule it.
I'm supposed/meant to be meeting John but I may be able to postpone that.
I was supposed/meant to have a work trip then, but it's been cancelled.

Saying no

Wednesday? I'm afraid not. I'm away overnight that night.
Tuesday's out for me, but Thursday would work.

Agreeing

Nine next Thursday, my place. OK, I think that'll work.
Let's pencil it in.
Sounds great.

FROM: PhilJames@xyzemail.com

TO: Oak Park Residents   CC:

SUBJECT: Summer street party update

Hi All,

The planning committee met recently to discuss plans for the upcoming summer street party. Various suggestions were made about entertainment. One proposal was to host an 'open mic' session so that local residents could demonstrate their talent, but not everyone agreed that this was a good idea. Another suggestion was to hire a band with a local reputation. The objection to this was that it would be difficult to choose a musical style that everyone would enjoy. We were unable to reach a final agreement.

We also discussed food. Several ideas were put forward, including asking a local restaurant to cater the event, but with several good choices, we found it difficult to choose one. The suggestion was also made that we could invite residents of Oak Park to work together to cook for the entire group, but that wasn't seen by everyone as a good option.

In the end, it was agreed that the best thing to do would be to create on online survey for residents to complete and share their views about plans for the party. When the survey is complete, I'll send a link. We'll make arrangements for the party based on the results.

Best regards,

Phil

WRITING A group email

6 Read the email. Answer the questions.

1 What suggestions were made about entertainment?
2 What suggestions were made about food?
3 What action did they agree to take to help come to an agreement?

Writing skill Impersonal language

7a Underline the phrases that the writer uses to avoid naming people directly when reporting what was said. Why was this technique used?

7b Rewrite the sentences from the email. Use the words given to make them impersonal.

1 Lucian proposed hiring a karaoke system.
(proposal) One _____ .

2 Justine didn't think it was a good idea.
(everyone/agree) Not _____ .

3 Harry said it would be difficult to limit the number of participants.
(objection) The _____ .

4 Leila suggested that we change the date.
(suggestion) The _____ .

5 Bill, Sara and Raul all said that more research was needed.
(agreed) It _____ .

8 21st **CENTURY OUTCOMES**

Work in groups of three. Have a five-minute meeting to plan a class party. Brainstorm the following topics and then make a decision about each one.

- Food
- Music
- Venue

9 Write a group email about it.

10 Exchange emails with another group. Is the message clear? Does it use impersonal language correctly?

READING

1 Read the article about Mellowcabs. Then say if each sentence below is true (T) or false (F).

1 Mellowcabs hopes to take market share from motorised taxis.
2 Mellowcabs offer the first two kilometres free, and after that, charge a small fare.
3 Every Mellowcab is fitted with a tablet computer.
4 Local landmarks will be tagged as triggers for auras.
5 Pedicabs have been popular in South Africa since the 1920s.
6 Du Preez and Breytenbach raised finance for their venture by selling shares.
7 Mellowcabs will not directly own all of the vehicles in its fleet.

2 Are there taxis similar to Mellowcabs in your area? Who uses them? Or do you think they would be popular if they were introduced? Why? / Why not?

Mellowcabs

One of the strongest positions a company can find itself in is to have no direct competitors, which is currently the case with South Africa's Mellowcabs. With an estimated 60 per cent of South African commuters travelling by taxi, it may be hard at first to understand how the company can claim to have no competition. But consider these facts:

- 65 per cent of urban journeys are shorter than four kilometres, and Mellowcabs is the only company that has made short distances its sector.

- The company is currently the only one that earns its money not from fares, but from advertising – so every ride is free.

- Unlike typical mainstream taxi companies, Mellowcabs alone uses fully electric vehicles with zero direct emissions, so they're environmentally friendly.

In addition to more traditional advertising on the cabs, each taxi also has an on-board tablet with location-sensing software, so as the taxi approaches shops or restaurants that are Mellowcabs' advertising clients, the tablet displays promotional offers for those businesses. The company plans to add augmented reality to its tablets, too. Passengers will be able to point the on-board tablet at a local landmark – a historical building, for example – and the tablet will display information about it. There will even be the option to choose different languages, so the tablet can be used as a kind of guidebook.

When co-founders, Neil du Preez and Kobus Breytenbach, started Mellowcabs in 2012, their aim was to develop the pedicab industry in South Africa. Pedicabs are bicycle taxis that have been operating in the cities of Europe and North America for at least twenty years, and in Asia for much longer, but not, until now, in South Africa. Du Preez and Breytenbach started Mellowcabs using their own money, most of it to manufacture the first eight vehicles, and also to pay their drivers and maintenance staff. The company wants to provide employment opportunities and is aiming for 60 per cent of their drivers and technicians to be young people and for at least fifteen per cent to be women. The company also has an owner-driver scheme that means some of the vehicles belong to the people who drive them.

Cities everywhere need clean, efficient transport for short journeys, so with any luck, the Mellowcabs idea will catch on and spread around the world.

EVERY MELLOWCAB:

- is made in South Africa

- has 110 km daily range

- has a solar panel on the roof, supplying up to 35% of the vehicle's charge

- conforms to international vehicle safety standards

- has a shell made from recycled plastic

- uses regenerative braking, which means the energy from the braking process is used to charge the battery

- features illuminated body panels to increase safety and display the adverts

- has pedals, not to directly power the vehicle, but to extend battery life

GRAMMAR

3 Complete the text with these words.

although	bound	by
considering	going	in spite of
provided	was	in view of the fact that
when	would later	was about

[1] _____ Tokyo merchant and cart manufacturer Akiha Daisuke put the first *jinrikisha* (literally 'human-powered vehicle') on sale in 1869, he probably had no idea he [2] _____ to start a personal mobility revolution. [3] _____ the idea was incredibly simple, it had the effect of shrinking cities. The business [4] _____ to become a runaway success first in Japan, then in the rest of Asia and eventually beyond.

The rickshaw, as it [5] _____ come to be known, reached Shanghai and Hong Kong in 1874, and by 1875, there were 100,000 of them on the streets of Tokyo alone. Its speed ([6] _____ you had a strong man pulling it), convenience, style and relatively low cost meant that it was [7] _____ to become a hit in the rapidly modernizing cities of Asia. In spite of its huge popularity around the turn of the twentieth Century, the cycle-powered version was soon [8] _____ to revolutionize things further.

[9] _____ that it was such an important innovation to a hugely popular mode of transport, it's amazing that no one knows who first got the idea of marrying the bicycle and the rickshaw to create the trishaw – also called a pedicab. The new hybrid vehicle almost certainly emerged in Singapore. [10] _____ the end of the Second World War, in 1945, the pedicab had almost completely replaced traditional rickshaws. And [11] _____ the fact that cars and motorcycles rule today's roads, the pedicab still has a place. It's estimated that as many as five million pedicabs still play a vital role in daily transport in India alone, and [12] _____ traffic problems and environmental concerns are a part of daily life, the future of the pedicab seems secure.

VOCABULARY

4 Choose the best options to complete the texts.

A pedicab business partnership proves that differences between people don't prevent a strong partnership.

Helena Roberts My business partner and I almost never [1] *see / look* eye to eye. If I say there's light at the end of the [2] *tunnel / cloud*, he says he can't see any hope in [3] *sight / view*. If I say the [4] *glass / bright side* is half full, he'll [5] *look / see* me in the eye and say no, it's half [6] *gone / empty*. However, as far as I can [7] *see / look*, we're going to stick together, because our differences are part of our success.

Jerry Bronski I [8] *oversee / look and see* the maintenance for our fleet of pedicabs. I need to keep them on the road, earning money, so it's part of my job to assume that if something [9] *can have a silver lining / bad can happen*, it will. I'm constantly [10] *on the lookout for / looking into* potential problems: worn tyres, loose nuts and bolts, and quite literally, [11] *rose-tinted / dark* clouds on the horizon – because the cloth coverings over the cabs need to keep passengers dry in all weathers. When it comes to vehicle maintenance, you can't [12] *wait and see / see about* what problems develop, you have to stop them before they arise.

DISCUSSION

5 Would Mellowcabs be a profitable business in your area? Consider the following questions.

- Are pedicabs already in use?
- Do many people need to make short journeys? If so, who?
- Are there tourists to your area who would use them? Why or why not?
- Would the climate make pedicabs an attractive option?

6 Would you invest in a local Mellowcabs business? Why or why not?

SPEAKING

7 Complete the conversation with these expressions. Then practise it with a partner.

I think	I was supposed	I was wondering
I'm around	let's	see you
we make it	work for you	

A: [1] _____ if you could make a meeting next week?

B: Sure, yeah, [2] _____.

A: Would next Tuesday at ten [3] _____?

B: That's not ideal, to be honest, but if [4] _____ midday, I can do that.

A: [5] _____ to be meeting Henry for lunch at 12.30, but that's been cancelled.

B: [6] _____ pencil it in.

A: OK, next Tuesday at twelve. [7] _____ that'll work.

B: Great! [8] _____ then!

CONTINUOUS ASPECT

Continuous verbs are made with *be + -ing*.

Name	Example
Present continuous	I**'m working** on a problem now.
Past continuous	I **was daydreaming** when the phone rang.
Present perfect continuous	They**'ve been talking** for hours.
Past perfect continuous	He **had been studying** for six hours when he took a break.
Future continuous	She**'ll be working** until she finishes the project.

The continuous aspect is used to describe actions that are in progress at a specific time and often connects an action in progress with a later point in time. It is usually used to refer to actions that are temporary and ongoing rather than permanent or completed. The continuous aspect can refer to a past, present or future action.

> Scientists **are scanning** people's brains as part of their research into daydreaming.
> We**'ll be writing** up our results tomorrow.
> We were exhausted. We**'d been working** since five in the morning.

Note that past continuous forms are often used in a sentence with the past simple to indicate that an ongoing action is interrupted by another shorter action.

> When he phoned yesterday I **was daydreaming**.

The continuous aspect is often used:

- to describe a new situation
  I've quit my old job and I**'m working** in a bakery, now.

- to describe a change, development or trend
  It**'s getting** harder to find good workers.
  The average temperature **had been increasing** for years.

- for a temporary, but repeated action
  My laptop **is making** a clicking noise.

Sometimes the choice of verb reflects the speaker's attitude.

Compare:

> I **went** to the gym every day when I was a student (and got really fit)
> I **was going** to the gym a lot last month (but then I got lazy and stopped going).

Note that we can't usually use the continuous when we describe how often something is repeated.

> I fell asleep three times on the bus yesterday. NOT ~~I was falling asleep three times on the bus yesterday.~~

With stative verbs

We rarely use the continuous form with verbs such as *believe, know, realize, suppose, understand, agree, remember, wish* etc. However, we sometimes use continuous forms if a dynamic use is intended. Compare:

> I **realize** you will be disappointed if you don't get accepted for the post.
> I**'m realizing** he's actually quite disappointed about this.

Note some verbs have a stative and a non stative use. Compare:

> I **think** Prague is a very interesting city.
> I**'m thinking** of visiting Prague next year.

We can also use the continuous to make statements, requests and questions with *hope, wonder* and *wish*, etc. less direct.

> I**'m hoping** you'll be able to help me.
> I **was wondering** if you might have ten minutes.
> **Are** you **wishing** we hadn't left the party so early?

This also works with non-stative verbs.

> I need a lift home. **Will** you **be leaving** soon, by any chance?

Special uses of the continuous

- to make complaints and criticisms, using *always* (and other words with a similar meaning)
  He's **always** coming to class late.
  She was **forever** forgetting to lock the door, and it really annoyed me.

Future

- to speculate about what people may be doing now
  His flight was delayed, so he**'ll** just **be arriving** now.

- to talk about planned events in the future
  We**'ll be heading** south on Wednesday. We can't leave before then.

Past

- to soften statements or questions. It is often used in informal speech to report what someone says.
  What were you saying? sounds more polite than What did you say?
  'Did you know Ella was buying a new flat?' 'Yes, she **was telling** us.'

- to make an action seem less significant. Compare:
  I **talked** to the headmaster yesterday.
  I **was talking** to the headmaster yesterday.

EXERCISES

1 Choose the best verb form to complete the sentences.

1 Sam had *been trying / tried* to phone you about six times before he finally got through.

2 I dropped my keys somewhere while I *was walking / walked* to work.

3 *I'm writing / I write* my final history essay right now, to hand in tomorrow.

4 Do you think you *'ll be living / live* in Barcelona a year from now?

5 *You're missing / You've missed* the bus twice this week, so leave a few minutes early today.

6 *He's always playing / He always plays* on his computer when he should be studying.

7 Fred *is always listening / always listens* to audio books while he drives to work.

8 I finally *was finishing / finished* reading War and Peace.

9 We haven't *tried / been trying* to go to the new cinema yet. Shall we go tonight?

10 I *wasn't thinking / didn't think* George's joke was funny.

2 Match the two parts of the sentences.

1 Can I call you back in fifteen minutes? I'm having a meeting

2 I was just shutting down my computer

3 She's been working on her proposal

4 We had been working for about twelve hours

5 They'll be staying here in Singapore

a for about six weeks, and it's nearly finished.

b when my boss asked me to do some more work.

c until the project is complete.

d at the moment.

e by the time Joe finally arrived.

3 Choose the best answer to each question.

1 Are you still thinking about hiring an assistant?
  a Yes, I definitely am.
  b Yes, I do.
  c Yes, I'm thinking.

2 What will they be doing right now?
  a They will have flown back.
  b They were flying back home.
  c I guess they'll be on the plane.

3 Had he been working all night when he finally left the office?
  a Yes, he had. He was looking pretty exhausted.
  b Yes, he was. But he said he'd finished.
  c Yes, he did. And it wasn't the first time.

4 George was telling us about your new house.
  a He said that? What happened then?
  b Oh, really? Yes, we were lucky to find it.
  c I know he is. I think he really likes it!

5 I heard you're teaching in Spain now.
  a Yes, you're right. I'm going there next month.
  b Yes, that's right. I started the job last month.
  c Yes, that's correct. I've been there for nearly twenty years.

6 And that's only the beginning!
  a Sorry, are you saying? The band is too loud!
  b Sorry, what will you be saying? It's the music!
  c Sorry, what were you saying? I didn't quite hear.

4 Complete the sentences using the correct continuous form of the verbs.

1 She ___*wasn't listening*___ (not listen) to the teacher because she was extremely tired.

2 This time next year, I _____ (work) in Australia.

3 They _____ (live) in New York for six years before they finally met their neighbours.

4 I _____ (spend) a lot of time this week preparing for my next trip.

5 We _____ (have) dinner when Beata's phone call came through.

6 If it's six o'clock, Luke _____ (arrive) in Singapore.

7 Larry _____ (drive) a lorry for the past fifteen years.

8 I _____ (travel) for three weeks when I realized my passport was out of date.

5 Complete the questions to which the sentences in Exercise 4 might be answers. Use the continuous form.

1 Why ___*wasn't she listening*___ to the teacher?

2 This time next year, _____ ?

3 How long _____ met their neighbours?

4 How _____ your time this week?

5 What _____ phoned?

6 What _____ right now?

7 How long _____ a lorry?

8 How long _____ out of date?

6 Correct the mistake in each sentence.

1 He's living in London since 2012.

_____

2 Right now, I try to repair my computer.

_____

3 This time last year, I'm working for Exxon.

_____

4 When she's graduating from university in two years, she'll be looking for her first job.

_____

5 I've been trying to find the office for 45 minutes when I finally got there.

_____

6 I had a nap when the phone woke me up.

_____

CAUSE AND RESULT

We can use a number of different verbs in English to show how one thing causes or is caused by another.

In sentences with *kills, gives rise to, causes, brings about, leads to, contributes to, makes, produces, fosters* the result follows the expression.

*Fog **results in** poor visibility.*

In sentences with *is a consequence of, results from, is the result of* and *arises from*, the result comes before the expression and the cause comes after.

*Poor visibility **is the result of** fog.*

Some verbs tend to be used when the speaker or writer feels that the result is negative, and others when the result is positive. Some can be used in either context.

Usually negative	Can be both / neutral	Usually positive
kills	gives rise to arises from is a consequence of causes brings about leads to contributes to makes produces results from results in is the result of stems from	fosters

*Long working hours **kill** employee motivation.*
*Long working hours **lead to** / **contribute to** reduced concentration.*
*A sense of dissatisfaction can **arise from** / **result from** having no security.*
*Many accidents on the job **are a consequence of** / **are the result of** workers being very tired.*
*Colder weather **gives rise to** minor health complaints.*
*Noise **causes** the most problems in open-plan offices.*
*The slight decrease in traffic **resulted from** schools being closed for the day.*
*The closure of the school **resulted in** a slight decrease in traffic.*
*This policy has **brought about** significant changes in employment practices.*
*Training often **produces** improved sales results.*
*Many studies have shown that being in work **contributes to** feelings of well being.*
*A relaxed work environment **fosters** good communication.*

We can also express cause and result using the conjunctions *since, as* and *because. Since* and *as* often go at the beginning of the sentence. *Since* is more formal than *as.*

***As** his daughter was ill, he took the day off.*
***Since** his child was ill, he was obliged to take a day's leave.*
*He stayed at home **because** his daughter was ill.*

The prepositions *due to, owing to, because of* and *on account of* can also be used to explain cause. Strictly speaking, *due to* is adjectival (so used only with a noun or pronoun), whereas *owing to* is adverbial (so used after a verb and where it could be replaced by *caused by*).

Compare:
***Due to** the flu epidemic, staff numbers were very low.*
*The high absenteeism was **owing to** the flu epidemic.*

In practice, many native speakers use *owing to, due to, on account of* and *because of* interchangeably.

*I missed the first day of the conference **owing to** / **due to** / **because of** / **on account of** severe flight delays.*

Thanks to is used to explain why something positive has happened.

***Thanks to** increased funding, we have been able to help 30 per cent more people this year.*

We can also express result using adverbs and adverbials: *for this reason, as a result, therefore* (formal), *consequently* (formal) *that's why,* and *thus* (very formal or literary) can all replace *so* to talk about the result of something you've just mentioned.

*It's been a very cold winter. **As a result** / **Therefore**, staff have not always been able to get into the office.*
*It was snowing heavily. **Thus**, it was decided to abandon the expedition.*

We can also use *thus* with a gerund to mean 'in this way'.

*It has been a very cold winter, **thus** leading to more work days missed.*

EXERCISES

1 Choose the best options to complete the sentences.

1 Too many meetings *kill / result from* motivation at work.
2 Success *leads to / is the result of* luck and hard work.
3 Bad weather usually *arises from people driving / makes more people drive* to work.
4 The failure of the business *fostered / was a consequence of* bad management.
5 Bonuses often *bring about / arise from* improved sales results.
6 The band's appearance in a cola advert *contributed to / was the result of* sales.

2 Complete the sentences with these expressions.

arise	bring	consequence
foster	kill	lead

1 Poor performance is a _____ of low investment.
2 Conflicts often _____ from poor communication.
3 Changes in management can _____ to improved results.
4 Flexitime can _____ a positive attitude among workers.
5 A big success will usually _____ about strong feelings of satisfaction.
6 Strong negative criticism can _____ creativity.

3 Match each sentence (1–6) with a possible ending (a–c).

1 Traffic in the town centre gives rise to
2 Severe traffic problems make
3 Traffic delays often result from
4 Unexpectedly high traffic volumes often produce
5 Traffic jams are often the result of
6 Road works often cause

a road works.
b commuter delays.
c people late for work.

4 Put the words in the correct order to make sentences.

1 hard / is / of / result / success / the / work
2 contributes / feelings / happiness / of / sunny / to / weather
3 you / trust / people / makes / honest / being
4 communication / foster / good / in / offices / open / spaces
5 consequence / management / low / of / is / a / productivity / poor
6 high / increased / lead / sales / sales / targets / to

5 Join the two phrases using the word in brackets.

1 bad diet, poor health (rise)
2 increased productivity, regular breaks (results)
3 back pain, bad posture (contributes)
4 lack of sleep, poor work performance (cause)
5 people angry, inappropriate phone use (make)
6 networking, increased opportunities (lead)

6 Rewrite the sentences using the word in bold.

1 He resigned as he was stressed. **account**
   He resigned on account of stress.
2 Due to an increased workload this year, I will no longer be able to play in the football team. **result**
3 She decided to quit her job because she wanted to spend some time travelling. **That's why**
4 Since he had taken early retirement, he wasn't able to draw his full pension. **Consequently**
5 I got a pay rise, so I've been able to start looking for my own flat at last. **thanks**
6 Only one of the team could be promoted, which resulted in tensions in the office. **thus**

7 Correct the mistake in each sentence.

1 Unreasonable demands from managers result unhappy employees.
2 Employee dissatisfaction consequences of low pay and poor working conditions.
3 Poor computer security rises to possible loss of data.
4 Company restructuring leads to employees feel insecure.
5 Constant negativity from management results to frustrated employees.
6 Training contributes a safer work environment.

INTENSIFYING ADVERBS

Adverbs modify adjectives, verbs or other adverbs to express time, place, degree or manner. Intensifying adverbs such as *extremely*, *totally* and *so* are a type of adverb of degree, which make the words they modify stronger.

> My holiday turned into a disaster **incredibly** quickly.
> I'm **quite** sure I'll never go there again.
> She disagreed with me **entirely**.

Note that some adverbs collocate more commonly with certain words than others. For example, it's more common to say *absolutely perfect* than to say *really perfect*. A good dictionary will provide the most common collocations.

We use different adverbs to intensify gradable and ungradable adjectives. The intensifier always goes directly before the adjective it modifies.

Gradable and ungradable adjectives

Gradable adjectives can be measured on a scale, e.g. *big*: a house can be more or less big. Ungradable adjectives, on the other hand, are not measured on a scale. They express only extreme or absolute qualities, e.g. *fantastic*, *empty*.

> Gradable: *I thought my flat was **pretty small**, but compared to John's, it's **quite big**.*
> Ungradable: *No one came to the concert. The theatre was **completely empty**.*

When used with an ungradable adjective, verb or adverb, *quite* means 'extremely'. With a gradable adjective, *quite* is not intensifying. See page 80.

> They were **quite** certain that there was a link between stress and health.
> Stress can **quite literally** make you ill.

Intensifying adverb + gradable adjective

extremely, highly, incredibly, really, so, very

> One **extremely interesting** finding was that even supposedly relaxing activities like going on holiday were never completely stress-free.
> We were incredibly **lucky**.

Intensifying adverb + ungradable adjective

absolutely, completely, entirely, quite, really, so, totally, utterly

> The results of their research made the connection **totally clear**.

Utterly is more commonly used with negative adjectives.

> Our fridge broke while we were on holiday, and when we got back, it was **utterly** disgusting.

Also note that *really* can be used with both gradables and ungradables.

> Gradable: *It's **really warm** in here.*
> Ungradable: *It's **really boiling** in here.*

Gradable and ungradable verbs

Verbs, like adjectives, can be gradable or ungradable. For example, *like* is gradable and *adore* is ungradable. You can like something a little or a lot, but *adore* is absolute.

> Gradable: *I **really like** James.*
> Ungradable: *We **absolutely adore** your cousin.*

The verbs most commonly modified by:

- **completely:** *be, have, change, agree, understand, ignore, go, remove, eliminate, lose, do, destroy, cover, satisfy, forget, disappear, get*

- **totally:** *be, agree, have, get, do, understand, change, feel, ignore, forget, lose, make, destroy, relax*

- **entirely:** *be, depend, make, base, focus, do, consist, rely, separate, go, build, disappear*

In sentences with a direct object, the intensifying adverb can go before or after the verb it intensifies, or at the end of the sentence.

> She **entirely** disagreed with him.
> She disagreed **entirely** with him.
> She disagreed with him **entirely**.

When used with negatives, they go before the verb:

> We **absolutely don't** want to cause any complications.

Utterly is more commonly used with negative verbs.

> In extreme cases, severe stress can **utterly destroy** a person's health, confidence and well-being.

Verbs commonly modified by *utterly: destroy, exhaust, disgust, baffle, confuse*

Negative intensifiers

We use these expressions to add negative emphasis.

> I had **no** experience **whatsoever**.
> They were **not (in) the least (bit)** interested in the local culture / not interested in the local culture **in the least**.
> The weather was **not at all** what I had expected.

EXERCISES

1 Choose the correct options to complete the sentences.

1 The holiday was stressful, but the views from the hotel were *quite / very* incredible!
2 I *utterly / really* don't want to talk about the problems we had.
3 Evan was *absolutely / extremely* right to ask for a refund.
4 The airline tickets must have been *totally / incredibly* expensive.
5 I agree *highly / entirely* with Kevin.
6 The tourist buses are always *really / completely* crowded.
7 I'm not *the least bit / whatsoever* interested in taking a city bus tour.
8 The food wasn't *very / in the least* what I expected.

2 Complete the conversation with these words. There is sometimes more than one possibility.

incredibly	the least bit	really
so	totally	very

A: You have to be ¹_____ lucky to get a cheap airline ticket these days.
B: I know. They've ²_____ gone up in price, haven't they? But I found a deal on the Internet that was so cheap I was ³_____ sure must be a mistake! I found two London to Hong Kong returns for 99 Euros.
A: I'm ⁴_____ jealous. When are you going?
B: Next month. But it isn't ⁵_____ perfect.
A: Oh, no? Why not?
B: It's a(n) ⁶_____ long journey. We have to change planes three times, and it takes 40 hours.
A: Really?! I'm not ⁷_____ interested in that kind of bargain. I'd rather pay more and fly direct!

3 Complete the sentences with the intensifiers.

1 We were _____ hungry when we left the hotel, and we were _____ starving by the time we got to the restaurant. **absolutely / very**
2 We felt _____ exhausted after three days of walking around New York, and I felt _____ tired the following week at work. **extremely / completely**
3 I was _____ confident in our tour guide, because some of the historical information he gave us was _____ incorrect. **n't so / utterly**
4 The food on the tour was _____ delicious, but I think some people found it _____ spicy. **totally / very**
5 The weather in Mexico was _____ hot, but we _____ roasted on the beach in Egypt. **absolutely / very**

4 Choose the best position in the sentence for the word in brackets.

1 The instructions were of no _____ value _____. (whatsoever)
2 I'm afraid his advice was _____ in the least bit _____ helpful. (not)
3 I _____ loved _____ that movie. (absolutely)
4 He said _____ they're hoping to change the system _____. (entirely)
5 His email was _____ surprising _____. (completely)
6 I've had _____ an _____ exhausting morning. (utterly)
7 The house fell apart _____ literally _____. (quite)
8 I don't _____ like _____ my new haircut. (really)

5 Match the two parts of the sentences.

1 They were very
2 We weren't at all
3 She absolutely
4 We've quite
5 I think we need to throw the plan away and start over

a happy with the accommodation.
b literally been running all day.
c tired after the long walk and slept for eighteen hours.
d entirely.
e doesn't need a new car.

6 Correct the mistake in each sentence.

1 The temperature at the beach was extremely boiling.

_____

2 We were utterly late for the plane, so we missed it.

_____

3 I had not fun whatsoever sitting around the hotel pool.

_____

4 The bungalow we stayed in was very perfect.

_____

5 I'm afraid I disagree with you quite about the hotel being comfortable.

_____

6 We had so a good time in Bali.

_____

PASSIVE REPORTING VERBS 1

We can form passive reporting structures like this:

- Subject + *be* + past participle of reporting verb + *to* infinitive.

This structure can be used with present, past or future reference.

> **They are said to be** the best surfers in the world.
> The ship's captain **was presumed to have died** in battle.
> (= It was presumed then) or
> The ship's captain **is presumed to have died** in battle.
> (= it is presumed now of a past event)
> The new energy source **is expected to be** cleaner.

These verbs are often used with this construction: *allege, assume, believe, consider, estimate, expect, find, know, prove, report, say, show, think, understand.*

We can use the passive voice to report actions and events. We use reporting verbs in the passive when:

- we don't know or cannot verify the source or agent of the information
  No injuries have been reported.

- we assume the reader or listener is not interested in who the agent or source is
  They are believed to have started exploring the cave at four in the morning.

- the agent or source is obvious from the context
  100 people **are known to have been arrested.**

- when you want someone to remain anonymous
  You've been reported to be driving without a licence.

► Exercises 1 and 2

PASSIVE REPORTING VERBS 2

We can also form passive reporting structures like this:

- *It* + *be* + past participle of reporting verb + (*that*) clause
  It is known (that) ancient people climbed mountains.

These verbs are often used with this construction: *agree, allege, announce, assume, believe, claim, consider, decide, estimate, expect, fear, hope, know, presume, report, say, suggest, think, understand.*

This construction can be also used with present, past or future reference.

> **It is said that** they **are** the best surfers in the world.
> **It was presumed that** the ship's captain **died** in battle.
> **It is expected that** the new energy source **will be** cleaner.

Notice the use of *There*.

> It is known that there are many more dangerous sports. →
> **There are known to be** many more dangerous sports.

► Exercises 3 and 4

QUALIFIERS

A qualifier is a word or phrase that intensifies or softens the word that comes after it.

Fairly modifies adjectives and adverbs. It means 'to a limited degree'.

> The chair was **fairly** easy to assemble.

Quite often suggests a higher degree than *fairly*. It can also qualify nouns and verbs.

> The instructions were **quite** confusing. I didn't really understand them.
> I **quite** enjoy working standing up.
> It was **quite** a comfortable chair.

With an adjective + noun, *quite* comes before *a/an*.

> The exercise ball came with **quite a** useful set of instructions.

Pretty also modifies adjectives and adverbs, and expresses a higher degree than *fairly* and *quite*. It can also suggest 'more than usual' and 'more than expected'. *Pretty* is slightly less formal than *quite* or *fairly*.

> I assembled the chair **pretty** quickly.

Rather is stronger than *quite*. It can modify adjectives, adverbs, nouns or verbs. It can express disappointment, criticism or surprise.

> It's **rather** uncomfortable.
> It was **rather** a mistake.

When qualifying an adjective + noun, *rather* can come before or after *a/an*.

> It was **rather a / a rather** low chair.

A bit, *slightly*, and *a little* soften adjectives, adverbs and verbs. They can make a criticism sound less direct. *A bit* is less formal than *slightly* and *a little*.

> The price seems **a bit / a little / slightly** high.
> The poor construction of the chair surprised me **a bit / a little / slightly**.
> The poor construction of the chair **slightly** surprised me.

A bit, *a little* and *slightly* can be used before comparative adjectives whereas *quite*, *fairly* and *pretty* cannot.

> The new chair is **slightly** better than the old one. (NOT ~~The new chair is quite better than the old one.~~)

When we use *a bit* or *a little* before a non-comparative adjective, the meaning is usually negative.

> He's **a bit** difficult to get along with. (Not ~~He's a bit nice.~~)

We can use *a bit of a/an* before a noun.

> It's **a bit of a** problem.

► Exercises 5–7

EXERCISES

1 Choose the correct options to complete the sentences.

1 The new CEO *is expected / will be* to make big changes.
2 Flying was *been shown / shown* to be safer than driving many years ago.
3 He *thinks / is thought* to have arrived already.
4 *There are / We are* believed to be ten people in the group.
5 The two men were alleged to *have / be* stolen more than a million dollars.
6 The city council is known *to planned / to be* planning major alterations to the town centre.

2 Match the two parts of the sentences.

1 Climbing hasn't always been understood to be
2 The surfing instructor is expected to arrive
3 There were reported to have been
4 BASE jumping is often assumed
5 The shuttlecock in badminton is known
6 BMX racers are often thought to have

a four bull riders injured in the event.
b to travel faster than the ball in any sport.
c a healthy pastime.
d after four o'clock this afternoon.
e a kind of addiction to fear.
f to be more dangerous that it really is.

3 Put the words in order to make sentences with passive reporting verbs.

1 known / it / is / that / climb / for / the feeling / of / danger / some people
2 has / reported / it / bad weather / that / cancelled / caused / the climb / been / to be
3 revealed / several days / was / the / two climbers / had / that / been / it /missing / for
4 believed / at first / it / that / climbing / would / become / wasn't / so popular
5 places / generally / in the past / it / were / mountains / felt / had / been / that / dangerous
6 feelings / commonly / that / it's / and / similar / excitement / are / known / fear

4 Complete the sentences with the correct form of the verbs.

1 It _____ that there are 3000 protestors in the street at this time. (estimate)
2 It is known that the company _____ creating 200 new jobs. (consider)
3 It _____ in 1954 that the club would open to women as well as men. (decide)
4 It wasn't widely known in the 1980s that the Internet _____ developed. (already / be)
5 It _____ that the new shopping centre will attract business from all over the region. (expect)
6 It isn't thought that many people _____ the band's first few performances. (attend)

5 Choose the best options to complete the sentences.

1 My new chair is *quite / a bit* comfortable.
2 We were pleased because they performed the work *reasonably / a little* skilfully.
3 Jamie has practised a lot and is now *slightly / rather* good at playing the piano.
4 Let's go by train. It's only *a bit / fairly* more expensive.
5 She lives in *quite / pretty* a big house.
6 It's *slightly / fairly* common these days to meet people who speak English.

6 Rewrite the sentences with a similar meaning using the qualifiers in bold.

1 It was a fairly hot day. **quite**
_____

2 Rather a long time had passed since his previous job. **fairly**
_____

3 The announcement slightly surprised me. **a little**
_____

4 The holiday cost rather a lot of money. **pretty**
_____

5 We had a little problem with the car. **a bit**
_____

6 It isn't very comfortable. **rather**
_____

7 Correct the mistake in each sentence.

1 Japanese is estimated to speak by more than 120 million native speakers.
_____

2 Vikings knew to have visited North America hundreds of years before Columbus.
_____

3 The new building is expected to be cost $20 million.
_____

4 Two students are believed to have climbing on to the roof of the building last night.
_____

5 The treasure is assumed by experts in the 1950s to have been lost at sea.
_____

6 20,000 are expected attend tomorrow night's concert.
_____

7 Getting my computer repaired turned out to be a bit nightmare.
_____

8 It was a quite useful meeting in Macau.
_____

SUBORDINATE CLAUSES

A clause is a group of words that contains at least a subject and a verb. A clause can be a full sentence, but is often just part of a sentence:

She sings. (a clause that is a full sentence)
You bring (a clause that isn't a full sentence)

When we want to combine two or more ideas in one sentence, we can use multiple clauses.

The tour bus arrived.
The locals held a welcome party.
*The tour bus arrived **and** the locals held a welcome party.*

When a clause could be a sentence on its own, it's called a main clause. Two main clauses can be joined into one sentence with a conjunction such as *and*, *but* or *or*.

We use subordinate clauses to give more information about a main clause. The subordinate clause doesn't make sense as a sentence on its own without the main clause, but the main clause makes sense without the subordinate clause. A subordinate clause can be joined to a main clause using a conjunction such as *when*, *because* or *although*. The clauses usually can go in either order:

***When** you get there, be sure to ask for a local guide.*
*Be sure to ask for a local guide **when** you get there.*

In writing, you may choose to order the clauses so that the most important information is at the end of the sentence. This can help to give it more impact.

Hal shouted for joy after being rescued. →
After being rescued, Hal shouted for joy.

Note that we use a comma after a subordinate clause when it begins the sentence.

The main clause and the subordinate clause can have different subjects.

*I haven't been to Laos, **although David** might have been.*
***We** had to borrow Leanne's map **because I** didn't have mine.*

Time
after, as, as soon as, before, by the time, every time (that), once, since, the first/last/next time (that), until, when, whenever, while
Contrast
although, even though, in spite of the fact that, regardless of the fact that, though, whereas, while
Precaution or provision
in case, in the event that
Condition
as long as, assuming (that), if, providing/provided (that), unless
Cause/reason
as, because, considering (that), given (that), in view of the fact that, since, in light of the fact that
Referring to other ideas, situations or information
as far as … (is concerned), as regards

Note the following:

In case is used to introduce something that might or might not be a factor.

***In case** you are unfamiliar with the idea of geotourism, the most popular definition of this very 21st-century concept is leisure travel that enhances the environment, culture, and the well-being of tourist destinations.*

We use *in case* to describe an action *before* a possible thing happens and *if* to describe an action *after* another possible thing happens.

Compare

*Take these pills with you **in case** you feel seasick on the journey.*
*You should take one pill **if** you feel seasick on the journey.*

In the event that can replace *in case* in a more formal context.

***In the event that** a tourist becomes ill, they should contact the tour guide.*

Given (that), considering (that), in view of the fact that (more formal), *as* and *since* refer to a factor that is already known in order to introduce another fact. *Considering* is usually used in a context that indicates some mismatch between the facts whereas *as* and *since* suggest one factor is usually the logical conclusion to another.

***Considering** global tourism is often blamed for ruining popular holiday destinations, the notion that tourism could save the world might seem surprising.*
*We expected to get good service, **as/since** we'd paid so much.*

Given that can be used in both examples above.

Provided/providing that means that one thing happens only if another happens. *Unless* is used to talk about something that only happens if something else *doesn't* happen.

Compare:

*Geotourism brings economic benefits to the hosts **provided that** businesses use local workers, services and supplies.*
*Geotourism brings economic benefits to the hosts **unless** businesses fail to use local workers, services and supplies.*

In spite of the fact that, although and *even though* are used to suggest that something is true as well as another factor which seems in conflict with it.

*But that's what geotourism's supporters claim, **in spite of the fact that** this is an apparent contradiction.*

With certain subordinating conjunctions, a pronoun subject + the verb *be* can be left out or replaced by an *-ing* form or past participle. These include *after, before, since, if, when, while, until, once, unless* and *although*. This happens in certain fixed expressions.

***If necessary**, we'll pay more for a more environmentally friendly holiday.*
***Unless told otherwise**, I'll assume you'll be on the ten o'clock flight.*
***When in doubt before buying a ticket**, thoroughly investigate travel offers that seem too good to be true.*

EXERCISES

1 Choose the correct options to complete the sentences.

1 *In spite of the fact that / Because* we're trying to save money, we didn't have a holiday this year.
2 The tour company cancelled the trip to the village *given that / even though* the locals said they were welcome.
3 I always travel with a map *in case / unless* I get lost.
4 You can stay in the country for three months *until / provided* that you have a visa.
5 *As far as / Although* using our own minibuses is concerned, everything is going very well indeed.
6 *Regardless / In view* of the fact that the reviews were negative, our experience at the lodge was excellent.

2 Match the two parts of the sentences.

1 Since we didn't have enough people,
2 Provided that we can get more than fifteen people,
3 Regardless of the fact (that) we asked for a local guide,
4 In the event that anyone gets separated from the group,
5 The next time we visit Brazil,
6 Whenever we can,

a return to the hotel.
b we stop and take photos.
c we'll go ahead with the trip.
d we cancelled the trip.
e we plan to spend a week living with a local tribe.
f the tour leader was from a different city.

3 Choose the correct position (a or b) for the word or expression in bold. Add any necessary punctuation.

1 **in spite of the fact that**
   (a) _____ many people expressed an interest in the museum
   (b) _____ very few people actually visited.
2 **so that**
   (a) _____ we'd like you to answer some questions
   (b) _____ we can figure out what went wrong.
3 **when**
   (a) _____ we think people learn a lot about themselves
   (b) _____ they travel.
4 **provided that**
   (a) _____ we save enough money
   (b) _____ we're going to take a holiday abroad next year.
5 **considering that**
   (a) _____ the tourists want to have an 'authentic' experience
   (b) _____ it's surprising that they complain about the lack of comfort.
6 **unless**
   (a) _____ no one will know about our services
   (b) _____ we advertise.

4 Join the two sentences together using the expressions in bold.

1 The trip was bad value. It cost over $10,000. **given that**
   _____
2 Everyone wakes up on time. We should be able to leave at six o'clock. **assuming that**
   _____
3 Our groups are usually limited to six people. We can make an exception this time. **although**
   _____
4 It rains. We put on our wet-weather gear. **whenever**
   _____
5 We'll cancel the trip. There's any bad behaviour. **in the event of**
   _____
6 There has been a large number of requests. Maybe we should add a second tour. **In view of the fact that**
   _____

5 Complete the sentences with these words.

before	doubt	going
necessary	once	otherwise

1 If _____, the guide will stop for a short break.
2 Please stay in the bus unless told _____ by a guide.
3 When in _____, ask for help.
4 When _____ into the jungle, be careful!
5 _____ registered, please find your room and take your things there.
6 _____ leaving, be sure to settle your hotel bill.

6 Correct the mistake in each sentence.

1 In view the fact that he cancelled a month before the trip, we'll refund his money.
   _____
2 As long you bring a good pair of boots, the walk shouldn't be too difficult.
   _____
3 Can you let us know as soon as you'll arrive?
   _____
4 The plans look great as I'm concerned.
   _____
5 Even the tourists weren't properly dressed for the weather, they had a great time.
   _____
6 This is the exit you use in case there will be an emergency.
   _____

FUTURE IN THE PAST

When we talk about the future from the perspective of the past, we use a range of structures, depending on whether we are talking about predictions or intentions, and on the level of certainty and immediacy.

would + infinitive without to

We use *would* and *would have* to:

- report ideas held in the past about the future
  *In the 1970s, some experts believed the world **would** be much colder by 2000.*
  *We thought Joe **wouldn't** arrive until midnight, but he came at eleven.*

- to describe something in the past as if seen as a future prediction
  *The 20th Century **would** be a time of extraordinary change.*

- hypotheses about different outcomes if the situation had been different, using the third or mixed conditionals
  *Airships and balloons **would have** become more common if hydrogen gas hadn't been so dangerous.*
  *I **wouldn't have** called you, but I didn't know who else to ask for help.*

This construction is also used in the passive voice.
  *You **would have been offered** the job, but you'd already taken another one.*

bound to + infinitive without to

We use *be bound to* to talk about past beliefs about what was almost certain to happen in the future:
  *Cars **were bound to** become more popular as the price went down.*
  *I **was bound** to find a job eventually.*

It also can be used in the passive voice.
  *The problem **was bound to be discovered**.*

about to + infinitive without to

We use *about to* to talk about things in the past that were going to happen in the immediate future, or on the point of happening.
  *The climbers were **about to** give up when they realized they'd reached the top of the peak.*
  *I **was about to** buy an MP3 player when a newer model came out.*

It is also commonly used in the passive voice.
  *The world record **was about to be broken**.*

likely/unlikely to + infinitive without to

We use *be likely / unlikely to* to talk about things in the past that were seen as probable or not probable.
  *They had no idea when Jim **was likely to** arrive.*
  *It **was unlikely to** be cold, so we didn't take any warm clothes.*

In the passive, it is formed like this:
  *The idea **was likely to be sold** for a lot of money.*

was/were going to + infinitive without to

We can use *was/were going to* in the following ways to talk about the future in the past:

- to make a prediction based on available information which may or may not have been fulfilled
  *It **was going to** be a very profitable investment.*

- to talk about an intention which may or may not have been fulfilled
  *I **was going to** take a job as a bus driver, but I decided to go to university instead.*

- to talk about a plan or arrangement which then changed
  *We **were going to** meet for lunch, but then Dave became ill.*

- to report a thought
  *I knew **I was going to need help**, but I didn't know who to ask.*

- in reported speech
  *I told you it **was going to** be sunny today!*

This construction is also used in the passive voice.
  *The rumour went around that a big discovery **was going to be made**.*

was/were to

We can use *was/were to*:

- instead of *was going to* or *would* to talk about something in the past as if seen as a future prediction
  *The 1900s **were to** bring even more world-changing events.*

- with *have* + past participle, to talk about a past plan or expectation, especially one that wasn't fulfilled
  *I **was to have** travelled to Stockholm, but the trip was cancelled at the last minute.*
  *They **weren't to have** arrived until midday, but the flight was early and came in at 10:30.*

- to report a past instruction
  *They said we **were to** let them know what time we were arriving.*

EXERCISES

1 Match the two parts of the sentences.

1 I was about to call Rick
2 Anna was bound to get lost
3 Vincenzo had no idea
4 It was going to
5 It was unlikely
6 They were going to

a when he was likely to arrive.
b buy an old car and drive across the USA
c on her way home.
d be a cold day, so we dressed warmly.
e when my phone rang.
f to end well.

2 Choose the correct options to complete the sentences.

1 As he left, Sam insisted he *would / will* wait ten minutes for Muriel, but no more.
2 Ben *is / was* unlikely to be in the office, but we tried phoning anyway.
3 From the start, it was *going to be / being* a very difficult project.
4 We didn't think we *have / would have* time to stop for lunch, so we took sandwiches with us.
5 I was about *to start walking / starting to walk* when the bus arrived.
6 Lisa was bound *to be / being* late, so we delayed the start of the meeting.

3 Complete the sentences with these words.

bound	have	to be
unlikely	weren't	would

1 Had we known you were coming, we _____ have waited for you.
2 The project was _____ to succeed because the team were the best in the business.
3 _____ you about to quit when the pay increases were announced?
4 We thought he was _____ to win the award, so we were delighted when he did.
5 It was going _____ a long and happy working relationship.
6 A grant was to _____ been given for the idea with the most potential.

4 Put the words in the correct order to make sentences.

1 at / have / met / midday / to / we / were
_____

2 a / be / built / going / laboratory / to / was
_____

3 finish / on / they / time / to / unlikely / were
_____

4 about / announced / be / invention / the / to / was
_____

5 best / bound / decision / make / she / the / to / was
_____

6 become / CEO / had / have / I / I / if / stayed / would
_____

5 Complete the second sentence using the words in bold, using future in the past, so that it means the same as the first.

1 The car probably wasn't going to start. **unlikely**
The car was unlikely to start.

2 It was almost time for us to leave. **about**
_____

3 I was sure we would find the wallet. **bound**
_____

4 It was probably going to rain. **likely**
_____

5 We expected him to arrive soon. **would**
_____

6 He had a plan to start a business. **going to**
_____

6 Correct the mistake in each sentence.

1 The party was bound being a success.
_____

2 At eight o'clock, we thought Jim won't arrive for another two hours, but he was there soon after nine.
_____

3 We were about start filming when Marta suddenly lost her voice.
_____

4 They're going to have a goodbye party for Sheila last Friday, but she didn't want one.
_____

5 When I saw the house, I knew Greg will like it.
_____

6 It was obvious that Amir is going to get a promotion after all his hard work.
_____

Audioscripts

Units 7–12

Audioscripts

Unit 7

🎧 **37**

1 I painted for 10 years, when I was offered a Fulbright to India. Promising to give exhibitions of paintings, I shipped my paints and arrived in Mahabalipuram.

2 This fishing village was famous for sculpture. So I tried bronze casting. But to make large forms was too heavy and expensive.

🎧 **38**

I went for a walk on the beach, watching the fishermen bundle their nets into mounds on the sand. I'd seen it every day, but this time I saw it differently – a new approach to sculpture, a way to make volumetric form without heavy solid materials.

🎧 **39**

I've been living in London for ten years, but I think I'd been living here for four years when I met Ella for the first time. We'd both been going to the same Spanish class for several weeks. We'd said hello to each other a few times, but never actually had a conversation. One week she wasn't there, and I realized I'd been daydreaming about seeing her and maybe asking her out. I was suddenly afraid she'd never come back again, and I thought I'd better do something if I ever saw her again! When she came to class the following week, I finally started a conversation with her, and I asked her out. We've been going out together ever since then, and in about six months, we'll be getting married.

🎧 **41**

M = Max, L = Lucy, D = Davina

M: Have you seen this picture?
L: Yeah, it's really weird, isn't it? Where was it taken?
M: In Belgium, near a place called Châtillon.
D: What do you think happened there?
M: I'm not really sure.
L: That's odd. There might've been some natural disaster – a forest fire, maybe? Or an earthquake that completely destroyed the road?
D: Something like that. I imagine the cars were just abandoned. It looks as though people had to run away quickly for some reason.
L: And they can't've been able to go back for them, right? Why would people leave so many cars and not go back for them?
M: I guess whatever happened, the cars couldn't be moved afterwards. Or it might not have been practical to move them.
D: How long have they been there?
M: They'd been there for about seventy years when this picture was taken.
L: Maybe something happened very suddenly. What if it was an alien invasion, and all the people were taken from their cars? That may have been why they could never go back!
M: Well, I hadn't thought of that, but …
D: Here's another idea, though. Maybe the cars weren't put there all at once.
M: What do you mean?
D: It looks like a traffic jam now, but maybe someone just dumped an old car in the forest, and then someone else added one. And the trees may have grown up around them. It might not have been a wooded area before.
L: I can imagine that. One by one, people just kept taking old cars out there and leaving them, perhaps.
D: So are the cars still there? Can people go and see them?
M: No, they're not. They were taken away a few years ago.

Unit 8

🎧 **44**

4 Kids get instant feedback about what works and what doesn't work.

5 business students are trained to find the single right plan, right? And then they execute on it. And then what happens is, when they put the marshmallow on top, they run out of time and what happens? It's a crisis. Sound familiar? Right. OK. What kindergarteners do differently is that they start with the marshmallow and they build prototypes.

🎧 **46**

J = Jane, R = Rudy, H = Helen

J: Shall I get us started? … OK, the product promotion for the organic drinks started to run last week, and we all know there were a lot of … issues. Big challenges, which we've talked about a lot already. I think we all agreed that coordination was the biggest challenge. Even though we were working on the same thing at the same time, we weren't always working together. We didn't have an administrator to support the project manager, and this led to some real problems. The leadership was there, but the teamwork was missing. I'd be interested in hearing your views about how we can do better next time. Rudy?
R: I think next time, the project manager really needs to facilitate more communication – especially when we develop a campaign or promotion. I'd really like to analyse …
H: Before you continue, can I just say …
J: I know you're dying to jump in, but can we just let Rudy finish?
H: Sure. Sorry.
R: I'd really like to analyse the way we do meetings.
J: Meaning … ?
R: We have really long meetings once a week, on Monday morning, and then everyone goes off and works all week. What if we had shorter meetings more often? Maybe even standing up meetings, so they don't last too long.
J: Interesting idea. What's your take on that, Helen?
H: That's just what I was going to say! I think the long meetings kill creativity. If we're going to work well as a team, we need more open, relaxed communication.
R: Yes, exactly. I'd like to suggest we start by focusing on administration …
…
J: Any more thoughts on improvements for next time, Rudy? Helen?
R: I think we've covered it.
H: No. Thanks. I think that's everything.
J: OK, if no one has anything else, I think we can stop there.

Review 4 (Units 7 and 8)

🎧 **48**

I love Boxcycle, mostly because the idea is just so simple. If you need cardboard boxes – say you're moving house – you can go on the Boxcycle website, type in your location and find used cardboard boxes that are available nearby. The site gives you a list that says roughly where the boxes are located, their size, and the price – which is cheaper than you would pay for new boxes. If you have boxes you don't need anymore, you just enter a description of them, the price, and your zip code, and people who want boxes can contact you via a message on the website. It couldn't be simpler, and it's great that you get a little money for your trouble! It's so much more energy efficient than using the boxes once and then sending them to the paper recycling centre, or worse, throwing them away.

Hipcycle is one of my absolute favourite online stores. All of the products on the site are things that have been made from materials that would otherwise have been thrown away. I recently bought some drinking glasses there that were made from old-style, green cola bottles. They're very heavy duty, and super stylish. The stuff on Hipcycle is appealing for so many reasons: it's handmade; it's made from junk that in many cases would have gone into landfill; and best of all, the products have a huge amount of character, unlike so much of the factory-produced stuff people sell these days. On the Hipcycle website, you can shop by material – old vinyl records, bicycle parts, glass, e-waste and so on – or you can shop by category – household goods, clothes, school and office supplies, et cetera. It's such a great idea!

I was very impressed when a company called Marriott Construction did a project near my home. It was a fairly big job, and my wife and I were concerned that it was really going to be disruptive with all the workers, materials and equipment coming and going. They were turning an old factory building into modern flats, but in the process, they had to knock down quite a few bits of the old building. Well, I can't say it wasn't a noisy, dusty project, but I think they did a great job, and were as considerate as possible of the people living in the area. I used to work in construction myself, and we always used to haul away loads of old material from sites like this, then bring in new material. But Marriott has a zero waste policy. One thing they did that really impressed me was that they crushed the material from the demolition and turned it into the temporary roadway they needed to build for the project, for the lorries to come and go. Keeping the material onsite meant a lot less lorry traffic in and out of the area – which meant less noise and less air pollution – and no doubt it saved the project money. We need to see more sensible solutions like this.

Unit 9

 49

It taught me – it gave me a greater appreciation, an understanding for the present moment.

 50

In fact, we spend more time looking after our cars, our clothes and our hair than we — OK, maybe not our hair, but you see where I'm going.

 51

1   But when you sit down and you watch the mind in this way, you might see many different patterns. You might find a mind that's really, sort of, restless and – the whole time.
2   You might find a mind that's very, sort of, dull and boring, and it's just, almost mechanical, it just seems it's as if you're getting up, going to work, eat, sleep, get up, work.

 53

Conversation 1
W1 = woman 1, M1 = Man 1

W1: Have you got a minute?
M1: Sure. What's up?
W1: I have a favour to ask.
M1: OK.
W1: I don't suppose you'd be willing to let me borrow that black leather jacket of yours? I'm going to a work party tomorrow night, and it would look really cool over my new dress …
M1: Tomorrow, huh … ?
W1: I can have it cleaned for you, if you want.
M1: That's a bit tricky, I'm afraid … . I was planning to wear it myself tomorrow night …
W1: Hmmm. All my jackets are either too warm or too summery. I wonder if that denim jacket of yours would …
M1: Yeah, I love that one. Unfortunately, a friend borrowed it a few weeks ago and hasn't returned it, so I can't …

Conversation 2
W2 = Woman 2, M2 = Man 2

W2: Could I have a word?
M2: Sure. What's on your mind?
W2: I have to apologize.
M2: For what?
W2: I said I was going to take care of the arrangements for Mr. Miyazaki's visit – I promised I'd do it yesterday and let him know, but I didn't get round to it.
M2: Don't worry, we still have some time. Can you deal with it today?
W2: Sure. I can sort it out straightaway.
M2: OK, do that, and let me know what you come up with …

Conversation 3
W3 = Woman 3, M3 = Man 3

M3: Sorry, but if you have a moment …
W3: Sure. What can I do for you?
M3: Actually, I've got a confession to make …
W3: A confession?
M3: The thing is … I left an office laptop on the train this morning. I've reported it as lost, but so far, no one has handed it in.
W3: Hmmm … that's a bit awkward.
M3: I know. There's a lot of stuff in there that we really don't want to share.
W3: You're right about that! OK, well, you did the right thing letting me know. But we're going to have to get in touch with the police and let them know what's happened. Would you please get on the phone as soon as possible …

Conversation 4
W4 = Woman 4, M4 = Man 4

W4: Excuse me?
M4: Yes?
W4: Sorry, but your van is blocking my way. The thing is, I need to get my car out. Would you mind … ?
M4: Oh, sorry, I'm just doing a delivery. I'll be here another five minutes.
W4: Would it be too much trouble to move your van two metres so I can get my car out?
M4: I won't be five minutes …
W4: Look, I'm sorry, but I'm running late and I really need to get going.
M4: Will you relax?
W4: I will when you've moved your van.
M4: All right, all right …

Conversation 5
M = Manager, D = David

M: What's on your mind, David?
D: It's my pay.
M: What about it?
D: Well, it hasn't been increased.
M: I see. We talked a bit about this when we had your six-month appraisal, but maybe the situation wasn't made clear to you at that time. The point is, you haven't had a pay increase yet.
D: I'm sorry, but I just don't think it's fair. Look, everyone can tell you don't like me. That's why you haven't given me a pay rise.
M: Whoa, hang on a second, David … It's a shame you feel unfairly treated, but this has nothing to do with my personal feelings. The thing is, you've been late to work every other day for the past six months. And not just a little late, but sometimes up to half an hour late. We've already spoken about this.
D: Well, I really don't think I've been late that often, but the point is I've done my job. I've done what I was supposed to do.
M: Not really, David. The thing is, being in the office during work hours is part of what you're supposed to do. Listen, we can work through this. Let's start tomorrow. Arrive on time – or a little early – every day for a month, then we'll meet again. That's the only way you're going to get anywhere with this. Agreed?
D: OK.

Unit 10

 55

My job at Twitter is to ensure user trust, protect user rights and keep users safe, both from each other and, at times, from themselves. Let's talk about what scale looks like at Twitter. Back in January 2009, we saw more than two million new tweets each day on the platform. January 2014, more than 500 million. We were seeing two million tweets in less than six minutes. That's a 24,900-per cent increase.

56

Now, the vast majority of activity on Twitter puts no one in harm's way. There's no risk involved. My job is to root out and prevent activity that might. Sounds straightforward, right? You might even think it'd be easy, given that I just said the vast majority of activity on Twitter puts no one in harm's way. Why spend so much time searching for potential calamities in innocuous activities? Given the scale that Twitter is at, a one-in-a-million chance happens 500 times a day. It's the same for other companies dealing at this sort of scale. For us, edge cases, those rare situations that are unlikely to occur, are more like norms.

57

A = Alex, C = Clare, J = Jenny

A: OK, the next part of the risk assessment is seating. Clare, you're taking care of that one, right?

C: Yes.

A: OK, so what have you got for seating? Is it *really* a hazard?

J: Well, it is if you fall off! … Seriously, can't we just order some regular office chairs?

C: Right, well, according to the Health and Safety Executive, seating is considered a workplace hazard because it can lead to back pain, and also to problems with arms – especially seating that isn't adjustable.

J: Well, that makes sense – it's easy to see how the wrong chairs could be bad for people. How high is the risk of people having back or arm problems?

C: For people working all day at a computer, the risk of back problems is actually fairly high if the seating isn't appropriate. So we need to choose our chairs carefully.

A: Well, we definitely want to get this right. What are the options?

C: I've been looking into the best computer chairs, and there are some pretty interesting options to choose from. Possibly the most obvious one is a conventional desk chair design – as long as it's good quality, and adjustable, which almost all of them are these days. If each worker can adjust their own chair, this lowers the risk of back and arm problems. People are used to this sort of chair, so they're popular.

J: OK, so that's basically what I said before, right? We just order some standard-issue office chairs?

A: Clare, what are the other options?

C: Ball chairs are big right now.

A & J: Ball chairs?

C: They're big balls filled with air, and you sit on them.

J: And this is a huge improvement on the office chair design that's been used successfully for hundreds of years around the world?

C: It's claimed that they make your lower back stronger and improve your sitting position. But a lot of the research says that there really isn't a big benefit with these and the risk of back pain is about the same as a standard chair.

A: So, in light of the research, ball chairs probably aren't the best option.

C: Agreed.

J: Well, I guess that leaves us with just plain old everyday office chairs, like I said before?

C: Not quite. Now, since sitting a lot increases the risk of back and arm problems, I looked into two standing options. The first is

basically a very high stool that you lean against. It's very basic and super lightweight, so on the plus side, the high stool isn't that expensive. The other isn't a chair at all, it's a standing desk.

J: But we wouldn't expect people to work standing up all day, would we?

C: No. Standing up regularly is very healthy, but actually, one downside of standing desks is that they increase the risk of leg problems – because you're on your feet all day. And of course a lot of people just don't like the idea of working all day standing up.

J: OK, good. So that's out. Which I guess brings us back to standard office chairs?

C: Not quite, Jenny. A final option that might do the job is kneeling chairs. A lot of people really like them.

J: You're kidding, right?

C: They're said to be good for keeping your back straight.

A: Any possible problems?

C: One drawback of these is that you become uncomfortable more quickly. Though they're pretty good for backs and arms, there's some risk of leg problems with these.

J: That doesn't sound very good.

C: On the plus side, they're adjustable. But a lot of people really don't like them just because they're so different.

A: Thanks, Clare. That was incredibly thorough.

J: It certainly was! All things considered, don't you think the choice is obvious?

 58

1   I love the idea of doing some fitness activities. I'd like to see yoga, aerobics, kung fu …

2   For ball sports, we should choose basketball, football or rugby.

Review 5 (Units 9 and 10)

59

The global financial crisis which began in 2007 eventually led to the failure of banks around the globe. It also resulted in changes in laws regulating the finance industry, to avoid such a catastrophe happening again. Since that time, an increasing number of the customers who felt betrayed by the banking system have taken their business out of the mainstream and into the sustainable – also called the ethical – banking sector. Today, we'll look at one sustainable banking success story: Triodos Bank.

Triodos opened for business in the Netherlands in 1980, and has since expanded to Belgium, Germany, Spain and the UK. Like any bank, it's a business and therefore needs to make a profit to survive. However, the company believes that they shouldn't earn income from any activity that harms the environment, promotes social inequality or injustice, or harms communities. This means that the company actively invests its customers' money in small to medium-sized businesses that the bank believes are a positive force in the world: fair trade enterprises, social housing, green energy projects, organic agriculture, and so on. Equally, it doesn't invest in businesses that can be linked to social or environmental harm, such as weapons manufacturers or producers of fossil fuels.

In the past, the relationship between ethics and profits was seen as either/or – a bank could be ethical, or it could be profitable, but it couldn't be both. But ethical banking has come of age, especially since the financial crisis. Nowadays, the financial returns from sustainable banking are competitive and the social, cultural and environmental returns are better understood and more greatly appreciated.

One key feature of Triodos is that its customers know how their money is being used. I'll tell you about three of them, just to give you a flavour.

Belle Vue Farm, in Wiltshire, UK, is owned by Joe and Izzy Dyke, who are the third generation to work on the 110-acre farm. In addition to raising organic produce, they offer holiday tents and weekly tours explaining the benefits of organic farming.

Key Driving Competences of Leuven, Belgium, knows that driving is essential in some businesses. Given the necessity of driving, the company believes that drivers can still reduce their impact on the environment by learning to drive more economically – and more safely. They've developed an in-car electronic monitoring system that measures drivers' behaviours and can help them alter their driving to reduce fuel consumption by up to 30%.

Graduates of Escuela del Actor, an acting school in Valencia, Spain, have performed in local, regional and national productions. In addition to training actors, the school also serves the community by organising shows and workshops for everyone, from young children to seniors.

In very practical ways, Triodos makes money work for positive change in society, the environment and culture – and everyone wins.

Unit 11

 62

But what does it look like to grow up in a place like that? I am an example of that. I was born in a little village called Gando. In Gando, there was no electricity, no access to clean drinking water, and no school. But my father wanted me to learn how to read and write. For this reason, I had to leave my family when I was seven and to stay in a city far away from my village with no contact with my family. In this place I sat in a class like that with more than 150 other kids, and for six years.

🎧 63

1 Although geotourism brings benefits to both the visitors and the hosts, some environmentalists feel that some parts of the world should be completely closed to tourism.
2 Considering that the local Masai people in Kenya have become a tourist attraction themselves, it may be worth re-thinking ecotourism.
3 By the time thousands of divers have visited a popular diving spot, damage has been done that can never be repaired.

🎧 64

C = Carly, M = Mike

C: Today, Mike, I'd like you to think about – and talk about – the future. But allow your thoughts free rein. I want to encourage you to explore what your dreams might be. So to begin with, we'll just forget about where you are now, and we won't worry about what feels reasonable or responsible or realistic or possible, we'll just get some ideas out there. I'd just like to hear a bit about some things that really excite you, or things you could envisage yourself doing in the future. Maybe think back to when you were a kid and you talked about what you wanted to do when you grew up. Think with that kind of freedom, that kind of openness.
M: OK, sure. Er … I've always fancied doing something with my hands. You know, making things?
C: OK, good. What sort of thing can you see yourself making?
M: You know, somehow I could see myself making furniture. I've never tried woodworking, so I have no experience with it, but I very much admire well-made furniture.
C: Forget about whether or not you'd be good at it. Let's just focus on the idea of making furniture.
M: OK.
C: So if money were no object, you think you might like to learn about furniture making?

M: Well, yeah. You know, if money were no object, I'd love to study furniture making … if we're not really thinking about what seems feasible or sensible.
C: OK, good.
M: One other thing: I could see myself spending some time in another country. I think languages are really interesting, and I'd love to learn to speak another language well. Going overseas would be a great way to do that.
C: Yes, I can see the appeal of that. Is there a language you're especially interested in?
M: Good question, and I'm not sure of the answer. I learned some Spanish at school, but I didn't carry on with it – my parents didn't really think it was important. … Wouldn't it be great to learn something really different from Spanish, like Chinese?
C: Chinese, wow! I can see you like a challenge!
M: Well, you said not to worry about what's actually possible, right?
C: Yes, right. And I wonder if you've ever thought about something like going abroad to study a craft? How about looking into woodworking courses in Spain or something like that?
M: I'd never thought about it, but why not?

Unit 12

🎧 66

So wouldn't it be amazing if our phones could see the world in the same way that we do, as we're walking around being able to point the phone at anything, and then have it actually recognize images and objects like the human brain, and then be able to pull in information from an almost infinite library of knowledge and experience and ideas.

🎧 70

Conversation 1
L = Linda, P = Phil

L: Hello?
P: Hi, Linda. Phil.
L: Oh, hi. How you doing?
P: Fine, thanks. You all right?
L: Yeah, fine, thanks. Busy.
P: Linda, I was wondering if you could make a meeting next week? We need to plan the summer street party.
L: This is great timing. I was supposed to have a work trip then, but it's been cancelled, so I'm around.
P: Would Wednesday work for you?
L: That should be OK. What time?
P: Evening? Eight o'clock? Here at my place.
L: Yeah, I can make that.
P: Great. See you then.
L: OK, bye.

Conversation 2
MD = Mr Dean, P = Phil

MD: Hello?
P: Hello, Mr Dean. This is Phil Johnson.
MD: Oh, hello Phil. How are you?
P: I'm very well, Mr. Dean. How are things with you?
MD: I can't complain. Now, what can I do for you?
P: As you know, I'm trying to organize a meeting with you and Linda Smith to plan the summer street party. Would next Wednesday at eight work for you?
MD: Wednesday? Weren't we going to meet on Tuesday night?
P: Yes, we were supposed to, but something came up for me, and now I can't make Tuesday.
MD: I'm afraid Wednesday won't work for me. I'm away overnight that night. We're going to see my daughter in Bristol. I could make Thursday.

P: Hmmm. Friday's definitely out for me, but Thursday would work. I'll have to get back to Linda, though. She was fine with Wednesday, but I'm not sure about Thursday. Anyway, let's pencil it in.

MD: That sounds good, Phil. Thank you.

P: Thank you, Mr Dean. Goodbye.

Conversation 3

L = Linda, P = Phil

L: Hello?

P: Linda, hi, Phil again.

L: Oh, hi, Phil.

P: I just spoke to Mr Dean. He can't make Wednesday next week, but he can make Thursday. Is that any good for you?

L: Hmmm. Thursday. Not ideal, to be honest. I was going to pick up some things in town, when the shops are open late. But if we make it nine instead of eight, I can manage that.

P: Nine next Thursday, my place … . OK, I think that'll work. I'll just have to confirm with Mr Dean. And I'll put an agenda together and email it through.

L: Sounds great, Phil. Thanks.

Communication activities

Unit 12.3 Exercise 9, Page 68
Student A

1   Read the scenario. You are an optimist. Try to convince
    your partner that it's a good idea for Matthew and Helena to
    buy the house. Consider:

- the size
- the price
- their salaries in the future
- holidays and other luxuries
- starting a family

Matthew and Helena are newlyweds who want to buy
a house. They have found a three-bedroom house that
they love. The price is only €250,000, which fortunately
is the maximum possible loan they can get considering
their current combined salaries. Paying back that amount
would mean they would need to limit the cost of holidays
and other luxuries, but it will be worth it. They don't have a
family now, and it will probably be a few years before they
want one. They're not sure whether they should buy the
house, or look for something different.

2   Can you and your partner agree on a 'realistic' course of
    action for the couple?

TED Talk transcripts

The transcripts use British English for all the talks, irrespective of the nationality of the speaker.

Any grammatical inaccuracies in the talks have been left uncorrected in the transcripts.

Unit 7 Taking imagination seriously

0.11   This story is about taking imagination seriously. Fourteen years ago, I first encountered this ordinary material, fishnet, used the same way for centuries. Today, I'm using it to create permanent, billowing, voluptuous forms the scale of hard-edged buildings in cities around the world. I was an unlikely person to be doing this. I never studied sculpture, engineering or architecture. In fact, after college I applied to seven art schools and was rejected by all seven.

0.49   I went off on my own to become an artist, and I painted for ten years, when I was offered a Fulbright to India. Promising to give exhibitions of paintings, I shipped my paints and arrived in Mahabalipuram. The deadline for the show arrived – my paints didn't. I had to do something. This fishing village was famous for sculpture. So I tried bronze casting. But to make large forms was too heavy and expensive. I went for a walk on the beach, watching the fishermen bundle their nets into mounds on the sand. I'd seen it every day, but this time I saw it differently – a new approach to sculpture, a way to make volumetric form without heavy solid materials.

1.36   My first satisfying sculpture was made in collaboration with these fishermen. It's a self-portrait titled 'Wide Hips.' (*Laughter*) We hoisted them on poles to photograph. I discovered their soft surfaces revealed every ripple of wind in constantly changing patterns. I was mesmerized. I continued studying craft traditions and collaborating with artisans, next in Lithuania with lace makers. I liked the fine detail it gave my work, but I wanted to make them larger – to shift from being an object you look at to something you could get lost in.

2.21   Returning to India to work with those fishermen, we made a net of a million and a half hand-tied knots – installed briefly in Madrid. Thousands of people saw it, and one of them was the urbanist Manuel Solà-Morales who was redesigning the waterfront in Porto, Portugal. He asked if I could build this as a permanent piece for the city. I didn't know if I could do that and preserve my art. Durable, engineered, permanent – those are in opposition to idiosyncratic, delicate and ephemeral.

3.02   For two years, I searched for a fibre that could survive ultraviolet rays, salt, air, pollution, and at the same time remain soft enough to move fluidly in the wind. We needed something to hold the net up out there in the middle of the traffic circle. So we raised this 45,000-pound steel ring. We had to engineer it to move gracefully in an average breeze and survive in hurricane winds. But there was no engineering software to model something porous and moving. I found a brilliant aeronautical engineer who designs sails for America's Cup racing yachts named Peter Heppel. He helped me tackle the twin challenges of precise shape and gentle movement.

3.54   I couldn't build this the way I knew because hand-tied knots weren't going to withstand a hurricane. So I developed a relationship with an industrial fishnet factory, learned the variables of their machines, and figured out a way to make lace with them. There was no language to translate this ancient, idiosyncratic handcraft into something machine operators could produce. So we had to create one. Three years and two children later, we raised this 50,000-square-foot lace net. It was hard to believe that what I had imagined was now built, permanent and had lost nothing in translation. (*Applause*)

4.45   This intersection had been bland and anonymous. Now it had a sense of place. I walked underneath it for the first time. As I watched the wind's choreography unfold, I felt sheltered and, at the same time, connected to limitless sky. My life was not

going to be the same. I want to create these oases of sculpture in spaces of cities around the world. I'm going to share two directions that are new in my work.

5.26   Historic Philadelphia City Hall: its plaza, I felt, needed a material for sculpture that was lighter than netting. So we experimented with tiny atomized water particles to create a dry mist that is shaped by the wind and in testing, discovered that it can be shaped by people who can interact and move through it without getting wet. I'm using this sculpture material to trace the paths of subway trains above ground in real time -- like an X-ray of the city's circulatory system unfolding.

6.07   Next challenge, the Biennial of the Americas in Denver asked, could I represent the 35 nations of the Western hemisphere and their interconnectedness in a sculpture? (*Laughter*) I didn't know where to begin, but I said yes. I read about the recent earthquake in Chile and the tsunami that rippled across the entire Pacific Ocean. It shifted the Earth's tectonic plates, sped up the planet's rotation and literally shortened the length of the day. So I contacted NOAA, and I asked if they'd share their data on the tsunami, and translated it into this. Its title: '1.26' refers to the number of microseconds that the Earth's day was shortened.

6.59   I couldn't build this with a steel ring, the way I knew. Its shape was too complex now. So I replaced the metal armature with a soft, fine mesh of a fibre fifteen times stronger than steel. The sculpture could now be entirely soft, which made it so light it could tie in to existing buildings -- literally becoming part of the fabric of the city. There was no software that could extrude these complex net forms and model them with gravity. So we had to create it.

7.35   Then I got a call from New York City asking if I could adapt these concepts to Times Square or the High Line. This new soft structural method enables me to model these and build these sculptures at the scale of skyscrapers. They don't have funding yet, but I dream now of bringing these to cities around the world where they're most needed.

8.05   Fourteen years ago, I searched for beauty in the traditional things, in craft forms. Now I combine them with hi-tech materials and engineering to create voluptuous, billowing forms the scale of buildings. My artistic horizons continue to grow.

8.31   I'll leave you with this story. I got a call from a friend in Phoenix. An attorney in the office who'd never been interested in art, never visited the local art museum, dragged everyone she could from the building and got them outside to lie down underneath the sculpture. There they were in their business suits, laying in the grass, noticing the changing patterns of wind beside people they didn't know, sharing the rediscovery of wonder.

9.02   Thank you. (*Applause*)

Unit 8 Build a tower, build a team

0.12   Several years ago here at TED, Peter Skillman introduced a design challenge called the marshmallow challenge. And the idea's pretty simple: Teams of four have to build the tallest free-standing structure out of twenty sticks of spaghetti, one yard of tape, one yard of string and a marshmallow. The marshmallow has to be on top. And, though it seems really simple, it's actually pretty hard because it forces people to collaborate very quickly. And so, I thought this was an interesting idea, and I incorporated it into a design workshop. And it was a huge success. And since then, I've conducted about 70 design workshops across the world with students and designers and architects, even the CTOs of the Fortune 50, and there's something about this exercise that reveals very deep lessons about the nature of collaboration, and I'd like to share some of them with you.

1.01　So, normally, most people begin by orienting themselves to the task. They talk about it, they figure out what it's going to look like, they jockey for power. Then they spend some time planning, organizing, they sketch and they lay out spaghetti. They spend the majority of their time assembling the sticks into ever-growing structures. And then finally, just as they're running out of time, someone takes out the marshmallow, and then they gingerly put it on top, and then they stand back, and – ta-da! – they admire their work. But what really happens, most of the time, is that the 'ta-da' turns into an 'uh-oh,' because the weight of the marshmallow causes the entire structure to buckle and to collapse.

1.44　So there are a number of people who have a lot more 'uh-oh' moments than others, and among the worst are recent graduates of business school. (*Laughter*) They lie, they cheat, they get distracted and they produce really lame structures. And of course there's teams that have a lot more 'ta-da' structures, and among the best are recent graduates of kindergarten. (*Laughter*) And it's pretty amazing. As Peter tells us, not only do they produce the tallest structures, but they're the most interesting structures of them all.

2.18　So the question you want to ask is: How come? Why? What is it about them? And Peter likes to say that none of the kids spend any time trying to be CEO of Spaghetti, Inc. Right? They don't spend time jockeying for power. But there's another reason as well. And the reason is that business students are trained to find the single right plan, right? And then they execute on it. And then what happens is, when they put the marshmallow on the top, they run out of time and what happens? It's a crisis. Sound familiar? Right. What kindergarteners do differently is that they start with the marshmallow, and they build prototypes, successive prototypes, always keeping the marshmallow on top, so they have multiple times to fix when they build prototypes along the way. Designers recognize this type of collaboration as the essence of the iterative process. And with each version, kids get instant feedback about what works and what doesn't work.

3.12　So the capacity to play in prototype is really essential, but let's look at how different teams perform. So the average for most people is around twenty inches; business school students, about half of that; lawyers, a little better, but not much better than that, kindergarteners, better than most adults. Who does the very best? Architects and engineers, thankfully. (*Laughter*) Thirty-nine inches is the tallest structure I've seen. And why is it? Because they understand triangles and self-reinforcing geometrical patterns are the key to building stable structures. So CEOs, a little bit better than average, but here's where it gets interesting. If you put an executive admin on the team, they get significantly better. (*Laughter*) It's incredible. You know, you look around, you go, 'Oh, that team's going to win.' You can just tell beforehand. And why is that? Because they have special skills of facilitation. They manage the process, they understand the process. And any team who manages and pays close attention to work will significantly improve the team's performance. Specialized skills and facilitation skills are the combination that leads to strong success. If you have ten teams that typically perform, you'll get maybe six or so that have standing structures.

4.30　And I tried something interesting. I thought, let's up the ante, once. So I offered a 10,000 dollar prize of software to the winning team. So what do you think happened to these design students? What was the result? Here's what happened: Not one team had a standing structure. If anyone had built, say, a one-inch structure, they would have taken home the prize. So, isn't that interesting? That high stakes have a strong impact. We did the exercise again with the same students. What do you think happened then? So now they understand the value of prototyping. So the same team went from being the very worst to being among the very best. They produced the tallest

structures in the least amount of time. So there's deep lessons for us about the nature of incentives and success.

5.21　So, you might ask: Why would anyone actually spend time writing a marshmallow challenge? And the reason is, I help create digital tools and processes to help teams build cars and video games and visual effects. And what the marshmallow challenge does is it helps them identify the hidden assumptions. Because, frankly, every project has its own marshmallow, doesn't it? The challenge provides a shared experience, a common language, a common stance to build the right prototype. And so, this is the value of the experience, of this so-simple exercise.

5.54　And those of you who are interested may want to go to MarshmallowChallenge.com. It's a blog that you can look at how to build the marshmallows. There's step-by-step instructions on this. There are crazy examples from around the world of how people tweak and adjust the system. There's world records that are on this as well.

6.11　And the fundamental lesson, I believe, is that design truly is a contact sport. It demands that we bring all of our senses to the task, and that we apply the very best of our thinking, our feeling and our doing to the challenge that we have at hand. And sometimes, a little prototype of this experience is all that it takes to turn us from an 'uh-oh' moment to a 'ta-da' moment. And that can make a big difference.

6.36　Thank you very much. (*Applause*)

Unit 9　All it takes is 10 mindful minutes

0.11　We live in an incredibly busy world. The pace of life is often frantic, our minds are always busy, and we're always doing something.

0.19　So with that in mind, I'd like you just to take a moment to think, when did you last take any time to do nothing? Just ten minutes, undisturbed? And when I say nothing, I do mean nothing. So that's no emailing, texting, no Internet, no TV, no chatting, no eating, no reading, not even sitting there reminiscing about the past or planning for the future. Simply doing nothing. I see a lot of very blank faces. (*Laughter*) My thinking is, you probably have to go a long way back.

0.51　And this is an extraordinary thing, right? We're talking about our mind. The mind, our most valuable and precious resource, through which we experience every single moment of our life, the mind that we rely upon to be happy, content, emotionally stable as individuals, and at the same time to be kind and thoughtful and considerate in our relationships with others. This is the same mind that we depend upon to be focused, creative, spontaneous, and to perform at our very best in everything that we do. And yet, we don't take any time out to look after it. In fact, we spend more time looking after our cars, our clothes and our hair than we – OK, maybe not our hair, but you see where I'm going.

1.38　The result, of course, is that we get stressed. You know, the mind whizzes away like a washing machine going round and round, lots of difficult, confusing emotions, and we don't really know how to deal with that, and the sad fact is that we are so distracted that we're no longer present in the world in which we live. We miss out on the things that are most important to us, and the crazy thing is that everybody just assumes, well, that's the way life is, so we've just kind of got to get on with it. That's really not how it has to be.

2.12　So I was about eleven when I went along to my first meditation class. And trust me, it had all the stereotypes that you can imagine, the sitting cross-legged on the floor, the incense, the herbal tea, the vegetarians, the whole deal, but my mom was going and I was intrigued, so I went along with her. I'd also seen a few kung fu movies, and secretly I kind of thought I might be able to learn how to fly, but I was very young at the time. Now as I was there, I guess, like a lot of people, I assumed that it was just an aspirin for the mind. You get stressed, you do some meditation. I hadn't really thought that it could be sort of preventative in nature, until I was about twenty, when a number of things happened in my life in quite quick succession, really serious things which just flipped my life upside down and all of a sudden I was inundated with thoughts, inundated with difficult emotions that I didn't know how to cope with. Every time I sort of pushed one down, another one would just sort of pop back up again. It was a really very stressful time.

3.12   I guess we all deal with stress in different ways. Some people will bury themselves in work, grateful for the distraction. Others will turn to their friends, their family, looking for support. Some people hit the bottle, start taking medication. My own way of dealing with it was to become a monk. So I quit my degree, I headed off to the Himalayas, I became a monk, and I started studying meditation.

3.39   People often ask me what I learned from that time. Well, obviously it changed things. Let's face it, becoming a celibate monk is going to change a number of things. But it was more than that. It taught me – it gave me a greater appreciation, an understanding for the present moment. By that I mean not being lost in thought, not being distracted, not being overwhelmed by difficult emotions, but instead learning how to be in the here and now, how to be mindful, how to be present.

4.15   I think the present moment is so underrated. It sounds so ordinary, and yet we spend so little time in the present moment that it's anything but ordinary. There was a research paper that came out of Harvard, just recently, that said on average our minds are lost in thought almost 47 per cent of the time. Forty-seven per cent. At the same time, this sort of constant mind-wandering is also a direct cause of unhappiness. Now we're not here for that long anyway, but to spend almost half of our life lost in thought and potentially quite unhappy, dunno, it just kind of seems tragic, actually, especially when there's something we can do about it, when there's a positive, practical, achievable, scientifically proven technique which allows our mind to be more healthy, to be more mindful and less distracted. And the beauty of it is that even though it need only take about ten minutes a day, it impacts our entire life. But we need to know how to do it. We need an exercise. We need a framework to learn how to be more mindful. That's essentially what meditation is. It's familiarizing ourselves with the present moment. But we also need to know how to approach it in the right way to get the best from it. And that's what these are for, in case you've been wondering, because most people assume that meditation is all about stopping thoughts, getting rid of emotions, somehow controlling the mind, but actually it's quite different from that. It's more about stepping back, seeing the thought clearly, witnessing it coming and going, emotions coming and going without judgement, but with a relaxed, focused mind.

6.04   So for example, right now, if I focus too much on the balls, then there's no way that I can relax and talk to you at the same time. Equally, if I relax too much talking to you, then there's no way I can focus on the balls. I'm going to drop them. Now in life, and in meditation, there'll be times when the focus becomes a little bit too intense, and life starts to feel a bit like this. It's a very uncomfortable way to live life, when you get this tight and stressed. At other times, we might take our foot off the gas a little bit too much, and things just become a sort of little bit like this. Of course in meditation – (Snores) – we're going to end up falling asleep. So we're looking for a balance, a focused relaxation where we can allow thoughts to come and go without all the usual involvement.

6.50   Now, what usually happens when we're learning to be mindful is that we get distracted by a thought. Let's say this is an anxious thought. So everything's going fine, and then we see the anxious thought, and it's like, 'Oh, didn't realize I was worried about that.' You go back to it, repeat it. 'Oh, I am worried. Oh, I really am worried. Wow, there's so much anxiety.' And before we know it, right, we're anxious about feeling anxious. You know, this is crazy. We do this all the time, even on an everyday level. If you think about the last time, I dunno, you had a wobbly tooth. You know it's wobbly, and you know that it hurts. But what do

you do every 20, 30 seconds? (Mumbling) It does hurt. And we reinforce the storyline, right? And we just keep telling ourselves, and we do it all the time. And it's only in learning to watch the mind in this way that we can start to let go of those storylines and patterns of mind. But when you sit down and you watch the mind in this way, you might see many different patterns. You might find a mind that's really restless and – the whole time. Don't be surprised if you feel a bit agitated in your body when you sit down to do nothing and your mind feels like that. You might find a mind that's very dull and boring, and it's just, almost mechanical, it just seems it's as if you're getting up, going to work, eat, sleep, get up, work. Or it might just be that one little nagging thought that just goes round and round and round your mind. Whatever it is, meditation offers the opportunity, the potential to step back and to get a different perspective, to see that things aren't always as they appear. We can't change every little thing that happens to us in life, but we can change the way that we experience it. That's the potential of meditation, of mindfulness. You don't have to burn any incense, and you definitely don't have to sit on the floor. All you need to do is to take ten minutes out a day to step back, to familiarize yourself with the present moment so that you get to experience a greater sense of focus, calm and clarity in your life.

9.08   Thank you very much. (Applause)

Unit 10 Protecting Twitter users (sometimes from themselves)

0.11   My job at Twitter is to ensure user trust, protect user rights and keep users safe, both from each other and, at times, from themselves. Let's talk about what scale looks like at Twitter. Back in January 2009, we saw more than two million new tweets each day on the platform. January 2014, more than 500 million. We were seeing two million tweets in less than six minutes. That's a 24,900-per cent increase.

0.53   Now, the vast majority of activity on Twitter puts no one in harm's way. There's no risk involved. My job is to root out and prevent activity that might. Sounds straightforward, right? You might even think it'd be easy, given that I just said the vast majority of activity on Twitter puts no one in harm's way. Why spend so much time searching for potential calamities in innocuous activities? Given the scale that Twitter is at, a one-in-a-million chance happens 500 times a day. It's the same for other companies dealing at this sort of scale. For us, edge cases, those rare situations that are unlikely to occur, are more like norms. Say 99.999 per cent of tweets pose no risk to anyone. There's no threat involved. Maybe people are documenting travel landmarks like Australia's Heart Reef, or tweeting about a concert they're attending, or sharing pictures of cute baby animals. After you take out that 99.999 per cent, that tiny percentage of tweets remaining works out to roughly 150,000 per month. The sheer scale of what we're dealing with makes for a challenge.

2.21   You know what else makes my role particularly challenging? People do weird things. (Laughter) And I have to figure out what they're doing, why, and whether or not there's risk involved, often without much in terms of context or background. I'm going to show you some examples that I've run into during my time at Twitter – these are all real examples — of situations that at first seemed cut and dried, but the truth of the matter was something altogether different. Details have been changed to protect the innocent and sometimes the guilty. We'll start off easy.

3.03   Let's look at spam. Here's an example of an account engaged in classic spammer behaviour, sending the exact same message to thousands of people. While this is a mockup I put together using my account, we see accounts doing this all the time. Seems pretty straightforward. We should just automatically suspend accounts engaging in this kind of behaviour. Turns out there's some exceptions to that rule.

Turns out that that message could also be a notification you signed up for that the International Space Station is passing overhead because you wanted to go outside and see if you could see it. You're not going to get that chance if we mistakenly suspend the account thinking it's spam.

3.45 OK. Let's make the stakes higher. Back to my account, again exhibiting classic behaviour. This time it's sending the same message and link. This is often indicative of something called phishing, somebody trying to steal another person's account information by directing them to another website. That's pretty clearly not a good thing. We want to, and do, suspend accounts engaging in that kind of behaviour. So why are the stakes higher for this? Well, this could also be a bystander at a rally who managed to record a video of a police officer beating a non-violent protester who's trying to let the world know what's happening. We don't want to gamble on potentially silencing that crucial speech by classifying it as spam and suspending it. That means we evaluate hundreds of parameters when looking at account behaviours, and even then, we can still get it wrong and have to re-evaluate.

4.44 Now, given the sorts of challenges I'm up against, it's crucial that I not only predict but also design protections for the unexpected. And that's not just an issue for me, or for Twitter, it's an issue for you. It's an issue for anybody who's building or creating something that you think is going to be amazing and will let people do awesome things. So what do I do? I pause and I think, how could all of this go horribly wrong? I visualize catastrophe. And that's hard. There's a sort of inherent cognitive dissonance in doing that, like when you're writing your wedding vows at the same time as your prenuptial agreement.(Laughter) But you still have to do it, particularly if you're marrying 500 million tweets per day. What do I mean by 'visualize catastrophe?' I try to think of how something as benign and innocuous as a picture of a cat could lead to death, and what to do to prevent that. Which happens to be my next example. This is my cat, Eli. We wanted to give users the ability to add photos to their tweets. A picture is worth a thousand words. You only get 140 characters. You add a photo to your tweet, look at how much more content you've got now. There's all sorts of great things you can do by adding a photo to a tweet. My job isn't to think of those. It's to think of what could go wrong.

6.19 How could this picture lead to my death? Well, here's one possibility. There's more in that picture than just a cat. There's geodata. When you take a picture with your smartphone or digital camera, there's a lot of additional information saved along in that image. In fact, this image also contains the equivalent of this, more specifically, this. Sure, it's not likely that someone's going to try to track me down and do me harm based upon image data associated with a picture I took of my cat, but I start by assuming the worst will happen. That's why, when we launched photos on Twitter, we made the decision to strip that geodata out. (Applause) If I start by assuming the worst and work backwards, I can make sure that the protections we build work for both expected and unexpected use cases.

7.20 Given that I spend my days and nights imagining the worst that could happen, it wouldn't be surprising if my world view was gloomy. (Laughter) It's not. The vast majority of interactions I see – and I see a lot, believe me – are positive, people reaching out to help or to connect or share information with each other. It's just that for those of us dealing with scale, for those of us tasked with keeping people safe, we have to assume the worst will happen, because for us, a one-in-a-million chance is pretty good odds.

8.02 Thank you. (Applause)

Unit 11 How to build with clay and community

0.11 I would like to show you how architecture has helped to change the life of my community and has opened opportunities to hope.

0.25 I am a native of Burkina Faso. According to the World Bank, Burkina Faso is one of the poorest countries in the world, but what does it look like to grow up in a place like that? I am an example of that. I was born in a little village called Gando. In Gando, there was no electricity, no access to clean drinking water, and no school. But my father wanted me to learn how to read and write. For this reason, I had to leave my family when I was seven and to stay in a city far away from my village with no contact with my family. In this place I sat in a class like that with more than 150 other kids, and for six years. In this time, it just happened to me to come to school to realize that my classmate died.

1.36 Today, not so much has changed. There is still no electricity in my village. People still are dying in Burkina Faso, and access to clean drinking water is still a big problem.

1.55 I had luck. I was lucky, because this is a fact of life when you grow up in a place like that. But I was lucky. I had a scholarship. I could go to Germany to study.

2.14 So now, I suppose, I don't need to explain to you how great a privilege it is for me to be standing before you today. From Gando, my home village in Burkina Faso, to Berlin in Germany to become an architect is a big, big step. But what to do with this privilege? Since I was a student, I wanted to open up better opportunities to other kids in Gando. I just wanted to use my skills and build a school. But how do you do it when you're still a student and you don't have money? Oh yes, I started to make drawings and asked for money. Fundraising was not an easy task. I even asked my classmates to spend less money on coffee and cigarettes, but to sponsor my school project. In real wonder, two years later, I was able to collect 50,000 U.S. dollars.

3.29 When I came home to Gando to bring the good news, my people were over the moon, but when they realized that I was planning to use clay, they were shocked.

3.45 'A clay building is not able to stand a rainy season, and Francis wants us to use it and build a school. Is this the reason why he spent so much time in Europe studying instead of working in the field with us?'

4.03 My people build all the time with clay, but they don't see any innovation with mud. So I had to convince everybody. I started to speak with the community, and I could convince everybody, and we could start to work. And the women, the men, everybody from the village, was part of this building process. I was allowed to use even traditional techniques. So clay floor for example, the young men come and stand like that, beating, hours for hours, and then their mothers came, and they are beating in this position, for hours, giving water and beating. And then the polishers come. They start polishing it with a stone for hours. And then you have this result, very fine, like a baby bottom. (Laughter) It's not photoshopped. (Laughter) This is the school, built with the community. The walls are totally made out of compressed clay blocks from Gando. The roof structure is made with cheap steel bars normally hiding inside concrete. And the classroom, the ceiling is made out of both of them used together.

5.37 In this school, there was a simple idea: to create comfort in a classroom. Don't forget, it can be 45 degrees in Burkina Faso, so with simple ventilation, I wanted to make the classroom good for teaching and learning. And this is the project today, twelve years old, still in best condition. And the kids, they love it.

6.08 And for me and my community, this project was a huge success. It has opened up opportunities to do more projects in Gando. So I could do a lot of projects, and here I am going to share with you only three of them.

6.28 The first one is the school extension, of course. How do you explain drawings and engineering to people who are neither able to read nor write? I started to build a prototype like that. The innovation was to build a clay vault. So then, I jumped on the top like that, with my team, and it works. The community is looking. It still works. So we can build. (Laughter) And we kept building, and that is the result. The kids are happy, and they love it. The community is very proud. We made it. And even animals, like these donkeys, love our buildings. (*Laughter*)

7.17 The next project is the library in Gando. And see now, we tried to introduce different ideas in our buildings, but we often don't have so much material. Something we have in Gando are clay pots. We wanted to use them to create openings. So we just bring them like you can see to the building site; we start cutting them, and then we place them on top of the roof before we pour the concrete, and you have this result. The openings are letting the hot air out and light in. Very simple.

7.59 My most recent project in Gando is a high school project. I would like to share with you this. The innovation in this project is to cast mud like you cast concrete. How do you cast mud? We start making a lot of mortars, like you can see, and when everything is ready, when you know what is the best recipe and the best form, you start working with the community. And sometimes I can leave. They will do it themselves. I came to speak to you like that.

8.34 Another factor in Gando is rain. When the rains come, we hurry up to protect our fragile walls against the rain. Don't confound with Christo and Jeanne-Claude. It is simply how we protect our walls. (*Laughter*) The rain in Burkina comes very fast, and after that, you have floods everywhere in the country. But for us, the rain is good. It brings sand and gravel to the river we need to use to build. We just wait for the rain to go. We take the sand, we mix it with clay, and we keep building. That is it.

9.19 The Gando project was always connected to training the people, because I just wanted, one day when I fall down and die, that at least one person from Gando keeps doing this work. But you will be surprised. I'm still alive. (*Laughter*)

9.39 And my people now can use their skills to earn money themselves. Usually, for a young man from Gando to earn money, you have to leave the country to the city, sometimes leave the country and some never come back, making the community weaker. But now they can stay in the country and work on different building sites and earn money to feed their family. There's a new quality in this work.

10.15 Yes, you know it. I have won a lot of awards through this work. For sure, it has opened opportunities. I have become myself known. But the reason why I do what I do is my community.

10.36 When I was a kid, I was going to school, I was coming back every holiday to Gando. By the end of every holidays, I had to say goodbye to the community, going from one compound to another one. All women in Gando will open their clothes like that and give me the last penny. In my culture, this is a symbol of deep affection. As a seven-year-old guy, I was impressed. I just asked my mother one day, 'Why do all these women love me so much?' (*Laughter*) She just answered, 'They are contributing to pay for your education hoping that you will be successful and one day come back and help improve the quality of life of the community.' I hope now that I was able to make my community proud through this work, and I hope I was able to prove you the power of community, and to show you that architecture can be inspiring for communities to shape their own future.

11.57 Merci beaucoup. (*Applause*) Thank you. Thank you. Thank you. Thank you. Thank you. Thank you. (*Applause*)

Unit 12 Image recognition that triggers augmented reality

0.12 So wouldn't it be amazing if our phones could see the world in the same way that we do, as we're walking around being able to point the phone at anything, and then have it actually recognize images and objects like the human brain, and then be able to pull in information from an almost infinite library of knowledge and experience and ideas?

0.31 Well, traditionally that was seen as science fiction, but now we've moved to a world where actually this has become possible.

0.36 So the best way of explaining it is to just show it. What you can see over here is Tamara, who is holding my phone that's now plugged in. So let me start with this. What we have here is a painting of the great poet Rabbie Burns, and it's just a normal image, but if we now switch inputs over to the phone, running our technology, you can see effectively what Tamara's seeing on the screen, and when she points at this image, something magical happens.

1.01 (*Laughter*) (*Bagpipes*) (*Bagpipes*) (*Applause*) (*Bagpipes*) Voice: Now simmer blinks on flowery braes ...

1.16 Matt Mills: Now, what's great about this is, there's no trickery here. There's nothing done to this image. And what's great about this is the technology's actually allowing the phone to start to see and understand much like how the human brain does. Not only that, but as I move the object around, it's going to track it and overlay that content seamlessly. Again, the thing that's incredible about this is this is how advanced these devices have become. All the processing to do that was actually done on the device itself.

1.47 Now, this has applications everywhere, whether in things like art in museums, like you just saw, or in the world of, say, advertising, or print journalism.

1.57 So a newspaper becomes out of date as soon as it's printed. And here is this morning's newspaper, and we have some Wimbledon news, which is great. Now what we can do is point at the front of the newspaper and immediately get the bulletin.

2.09 Voice: ... To the grass, and it's very important that you adapt and you, you have to be flexible, you have to be willing to change direction at a split second, and she does all that. She's won this title.

2.20 MM: And that linking of the digital content to something that's physical is what we call an aura, and I'll be using that term a little bit as we go through the talk.

2.28 So, what's great about this is it isn't just a faster, more convenient way to get information in the real world, but there are times when actually using this medium allows you to be able to display information in a way that was never before possible.

2.41 So what I have here is a wireless router. My American colleagues have told me I've got to call it a router, so that everyone here understands – (*Laughter*) – but nonetheless, here is the device. So now what I can do is, rather than getting the instructions for the device online, I can simply point at it, the device is recognized, and then –

3.03 Voice: Begin by plugging in the grey ADSL cable. Then connect the power. Finally, the yellow ethernet cable. Congratulations. You have now completed setup.

3.15 (*Laughter*) MM: Awesome. Thank you. (*Applause*)

3.20 The incredible work that made that possible was done here in the U.K. by scientists at Cambridge, and they work in our offices, and I've got a lovely picture of them here. They couldn't all be on stage, but we're going to bring their aura to the stage, so here they are. They're not very animated. (*Laughter*) This was the fourth take, I'm told. (*Laughter*)

3.45 OK. So, as we're talking about Cambridge, let's now move on to technical advancements, because since we started putting this technology on mobile phones less than twelve months ago, the speed and the processor in these devices has grown at a really phenomenal rate, and that means that I can now take cinema-quality 3D models and place them in the world around me, so I have one over here. Tamara, would you like to jump in?

4.14 (*Music*) (*Dinosaur roaring*) (*Laughter*) MM: I should leap in. (*Music*) (*Dinosaur roaring*) (*Applause*)

4.33 So then, after the fun, comes the more emotional side of what we do, because effectively, this technology allows you to see the world through someone's eyes, and for that person to be able to take a moment in time and effectively store it and tag it to something physical that exists in the real world. What's great about this is, the tools to do this are free. They're open, they're available to everyone within our application, and educators have really got on board with the classrooms. So we have teachers who've tagged up textbooks, teachers who've tagged up school classrooms, and a great example of this is a school in the U.K. I have a picture here from a video, and we're now going to play it.

5.09   Teacher: See what happens. (*Children talking*) Keep going.

5.17   Child: TV. (*Children react*)

5.21   Child: Oh my God.

5.22   Teacher: Now move it either side. See what happens. Move away from it and come back to it.

5.28   Child: Oh, that is so cool.

5.31   Teacher: And then, have you got it again?

5.34   Child: Oh my God! How did you do that?

5.38   Second child: It's magic.

5.41   (*Laughter*) MM: (*Laughs*) So, it's not magic. It's available for everyone to do, and actually I'm going to show you how easy it is to do by doing one right now.

5.50   So, as sort of — I'm told it's called a stadium wave, so we're going to start from this side of the room on the count of three, and go over to here. Tamara, are you recording? OK, so are you all ready? One, two, three. Go!

6.01   Audience: Whooooooo!

6.05   MM: Fellows are really good at that. (*Laughs*) (*Laughter*)

6.08   OK. Now we're going to switch back into the Aurasma application, and what Tamara's going to do is tag that video that we just took onto my badge, so that I can remember it forever.

6.21   Now, we have lots of people who are doing this already, and we've talked a little bit about the educational side. On the emotional side, we have people who've done things like send postcards and Christmas cards back to their family with little messages on them. We have people who have, for example, taken the inside of the engine bay of an old car and tagged up different components within an engine, so that if you're stuck and you want to find out more, you can point and discover the information.

6.47   We're all very, very familiar with the Internet. In the last twenty years, it's really changed the way that we live and work, and the way that we see the world, and what's great is, we sort of think this is the next paradigm shift, because now we can literally take the content that we share, we discover, and that we enjoy and make it a part of the world around us. It's completely free to download this application. If you have a good Wi-Fi connection or 3G, this process is very, very quick.

7.15   Oh, there we are. We can save it now. It's just going to do a tiny bit of processing to convert that image that we just took into a sort of digital fingerprint, and the great thing is, if you're a professional user, – so, a newspaper – the tools are pretty much identical to what we've just used to create this demonstration. The only difference is that you've got the ability to add in links and slightly more content. Are you now ready?

7.34   Tamara Roukaerts: We're ready to go.

7.35   MM: OK. So, I'm told we're ready, which means we can now point at the image, and there you all are.

7.40   MM on video: One, two, three. Go!

7.46   MM: Well done. We've been Aurasma. Thank you. (*Applause*)

Communication activities

Unit 10.3 Exercise 1, page 46

Answers

1e Being struck by lightning in your lifetime (1 in 3,000)
2b Being injured by a toilet this year (1 in 10,000)
3a Being killed by a bee sting (1 in 6 million)
4d Being attacked by a shark (1 in 11.5 million)
5c Being killed by an asteroid impact (1 in 74,817,414)

Unit 12.3 Exercise 9, Page 68

Student B

1 Read the scenario. You are a pessimist. Try to convince your partner that it's a bad idea for Matthew and Helena to buy the house. Consider:

- the size
- the price
- their salaries in the future
- holidays and other luxuries
- starting a family

Matthew and Helena are newlyweds who want to buy a house. They have found a three-bedroom house that they love, but it's expensive at €250,000. This amount is the maximum possible loan they could get considering their current combined salaries. Paying back that amount would mean they would need to limit the cost of holidays and other luxuries – and they both love traveling and relaxing. They don't have a family now, but they probably want to start one in the next few years. They're not sure whether they should buy the house, or look for something different.

2 Can you and your partner agree on a 'realistic' course of action for the couple?

Wordlist

Word class abbreviations:

The following abbreviations are used in the word list: n = noun, v = verb, adj = adjective, adv = adverb, phr = phrase, phr v = phrasal verb

Unit 7

Pages 8-9

airspace (n)

billow (v)

bronze (n)

bundle (v)

casting (n)

ephemeral (adj)

fabric (n)

fastening (n)

idiosyncratic (adj)

inviting (adj)

knot (n)

lace (n)

medium (n)

mound (n)

natural fibre (n)

pay tribute to (something) (phr)

point of focus (n)

reshape (v)

volumetric (adj)

Pages 10-11

accomplishment (n)

authentic (adj)

bland (adj)

craftsperson (n)

mesmerized (adj)

ripple (v)

shift (v)

waterfront (n)

Pages 12-13

(somebody's) mind wander (phr)

daydream (v)

drawback (n)

routine (adj)

test subject (n)

Pages 14-15

be in two minds about (something) (phr)

bear (something) in mind (phr)

blow your mind (phr)

ease your mind (phr)

experimental (adj)

give (somebody) peace of mind (phr)

have something on your mind (phr)

keep an open mind (about something) (phr)

measurable (adj)

outcome (n)

put your mind to (something) (phr)

see (something) in your mind's eye (phr)

visualize (v)

Pages 16-17

alien (adj)

allegedly (adv)

artefact (n)

by all accounts (phr)

magnetic (adj)

occurrence (n)

quote (v)

reportedly (adv)

seemingly (adv)

speculation (n)

supposedly (adv)

Unit 8

Pages 18-19

absorb information (phr)

assign (v)

collaboration (n)

continually (adv)

executive admin (n)

facilitation (n)

innovative (adj)

iterative (adj)

kindergartener (n)

practitioner (n)

skilful (adj)

Pages 20-21

assemble (v)

high stakes (n)

jockey for power (phr)

orient (v)

participant (n)

significance (n)

sketch (v)

ta-da (phr)

trial and error (phr)

uh-oh (phr)

up the ante (phr)

Pages 22-23

(be) the consequence of (something) (phr)

acute (adj)

arise from (something) (v)

bring (something) about (phr v)

foster (v)

give rise to (something) (phr)

kill (stop something) (v)

migraine (n)

neck strain (n)

pull a 'sickie' (phr)

recurring (adj)

repetitive strain injury (n)

Pages 24-25

anticipate (v)

bond (v)

do your fair share of (something) (phr)

enhance (v)

feel a part of (something) (phr)

go the extra mile (phr)

have a sense of belonging (phr)

motivate (v)

pull your weight (phr)

share the load (phr)

team player (n)

team-building (n)

Pages 26-27

abrupt (adj)

administration (n)

administrator (n)

as a consequence (phr)

coordination (n)

debriefing (n)

deliver (v)

expertise (n)

host (v)

invite (ask officially) (v)

jump in (phr v)

leadership (n)

lose money (phr)

project manager (n)

signal (v)

take the time to (do something) (phr)

teamwork (n)

your take on (something) (phr)

Pages 28-29

cramped (adj)

degrade (v)

discarded (adj)

downcycling (n)

edge (n)

ever-growing (adj)

eye-catching (adj)

immediate (closest) (adj)

junk (n)

noticeable (adj)

upcycling (n)

Unit 9

Pages 30-31

accessible (adj)

clarity (n)

focused (adj)

frantic (adj)

inundate (v)

meditate (v)

meditation (n)

mindful (adj)

monk (n)

preventative (adj)

restless (adj)

spontaneous (adj)

Pages 32-33

(be) overwhelmed by (something) (adj)

clarity (n)

framework (n)

illustrate (v)

intense (adj)

jargon (n)

nagging (adj)

reminisce (v)

research paper (n)

take your foot off the gas (phr)

wobbly (adj)

Pages 34-35

mild (adj)

moderate (adj)

no (something) whatsoever (adv)

quite literally (phr)

undeniable (adj)

utterly (adv)

Pages 36-37

(be) in over your head (phr)

(be) on your toes (phr)

(be) up to your eyeballs in (something) (phr)

(something) makes your blood boil (phr)

a pain in the neck (phr)

a shot in the arm (phr)

alert (adj)

awareness (n)

be a weight off your shoulders (phr)

burst (n)

chronic (adj)

clinical (adj)

exposure (n)

get cold feet about (something) (phr)

get something off your chest (phr)

immune system (n)

keep your chin up (phr)

let your hair down (phr)

nutrition (n)

thoughtfully (adv)

thrill (n)

vaccination (n)

Pages 38-39

cover for (somebody) (phr v)

spark (v)

version (n)

Unit 10

Pages 40-41

calamity (n)

cut and dried (phr)

give voice to (something) (phr)

globe (n)

innocuous (adj)

legal battle (n)

open (adj)

prenuptial agreement (n)

root out (something) (phr v)

social network (n)

stake (n)

Pages 42-43

(be) in harm's way (phr)

bystander (n)

gloomy (adj)

landmark (n)

odds (n)

parameter (n)

phishing (n)

put forward (something) (phr v)

spam (n)

wedding vow (n)

Pages 44-45

BASE jumping (n)

lacrosse (n)

measure (judge) (v)

skydiving (n)

softball (n)

white-water rafting (n)

Pages 46-47

antidepressant (n)

asteroid (n)

be a one-in-a-million chance (phr)

bee sting (n)

consumption (n)

follow your heart (phr)

gut instinct (n)

impact (n)

increase the likelihood of (something) (phr)

intuition (n)

make matters worse (phr)

medication (n)

pose a threat to (something) (phr)

produce (n)

reduce the odds of (something) (phr)

run the risk of (something) (phr)

sceptical (adj)

statistically (adv)

the chances of recovering from (something) (phr)

Pages 48-49

all things considered (phr)

downside (n)

drawback (n)

in light of (something) (phr)

on the plus/minus side (phr)

Pages 50-51

(financial) return (n)

engage in (something) (phr v)

ethical (adj)

interest rate (n)

mainstream (adj)

philosophy (n)

regulation (n)

sector (n)

sustainable (adj)

Unit 11

Pages 52-53

cast (v)

clay (n)

compress (v)

flatten (v)

fragile (adj)

harden (v)

profound (adj)

prototype (n)

structure (building) (n)

ventilation (n)

Pages 54-55

(be) over the moon (phr)

fundraising (n)

gravel (n)

motivation (n)

photoshopped (adj)

privilege (n)

scholarship (n)

shape (v)

Pages 56-57

(be) concerned with (something) (adj)

environmentalist (n)

given that (something) (phr)

heritage (n)

in the event that (something) (phr)

in the foreseeable future (phr)

indigenous (adj)

inevitable (adj)

ranch (n)

sample (v)

unspoiled (adj)

vineyard (n)

widespread (adj)

Pages 58-59

(be) on the lookout for (something) (phr)

as far as I can see (phr)

constitute (v)

inward (adj)

look (someone) in the eye (phr)

look and see (phr)

look into (something) (phr v)

look up to (somebody) (phr v)

master (v)

necessity (n)

overlook (v)

oversee (v)

portray (v)

pursue (v)

see about (something) (phr v)

see eye to eye about (something) (phr)

visionary (n)

wait and see (phr)

Pages 60-61

adulthood (n)

asset (n)

endorsement (n)

envisage (v)

honoured (adj)

if money were no object (phr)

life coach (n)

persuasive (adj)

proactive (adj)

strength (n)

Unit 12

Pages 62-63

augmented reality (n)

blend (v)

cutting-edge (adj)

label (v)

overlay (v)

recognition (n)

tag up (phr v)

trigger (v)

Pages 64-65

advancement (n)

animated (adj)

lightweight (adj)

modified (adj)

overly (adv)

paradigm shift (n)

phenomenal (adj)

rate (v)

repetitive (adj)

router (n)

seamlessly (adv)

trickery (n)

Pages 66-67

commonplace (adj)

fake (adj)

revolutionize (v)

Pages 68-69

every cloud has a silver lining (phr)

light at the end of the tunnel (phr)

look on the bright side (phr)

mindset (n)

optimist (n)

pessimist (n)

realist (n)

realistically (adv)

see (something) through rose-tinted glasses (phr)

see clouds on the horizon (phr)

the glass is half full/empty (phr)

Pages 70-71

pencil (something) in (phr)

put forward (something) (phr v)

Pages 72-73

(company) share (n)

fleet (n)

market share (n)

motorised (adj)

venture (n)

Keynote

ADVANCED Workbook

Contents Split B

NGL.Cengage.com/Keynote

PASSWORD keynoteStdt#

Paula Mulanovic
Mike Harrison
Sandy Millin

7 Imagination

7.1 Taking imagination seriously

TEDTALKS

'I try to imagine my goal as a reality, and then work backwards to figure out all the steps I need to take to make it so,' says **JANET ECHELMAN**. This imagination dreamed up, for example, *Unnumbered Sparks*, a 745-foot net sculpture which would billow in the wind and come alive at night with light and digital designs powered by the public. Her career has been as fluid and varied as her art. Although originally rejected by seven universities, she has since studied art at Harvard University, and has an MA in counselling psychology. She has been awarded residencies, grants and scholarships in Europe and Asia, including the Fullbright Senior Lectureship and the Guggenheim Fellowship. When she began painting she listened attentively to her inner voice; she drew and wrote using her less dominant hand to access creative ideas that might otherwise never come into being. A stroke of fate changed her chosen media from paint to fibre; the knotting and sculpture she now does requires both hands.

She has exhibited prolifically across the globe and the awards she has won have been for architecture and structural engineering as well as in art and design. She's worked with and learned from fishermen, engineering firms, software engineers, industrial weavers and experts to bring what she imagines to life. For example, to make *Unnumbered Sparks*, which was designed and built to celebrate TED's thirtieth year, she collaborated with Aaron Koblin, another TED speaker and a digital media artist. The huge, interactive structure was suspended outside the Vancouver Conference Centre where TED 2014 was held, making something truly original that brought together the man-made, the natural and the public.

Janet Echelman

CAREER PATHWAYS

1 Read the text. Answer the questions.

  1 How does Janet Echelman use her imagination in her work?
  2 What is distinctive about *Unnumbered Sparks*?
  3 What did she study at university?
  4 What does she use to help access her creativity?

TED PLAYLIST

2 Other TED speakers are interested in topics similar to Janet Echelman's TED Talk. Read the descriptions of four TED Talks at the top of page 105. In your opinion, which is the best title for this playlist, a, b or c?

  a Storytelling and technology
  b Art and imagination's limitations
  c Stories and art that stretch the imagination

3 Complete the six-word summary (1–4) that corresponds to each talk in the TED playlist. Use these words.

between	carpet	everywhere	pushing

  1 An imaginative artist's magic _____ ride.
  2 _____ the envelope of boundless creativity.
  3 Depicting everything and _____ in paper.
  4 Imagination lies _____ truth and lies.

4 Match the verbs (1–5) with their collocates (a–e). Check your answers in the playlist descriptions.

  1 to colour   **a** disbelief
  2 to push   **b** characters and stories
  3 to depict   **c** someone on a fantastic journey
  4 to launch   **d** boundaries
  5 to suspend   **e** one's life experiences

5 Which talk would you most like to see? Why? Watch the talk at TED.com.

▶ **Raghava KK: My 5 lives as an artist**

Raghava KK is an artist who's lived and travelled around the world, changing his art along the way. His life experiences have driven his artistic reincarnations and in turn these reincarnations have coloured his life experiences. As cartoonist, painter, realist, thinker and family guy, he's been both media darling and media outcast. His honest and vulnerable talk details all five of Raghava KK's artistic chapters so far, warts and all, and contains all the drama, emotion and colour of a Bollywood film.

▶ **James Cameron: Before Avatar … a curious boy**

James Cameron is a director of blockbuster films like *Titanic, Avatar* and *Terminator*, as well as an underwater explorer and science-fiction fanatic. His curiosity has led him to explore the world and these three passions. In his personal talk he tells us how film-making puts stories and pictures together to push boundaries to create a new reality.

▶ **Béatrice Coron: Stories cut from paper**

Béatrice Coron glides onto the TED stage in a full-length paper-cut cape that contrasts dramatically with her plain black clothing beneath, providing a stunning demonstration of her work as a papercutting artist. Coron uses scissors, paper and other materials to depict characters, stories and entire worlds in amazing and imaginative detail.

▶ **Mac Barnett: Why a good book is a secret door**

Mac Barnett believes that children are in many ways the most imaginative and serious of all readers, and he writes books that launch them on fantastic journeys: to worlds that include, for example, trading phone messages with pet blue whales. He's an award-winning writer with a penchant for the zone where disbelief is suspended and fiction can escape the page and enter the real world.

AUTHENTIC LISTENING SKILLS Inferring meaning from context

6 🎧 **2 1** You are going to hear a podcast in which a member of the *Keynote* team talks about James Cameron's TED Talk, *Before Avatar … a curious boy*. Complete the sentences. Then listen and check your answers.

1 This talk has personal _____ for me and not only me, but for any professional.
2 Everyone has some degree of motivation for choosing what they do for a _____ and in this talk James Cameron revealed some personal reasons why he made particular film choices.
3 James Cameron has an easy, confident way of talking, without relying on emotional outbursts and high-pitched statements for his audience's _____ .
4 This confidence may come in part from Cameron's phenomenal business success, but I think it's also based on his _____ in what he does.
5 This belief is impersonal and fact-based, in other words, he disconnects his ego from his work when he talks about it, and he isn't the block-buster _____ but a man doing a job and living a life.

LISTENING

7 🎧 **2 2** Listen to the full podcast. Are these statements true (T) or false (F)?

1 James Cameron uses a lot of exciting visuals in his talk. ☐
2 Doruk describes Cameron as having been fascinated by nature as a child. ☐
3 Cameron was always keen to learn about and explore unknown worlds. ☐
4 His dream was to go scuba diving in California. ☐

8 🎧 **2 2** Listen again and answer the questions.

1 What two areas was Cameron especially interested in as a child, which influenced his later work?
2 When making *Titanic*, how did he legitimately use the film's production to realize a personal dream?
3 What technology did Cameron want to use in *Titanic* and why?
4 What does Doruk see as the message of the talk?

VOCABULARY IN CONTEXT

9 Read the extracts from the podcast. Choose the correct meaning of the words in bold.

1 I found that Cameron's way of talking was especially **compelling** because of his lack of ego …
   a memorable ☐   b undeniable ☐
   c interesting and exciting ☐
2 He was also an **avid** reader of science fiction and read for at least two hours a day.
   a secret ☐   b quick ☐   c keen ☐
3 He would spend time drawing – as a **creative outlet**.
   a exercise ☐   b means of expression ☐
   c hobby ☐
4 … making a film about it was the perfect **vehicle** to do this.
   a disguise ☐   b way ☐   c car ☐
5 This was the part that particularly **grabbed me** …
   a caught my attention ☐   b made me laugh ☐
   c puzzled me ☐

105

GRAMMAR The continuous aspect

1 Match the headings 1–5 with sections A–E of the text.

1 Daydreaming makes you forget what you ¹*did /were doing*. ☐

2 Daydreaming turns off other parts of the brain. ☐

3 You daydream less as you get older. ☐

4 Daydreaming makes you more creative. ☐

5 Your brain, not your mind, ²*controls / is controlling* your daydreams. ☐

2 Choose the best options (1–8) to complete the text.

Five surprising facts about daydreaming
By Christine Dell'Amore, National Geographic

Here are some interesting facts about daydreaming you ³*may not have known / may have not been knowing*.

A

Daydreaming is often about anticipating the future, dreaming of what you ⁴*will be doing / are doing*, notes Peter Delaney, a psychologist at the University of North Carolina, Greensboro. Later in life, daydreaming decreases as the future shrinks.

B

If people are asked to daydream about the past, for instance, they tend not to remember what they ⁵*were working on / worked on* before the daydream started.

C

Our brain has two key systems: an analytic part that helps us make reasoned decisions, and an empathetic part that allows us to relate to others. Our mind uses one system at a time and ⁶*is requiring / requires* the energy from the other one to complete the task at hand.

D

The physical and the conscious are like different aspects of the same thing, like the software and hardware of a computer. As we learn new things the connections between nerve cells ⁷*are constantly changing / constantly change*.

E

When daydreaming, the brain accesses information that was dormant or out of reach, notes Eugenio M. Rothe, a psychiatrist at Florida International University. It may make an association between bits of information that the person ⁸*had never considered / had never been considering* in that particular way.

3 🔊 2 3 Complete the conversation with the correct continuous form. Then listen and check your answers.

A: ¹_____ (you / daydream) when I came in?

B: Oh dear. Yes, I was. Actually, I ²_____ (think) about my holiday next week.

A: I heard we daydream less when we get older. Do you think there's anything in it?

B: ³_____ (you / be) cheeky and saying I'm too old to daydream?

A: Of course not! I ⁴_____ (not imply) anything of the sort. I ⁵_____ (just / wonder).

B: I ⁶_____ (daydream) since I was at school, though.

A: Yeah, I ⁷_____ (always / get caught) daydreaming, too, especially in French. It was so boring. What made you start daydreaming this time?

B: Not sure. Maybe it's to do with the report I ⁸_____ (read) all morning!

A: Oh, that report's next on my to-do list. I ⁹_____ (probably / daydream) myself soon.

4 Complete the sentences with the correct continuous form of the verbs in brackets, using contracted forms where you can. More than one answer may be possible.

1 He _____ (work) in the research team for two years before he was asked to lead it.
2 They _____ (come) over from head office to meet the new manager, once she's settled in.
3 We _____ (go) to Greece on holiday ever since I can remember.
4 I _____ (work) in the garden when the news of the disaster broke.
5 You could tell he _____ (not / listen); he was still working out the finances in his head.
6 She _____ (exhibit) in Australia and New Zealand later in the year; she's a very sought after artist.
7 He _____ (dream) of going abroad when the chance for an exchange came up.
8 She _____ (hope) to do some research into cognitive processing next year.

5 Choose the best options to end each sentence.

1 I'm working in London *for the summer / since 2004*.
2 She's waiting for the response from her interview *last week / next week*.
3 He hadn't ever been sailing *last year / before last year*.
4 They were planning to arrive this evening, *until they've been delayed / but there's a strike*.
5 By then she'll be living in Spain – *she's moving this week / she moved last week*.
6 They were just signing the contract *when they heard the news / when they were leaving*.
7 They're implementing the project in Sweden *every year / before the end of the year*.
8 She's been attending training courses there *ever since I can remember / last year*.

6 Choose the best answer (a, b or c) for each question.

1 How long have they been renting out their place on Airbnb?
   a Last week they started.
   b About a year now.
   c More regularly.
2 Is there someone staying there now?
   a I'm not sure, you'd have to ask them.
   b There's someone who will stay every June.
   c No, no one stayed last week.
3 Will anyone be using it over the holidays or can we stay there again?
   a Their parents won't stay.
   b That would be nice, wouldn't it? We'll have to see.
   c I think so.
4 Were you still living at home or were you there when there was that huge storm?
   a Yes, I did.
   b Yes, I stayed there.
   c Yes, I was there. It was awful actually.

5 How long had they been renting it for before we went there?
   a Not long, about six months.
   b In 2013.
   c Six months previously.

GRAMMAR EXTRA! Adverbs of certainty

7 Complete the sentences with the correct adverbs of certainty.

1 We'll *probably / maybe* be renting a car for the whole summer.
2 Future generations will *maybe / definitely* be living longer.
3 Most of us will *probably / surely* be living in megacities in 30 years' time.
4 We'll *perhaps / undoubtedly* be shopping online more over the next decade.
5 Businesses will *maybe / certainly* be using and sharing more through open source in the future.
6 Higher life expectancy means people will *definitely / perhaps* be needing more support and services in coming years.
7 There *most probably / maybe* won't be many mono-ethnic workforces in existence over the next 20 years.
8 People will *surely / maybe* start to take better care of the environment in the near future.

PRONUNCIATION /ŋ/ sound

8 🎧 2 4 Underline the words that have a /ŋ/ sound. Then listen and check your answers.

1 How long have they been renting their place on Airbnb?
2 Is there someone staying there now?
3 Will anyone be using it over the holidays or can we stay there again?
4 Were you still living at home or were you there when there was that huge storm?
5 How long had they been renting it for before we went there?

DICTATION

9 🎧 2 5 Listen to someone talking about getting a good idea. Complete the paragraph.

Well, they say that daydreaming makes you more creative. I remember one time _____ the details of a presentation. _____ in the final section and needed a way of bringing them together. _____ and nothing had worked. Then _____ but actually _____ , daydreaming and sort of allowing my mind to freewheel. Suddenly there it was, _____ .
It just popped into my head from nowhere. The perfect solution.

READING

1 Read the introductory paragraph. Match each term (1–6) with the best definition (a–f).

A personal vision behind each event

With an emphasis on global cuisine and a passion for incorporating plentiful Vermont fresh food and products, Susanna's Catering provides a fully-insured service that combines outstanding quality ingredients, a wealth of experience, bold imagination and impeccable service for any size event in the greater Stowe, Vermont region. Susanna is a member of the Vermont Fresh Network and can provide a tailor-made service to perfectly orchestrate your special event.

Interview with the chef

In what way can the food served by Susanna's Catering be called [1] _____ ?

Susanna Keefer is the chef and founder of Susanna's Catering. She says that her food is locally sourced but globally inspired and delicious. She grew up in the UK, has worked on hotel canal boats in France, sailed the seven seas as a private chef on yachts and travelled extensively in Asia and Australia. Based for the last twenty years in Vermont, USA, she has been catering for weddings and many other events. Beginning as a start-up out of her own kitchen, she now employs eight full-time staff and rents business premises.

How important is the [2] _____ **to the success of the event?**

Every customer event is a culinary work of art designed to fulfil the expectations of the client and their guests. Each menu is original and made to order. Everything starts with the client – almost half are referrals, repeat customers or have been guests at other events. In the first consultation on the phone or in the tasting kitchen, Susanna and the client get to know each other and Susanna finds out about the event and the client's vision and expectations. She listens carefully to how they see the food fitting the overall concept.

Where does the local [3] _____ **come in?**

Great food engages all the senses, and the vision for each party is how the guests can enjoy it best. When a clear idea has been established, Susanna starts to add her own ideas. Working with illustrated lists of appetizers, starters, main courses and desserts, dishes and ingredients are

1	global cuisine	a	back-up in case of loss or damage
2	Vermont Fresh Network	b	original ideas
3	fully-insured service	c	foods and recipes from around the world
4	bold imagination	d	planning an event to suit the individual client
5	impeccable service	e	community that produces locally grown food
6	tailor-made service	f	smart and friendly staff

2 Read the interview and complete the questions (1–5) with five of the phrases from Exercise 1.

3 Read the interview again. Are these statements true (T) or false (F)?

1 The chef has worked on water and land internationally. ☐

2 The client's idea drives the menu creation. ☐

3 Clients start by looking at pictures of dishes online to create their own menu and then meet someone from Susanna's Catering. ☐

4 Most of the food is sourced from abroad. ☐

5 Highlights from Susanna's travels contribute to the mix. ☐

6 Staff have to learn about the food they serve in order to train new recruits. ☐

selected that appeal. The menu is developed after taking any dietary considerations into account, such as vegetarians, people with gluten or nut allergies. Susanna's Catering is a member of a local organization of farmers, producers and chefs whose aim is to promote rural identity and locally grown food. Most of the ingredients she uses are locally sourced and many are organic.

Where can we see Susanna's [4] _____ **in action?**

She says: 'The inspiration and imagination comes from everything I've experienced and collected from my travels. I can still see things in my mind's eye, remember the smell, taste and feel of things: markets in France, seafood in South Africa, spices in India, cakes and sweets in the Caribbean. The exciting thing is to bring the right elements from abroad to flavour and complement the rich local produce we have here. That's the magic.'

How does [5] _____ **add to the experience?**

The chef and catering team tease out some details from their clients that are personal; for example, if it's a wedding, where a couple met or where they go on holiday, and bring it out in the menu in some way. Nowadays people often marry and celebrate across cultures rather than within them. Stationed buffets create islands of the individual cultures, like a street food cart from India with all the dishes presented on it, or an English afternoon-tea table. These things make the event more interactive and exciting. The service staff are a tightly knit team and know everything about the food, so they can provide additional information as they serve the meals and help bring the whole experience alive – with a smile.

VOCABULARY Expressions with *mind*

4 Match 1–8 with a–h to complete the expressions with *mind*.

1 to put		**a** of mind
2 to bear		**b** your mind's eye
3 to blow someone's		**c** your mind to it
4 to give someone peace		**d** minds
5 to keep		**e** someone's mind
6 to ease		**f** something in mind
7 to be in two		**g** an open mind
8 to see something in		**h** mind

5 Complete the sentences with the correct form of the expressions from Exercise 4.

1 If I don't _____ , I'll never finish this presentation before the deadline.

2 Please _____ when applying for positions that due to the high demand we are not able to reply to unsuccessful candidates.

3 He was _____ about accepting the promotion; it was more responsibility but it would require relocating.

4 The high salaries of the board members and CEOs can _____ if you compare them to what a normal worker earns!

5 It can be difficult to _____ about the candidates; it's easy to be influenced by factors such as your first impressions and personal preferences.

6 It would _____ to know that you are going to be able to get the figures ready in time for my meeting.

7 If you can _____ the finish line _____ when you run a marathon it makes it easier.

8 He was leading a difficult project but working with a reliable team _____ .

WORDBUILDING Verbs with two past participles

6 Write the infinitive of the verb. Then match each past participle with its meaning (a or b).

1 *hang* hanged **a** put a picture on the wall
hung **b** killed with a rope around the neck

2 _____ been **a** travelled to and returned from
gone **b** being no longer present

3 _____ costed **a** calculated the cost for accounts
cost **b** was priced at

4 _____ laid **a** was horizontal at night
lied **b** not told the truth

5 _____ shined **a** produced light
shone **b** polished (of metal or leather)

7 Complete the sentences with the correct past participle from Exercise 6.

1 It seemed as though I had barely _____ my head on the pillow when the alarm rang.

2 My grandfather has always _____ his shoes and pressed his shirts himself.

3 He's not here. He's _____ to head office to attend the training programme.

4 He had _____ to the Personnel Manager about his absence and so was given a warning about not telling the truth.

5 They have _____ all projects completed this year to help calculate the budgets for next year.

6 He's _____ to Italy several times but he still can't speak the language.

7 If I'd known how much it had _____ , I wouldn't have asked him to get it.

8 The last time a person in Britain was _____ was in 1964.

9 She had _____ her jacket on the back of the chair but only remembered it later.

10 The moon has _____ brighter than ever tonight. Is it a supermoon?

WORD FOCUS *eye*

8 Match the idioms (1–6) with the meanings (a–f).

1 to keep an eye on		**a** to see something without special equipment
2 to be up to one's eyes in		**b** to become aware of the truth of
3 to see something with the naked eye		**c** to be very attractive or unusual
4 to open one's eyes to		**d** to be overwhelmed by the quantity of
5 to be eye-catching		**e** to do something easily
6 to do something with your eyes shut		**f** to look after

9 Complete the sentences with the correct form of the idioms from Exercise 8.

1 Can you _____ the new intern until I get back and make sure she's got enough to do and answer any of her questions?

2 The company logo _____ really _____ . Everyone noticed it straight away.

3 On a clear day you can _____ the cathedral _____ from the top floor of the building.

4 I don't know anyone who isn't _____ work, do you?

5 He's driven that road so often he could almost _____ it _____ .

6 That documentary really _____ the issues for women in developing countries.

109

SPECULATING

1 Nicky didn't arrive at work today. Why might she be missing from the office? Write explanations using the prompts and the words in brackets.

1 I / she / holiday (expect) ☐

2 I / she / training course (imagine) ☐

3 She / ill (must) ☐

4 One of her children / ill (might) ☐

5 She / stuck in traffic (probably) ☐

6 She / overslept (may) ☐

2 🎧 **2 6** Listen to a conversation about why Nicky isn't at work. Tick (✓) possible reasons in Exercise 1 that you hear and write the exact words of two additional speculations.

1 _____

2 _____

3 🎧 **2 7** Listen to the explanation and complete the sentences using the prompts in brackets.

1 She called us using someone else's phone so … (she / can't / her phone / with her)

_____

2 There were no casualties so … (everyone / must / left the building / in time)

_____

3 They couldn't re-enter the building so … (it / likely / serious fire)

_____

4 She's suffering from shock so … (I / guess / need a day off)

_____

5 They were up all night so … (the children / probably / tired)

_____

6 The firemen … (bound / find cause / by now)

_____

PRONUNCIATION Contraction with *have*

4 🎧 **2 8** Do you think *have* is contracted or not in these sentences? Listen and check your answers.

1 They must *have / 've* been really worried.

2 How dreadful. They may *have / 've* had to leave quickly in the middle of the night.

3 They might *have / 've* been worried the fire would spread to their building.

4 I imagine they can't *have / 've* had much with them, just what they might *have / 've* grabbed.

5 Sounds lucky, the fire and smoke are likely to *have / 've* spread really fast.

6 I expect the boys would *have / 've* probably enjoyed watching the firemen, as long as everyone was safe.

5 🎧 **2 9** Put the words in the correct order to make phrases for agreeing or disagreeing with a speculation. Use appropriate contractions. Then listen and check your answers.

1 be / right / can / not / that

_____

2 onto / think / you / I / something / there / are

_____

3 convinced / am / not / I / entirely

_____

4 certainly / way / that / looks / it

_____

5 does / that / at / all / likely / me / to / seem / not

_____

6 seems / that / a / explanation / likely

_____

WRITING Neutral reporting

6 Put the letters in the correct order to complete the sentences with neutral reporting words.

1 *deeporrytl* = said to be true by someone else
He _____ left two hours ago, but we've not heard from him.

2 *eleiveb* = have a strong feeling something is true
We _____ that dissatisfaction is the main reason for absenteeism.

3 *licma* = say something is true
She tried to _____ that her lateness was due to a train delay but it turned out to be untrue.

4 *plaarenpty* = it has been heard, but there's no evidence
_____ salaries are going to increase next year but at the moment it's just a rumour.

5 *aisd ot* = some people think it's true
Checking email just twice a day is _____ improve productivity at work.

6 *geaedlllly* = it has been rumoured to be true
The CEO is _____ retiring earlier than planned, I heard on the grapevine.

7 *ecpualtions* = discussion of ideas
There is a lot of _____ about the reasons for his resignation. He needs to set the record straight.

8 *yb lal cunacots* = it's widely believed to be true
Working life is _____ becoming more, not less, stressful.

7 Read the article. Choose the correct options to complete the text.

[1]*Speculation / Believe* is mounting for the upcoming annual inter-departmental relay run. Each department elects a team of five to run the twenty-kilometre course, but, as tradition dictates, members of each team are not announced until the day of the race. A source close to the author [2]*said to / reportedly* witnessed the Research and Development department's team practising, which seemed to include the whole department. This [3]*claimed / is believed* to be either a tactic or a case of keeping as many options open as possible. The R&D department are [4]*speculation / by all accounts* strong contenders for winning, having finished in the top three for the last three years. The marketing team are [5]*said to / apparently* be this year's favourites due to the low average age and the high number of marathon runners in the department. The top management have [6]*allegedly / claimed* been keeping to a strict diet to better their chances. Kitchen staff [7]*claim / believe* to have removed all but the healthiest choices from the menus. Elsewhere, large mysterious boxes have arrived, [8]*apparently / said* containing exercise bicycles so department meetings can be conducted while improving fitness simultaneously. The countdown has started.

8 Read the report of the event and correct one mistake in each sentence.

1 The day of the race dawned with much excitement by each accounts.
_____

2 Management claiming to have been called away on business but managed to attend at the last minute.
_____

3 Kitchen staff alleged weren't competing at all and then surprised everyone by finishing third.
_____

4 The IT department, who are belief to dislike sport, walked much of the course with good humour.
_____

5 The Communications team are say to be generally unfit, but daily training paid off.
_____

6 As predicted, the winning team were R&D, despite much speculate as to who would actually run.
_____

9 Use the notes and the words in brackets to write another short report for the company magazine that will go to customers as well as staff.

1 Manufacturing companies not fit – trying reverse trend. / (reportedly)
Manufacturing companies are reportedly not the fittest but we're trying to reverse the trend.

2 When employees physically fit – positive effect business. (allegedly)
_____

3 Top management – this the reason start annual relay race five years ago. (quoted as saying)
_____

4 The race strengthens corporate identity, provides year-long entertainment, fun. (by all accounts)
_____

5 Tactics build throughout year – departments bond through training outside working hours. (speculation)
_____

6 Almost certain R&D department win every time, as this year. But some surprises in innovative tactics and other positions. (said)
_____

7 Total 250 employees, friends, family attend race summer party – weather, drinks and snacks provided. (apparently)
_____

8 Possibly highlight corporate year. (believe)
_____

YOUR IDEA

1 Read the paragraphs about *Using your imagination*. Match the paragraphs with the photographs (a, b, c).

1 My sister and I were little terrors, honestly. I'm not sure how Mum and Dad put up with us. We were always building things using our bed sheets. I remember one time we made this massive structure between our beds – we shared a bedroom, you see. We used our pillows and duvets to make walls. Then we would defend our 'fort' from everybody, including our parents! ☐

2 I think it's a phase that everyone goes through when they're young. You have wild dreams about what you're going to be when you grow up. I think it's a key thing for children to use their imagination like this and have crazy ambitions, however unlikely they are. My parents were great. They bought a load of dressing-up stuff for me. I would always put on an astronaut costume and pretend that I was going into space! ☐

3 I'm a big believer in the importance of being creative and imaginative. I think it's vital in order to develop fully as a human being. I get quite annoyed by the focus at school on children learning facts and preparing for tests. That's why I decided to set up a storytelling club for the children at my school. Every Wednesday, after the last lessons of the day, a group of teachers and students get together in one of the lounge areas we have – in the library or common room – and we tell each other stories. It's brilliant! ☐

a

b

c

2 Write notes about a time when you use, or have used, your imagination. If you can't think of something from your own experience, write about someone you know. Think of several ideas so you can choose the best one.

_____

_____

_____

_____

3 Choose one thing from your list. Answer these questions about it.

1 Where and when do/did you do it?

_____

2 Who do/did you do it with? Or is it something you do/did alone?

_____

3 How does/did it make you feel?

_____

4 Practise talking about using your imagination. Try to …
- include yourself in the talk as part of the story.
- use your own natural voice – imagine you are having a conversation with the audience.
- stay physically relaxed – move as you normally would but not so much that it is a distraction.

ORGANIZING YOUR PRESENTATION

5 Match the four steps of a presentation with two examples of useful language (a–h).

1 Greet and welcome the audience, and introduce yourself ☐☐

2 Tell a story or set a scene about using your imagination ☐☐

3 Talk about the benefits of using your imagination ☐☐

4 Thank the audience and finish the talk ☐☐

a Hi, I'm Tim Robson. It's wonderful you can all be here today.

b When I was younger, …

c It's so important for developing your creativity.

d I've always loved creating …

e Hello, and thanks for coming along. My name's Charlotte Smith.

f Thank you for taking the time to listen.

g There is proof that children who play make-believe games are better at problem solving.

h Thank you so much for listening today.

YOUR PRESENTATION

6 Read the useful language on the left and make notes for your presentation.

1 Greet and welcome the audience, and introduce yourself Hi, I'm … . It's wonderful you can all be here today. Hello, and thanks for joining me. My name's … Welcome, everyone. I'm …	
2 Tell a story or set a scene about using your imagination When I was younger, … I always used to … We would often …	
3 Talk about the benefits of using your imagination People say that … It's possible to … It's so important for … Using your imagination …	
4 Thank the audience and finish the talk Thank you so much … Thank you for …	

7 Film yourself giving your presentation or practise in front of a mirror. Give yourself marks out of ten for …

- including yourself in your talk.   ☐ /10
- using your voice naturally.   ☐ /10
- staying physically relaxed during your talk – not moving around too much.   ☐ /10
- following the four steps in Exercise 6.   ☐ /10
- using correct grammar.   ☐ /10

8 Working together

8.1 Build a tower, build a team

TEDTALKS

It might be more appropriate to sketch a picture than to write a text about the designer and author, **TOM WUJEC**; he's such a visual thinker and communicator. He was born in Canada where he still lives and works. Although he now works in the fields of design and visual thinking, he originally studied Astronomy and Psychology at the University of Toronto. He worked first at McLaughlin Planetarium in Toronto as a producer, lecturer and writer. His next career step took him to the Royal Ontario Museum, where he was Creative Director and he designed and built interactive exhibits for the museum's diverse collection of fossils and dinosaurs, and modern discoveries. Wujec says that it was during his time at the museum that he really learned to think in images, although he'd been a student of visual thinking for many years. He now teaches these skills to others.

TED has played a key role in Tom Wujec's professional career since he attended his first TED conference in 1994. In addition to giving seven TED Talks, he's also been a visual artist and host at TED conferences, and he lists TED among his clients. He is the author of four books on design and creativity and is working on his fifth, *Wicked Problem Solving*. Currently, he's a fellow at Autodesk where he once designed and marketed their software and design products – one of which won an Academy Award. When asked in an interview what makes him tick, he said that he's a passionate learner, insatiably curious and loves to share ideas in a visual, tangible and persistent way.

Tom Wujec

CAREER PATHWAYS

1 Read the text. Answer the questions.

1 Why does the writer suggest it could be appropriate to describe Tom Wujec's ideas pictorially?
2 What might be seen as surprising about what he studied?
3 What work led him to think visually?
4 How has he been involved with TED?
5 What was he working on at the time of this article?

TED PLAYLIST

2 Other TED speakers are interested in topics similar to Tom Wujec's TED Talk. Read the descriptions of the four TED Talks at the top of page 115. In your opinion, which is the best title for this playlist, a, b or c?

a Forging new networks
b Collaboration drives innovation
c Making change happen faster

3 Complete the six-word summary (1–4) that corresponds to each talk in the TED playlist. Use these words.

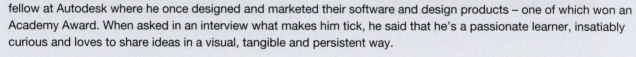

collaboration	complex	create	origin

1 Coffee shops _____ of new innovations.
2 Leading innovation to _____ collective genius.
3 Producing positive outcomes from close _____.
4 Making _____ systems work with checklists.

4 Match the verbs (1–5) with their collocates (a–e). Check your answers in the playlist descriptions.

1 to come up with   a insights
2 to gain   b connect in unexpected ways
3 to urge people to   c a positive mindset
4 to make a case for   d a checklist
5 to devise / implement   e new ideas

5 Which talk would you most like to see? Why? Watch the talk at TED.com.

Steven Johnson: Where good ideas come from

Steven Johnson examines how coffee houses may have been the hub of some of history's most significant innovations in science and technology. He uses fascinating examples to reveal that it is not a single 'Eureka moment', but a series of events and connections that contribute to making a breakthrough discovery. Johnson believes it's as important to share and connect new ideas as it is to come up with and protect them.

Linda Hill: How to manage for collective creativity

Linda Hill shares the insights she's gained from a decade's work observing creative processes at leading companies in twelve different industries. She's a business professor who uses ethnographical methods to study leadership in innovation. Using well-known companies as case studies, she presents surprising and paradoxical findings in skilful and memorable ways.

Kare Anderson: Be an opportunity maker

Kare Anderson is a columnist for *Forbes* who writes about research-based methods for, and benefits of, becoming more deeply connected. In her talk, she urges us all to connect in unexpected ways for the greater good. Using examples from her own experiences, she makes a powerful case for a positive collective mindset.

Atul Gawande: How do we heal medicine?

A surgeon and a public health journalist, Atul Gawande takes the question of 'How can we get good at doing what we do?' and answers it on many different levels. He explains how relatively simple changes can help us manage complex problems successfully. He describes innovations he has introduced in his own hospital, such as devising and implementing checklists for surgical teams, that have had a huge impact on the reduction of death rates.

AUTHENTIC LISTENING SKILLS
Understanding contrastive stress

6 🎧 2 10 You are going to hear a podcast in which a member of the *Keynote* team talks about Atul Gawande's TED Talk, *How do we heal medicine?* Listen to the extracts from the podcast. Underline the pairs of contrasting words or phrases that are stressed.

1 Gawande is able to take a step back from the detailed work of his job as a practising doctor to look at medicine as a whole.

2 He sets out to provide clarity to problems that show bewildering complexity.

3 … in 1970 the average hospital visit required care from two full-time clinicians. By the end of the twentieth century the number had risen to fifteen.

4 Gawande's message is an important one: medicine is broken but there are answers to its problems so it can be fixed.

LISTENING

7 🎧 2 11 Listen to the full podcast. Answer the questions.

1 What does the podcaster like about the way the information is presented?

2 According to Daniel, what does Gawande identify as the source(s) of complexity?

3 Which industries informed Gawande's solutions for managing complex systems?

4 What is Daniel's personal interest in medicine?

8 🎧 2 11 Try to complete the sentences from the podcast. Then listen again and check your answers.

1 Progress in medicine means _____ procedures and _____ drugs are available.

2 Three statistics show that the systems are failing: _____ heart patients and _____ stroke patients don't get appropriate care and _____ get sick while in hospital.

3 The three skills Gawande describes are: _____ _____ and _____ .

4 Gawande discovered _____ when studying other high-risk industries.

5 When he implemented them in some hospitals, they _____ in every case and cut death rates by _____ .

VOCABULARY IN CONTEXT

9 Read the extracts from the podcast. Choose the correct meaning of the words in bold.

1 I like to see the **bigger picture** on …
   a whole situation ☐   b the visual aspects ☐
   c the facts ☐

2 … the number of **clinicians** required now and in the past …
   a doctors who do research ☐   b staff who work in pharmacies ☐   c doctors with patient contact ☐

3 In the next part of the talk, he outlines the **methodology** to find these solutions using three skills: …
   a principles used ☐   b medical philosophy ☐
   c personal beliefs ☐

4 … Gawande decided to look at other high-risk industries to see how they **tackled** complex systems.
   a observed ☐   b dealt with ☐   c forced ☐

5 … my daughter, who's eleven, was **diagnosed with** a rare genetic condition called cystic fibrosis.
   a identified as having ☐   b caught by ☐
   c developed ☐

8.2 Having an off day?

GRAMMAR Cause and result

Teambuilding workshop

Our small team of six don't work together as well as we could, a recent audit revealed. We were rather surprised; we thought we were good at collaborating. As part of the audit recommendations, we all took part in a facilitated workshop which included various team-building activities. The first session involved ¹_____, which was to identify the strengths and weaknesses of our collaboration. The boss had a personal aim which was to participate and observe the team's iterative process in action while doing a task that had a clear outcome. Later we would identify some key issues that needed changing. Only time will tell whether the ²_____ will improve our overall collaboration and productivity. During the teambuilding workshop itself we worked inside and outside in various formations. Although some of the team, including myself, were initially quite sceptical, it built rapport and we enjoyed ³_____ in a competitive task. We were very motivated to be the winning team! The ensuing feedback session proved to be very enlightening and has helped us tighten our processes. We'll work towards eliminating steps we agree are no longer necessary and communicating more closely. I would recommend taking part in this workshop – it enabled us to focus on our work as a team and it was enjoyable.

1 Complete the text with the phrases (a–c).

   a achieving short-term targets
   b setting a clear goal
   c successful completion of targets and goals

2 Rewrite these sentences about the team-building event using the cause and result phrases in brackets.

   1 Our small team of six don't work together as well as we could, a recent audit revealed. (result in / revelation that)
   A recent audit _____ .

   2 As part of the audit recommendations, we all took part in a facilitated workshop. (to be the consequence of)
   Taking part in _____ .

3 The boss participated and later proposed changes in some key areas. (lead to / proposals)
The boss's observations _____ .

4 Although some of us were initially quite sceptical, the workshop built rapport. (foster)
Despite our _____ .

5 The ensuing feedback session has helped us tighten our processes. (contribute to)
The feedback session _____ .

6 We'll work towards communicating more closely. (bring about / communication)
The workshop will _____ .

3 Choose the correct options to complete the sentences.

1 The team-building activity *was due to / brought about* a relaxed atmosphere and some fun.
2 The team with no manager won, which *caused / resulted from* some disappointment to management!
3 The tasks *are the result of / gave rise to* a useful context in which to assess collaboration.
4 An increased appreciation of everyone's contribution *stemmed from / brought about* the successful workshop.
5 Stronger rapport in the team *resulted in / resulted from* working and laughing together in the workshop.
6 A lack of communication *contributes to / arises from* some work tasks having to be done twice and others being neglected.
7 The facilitator *killed / fostered* better communication through debriefing and progress reporting.
8 Ultimately the workshop *resulted in / arose from* decisions to redefine working groups and optimize processes.

GRAMMAR EXTRA! *so / such … that +* clause

4 *So* and *such* are intensifiers used in combination with *that* to indicate a result. Write two sentence beginnings (use *so* in a and *such* in b). Keep the meaning the same. You may have to change or add some words.

1 (Bad storm) … the police and fire brigade were out dealing with fallen trees and flooding most of the night.
   a *The storm was so bad that*
   b *It was such a bad storm that*
2 (Cheap flights) … the New York trip has become considerably more realistic.
   a _____
   b _____
3 (Large order) … we'll have to employ some temporary staff to manage it.
   a _____
   b _____
4 (Good presentation) … he was promoted.
   a _____
   b _____
5 (Workshop a success) … she held an extra one.
   a _____
   b _____
6 (Travelling rush hour time-consuming activity) … the company started flexitime and home-working days to deal with it.
   a _____
   b _____
7 (Serious setback caused by IT problems) … they had to extend the project deadline by a week.
   a _____
   b _____

8 (Many complaints)… they had to remove the product from the shelves.
   a _____
   b _____
9 (Very popular product) … we had to increase orders.
   a _____
   b _____

PRONUNCIATION Voicing in final consonants

5 ∩2 12 In each pair, underline where there's a shorter vowel sound before an unvoiced final consonant. Then listen and check your answers.

1 worksho**p**   workroo**m**
2 share**d**   shu**t**
3 la**ck**   la**g** behind
4 wor**k**   wor**d**

6 ∩2 13 Listen and repeat. In each sentence underline the final consonant sound in bold that is voiced.

1 It was brought about by ba**d** manageme**nt**.
2 Plea**s**e cut u**p** your old credit card on receipt of your new one.
3 She asked me to co**m**e ba**ck**.
4 He wasn't able to produ**c**e any I.**D**.

DICTATION

7 ∩2 14 Listen to someone talking about a way to achieve big goals. Complete the paragraph.

When I have to achieve big goals, and _____

_____ 'eating an elephant model'. Creighton Abrams, a US army general, came up with it and, _____ .

The fact that the originator was in the army _____

_____ .

Given the elephant's large size, the idea is that _____

_____ .

Otherwise, reaching a big goal might seem unobtainable _____ .

Last year, before moving premises, we agreed to throw away any unwanted papers and files. _____

_____

enormous task successfully was to deal with it bit by bit.

_____

and cleared the way for the move. As Abrams said: 'When eating an elephant, take one bite at a time'.

8.3 How *not* to motivate people

READING

1 Are these statements true (T) or false (F)? Read the article and check.

1 Bhutan broke a World Record in 2001. ☐
2 Bhutan is a small country in the Himalayas. ☐
3 It's a well-known trekking destination. ☐
4 Football is the national sport in Bhutan. ☐

2 Read the article again and answer the questions.

1 What kinds of motivation are described?
2 What made the team one of the weakest in the world?
3 What did the players say about being bottom of the league?
4 How does the country restrict modern influences?
5 Why does Bhutan measure Gross National Happiness?
6 Why didn't they have a strong national team after the early 80s?

Motivating Bhutan's national **football team**

If you were coaching the players in a national football team that was bottom of the world league, how would you motivate them? Would you pay them bonuses for every goal? Or would you make everyone feel they had something to contribute? Do you believe in external or extrinsic motivators like money and fame, or in internal or intrinsic motivation coming from the task itself and wanting to do it well? Up until recently, Bhutan was bottom at place 209 in FIFA's ranking, with a reputation of being one of the weakest teams in the world. They are relatively new to the game, having only started playing internationally in 1982. Since then they have only won four times in 33 years. In 2000, they broke the Guinness World Record for the team with the most goals against them when a match against Kuwait resulted in a score of twenty-nil.

Bhutan's team captain Karma Shedrup Tshering is quoted as saying 'Everyone was talking about us being at the bottom but we didn't feel any pressure because you can only go one way from there and that's upwards.'

The word 'Bhutan' roughly translates as 'land of the thunder dragon', originating from the storms and landslides that are typical there. This small kingdom, a little bigger than Taiwan or Belgium, is situated in the eastern part of the Himalayas. The capital city Thimphu is a giddy-making 2,648 metres above sea level and this may be one reason why the team has never lost a football game at home.

Western and modern influences have been allowed into the country only slowly and in a controlled manner. Although Bhutan is a popular trekking destination, tourism is permitted exclusively through authorized package tours. Television and the Internet were not available there until 1999. Bhutan is the only country to measure happiness at a country level. 'Gross National Happiness' (GNH), a term coined by former king, Jigme Dorji Wangchuk, in 1972, aims to help people strike a balance between material and spiritual concerns.

Archery is the national sport but football has slowly grown in popularity, arriving with foreign teachers recruited into schools in the 1950s. In the early 80s, there was a strong national team but no players to succeed them once they had retired and, although the government supported football, there were other priorities to invest in, like health and education. Bhutan became a member of FIFA in 2000 and now receives some funding.

The team is ever optimistic despite the infamous game with Kuwait. The current national coach, Chokey Nima, was a player in that match and everyone there knows that nothing motivates quite like a beating like that. In March 2015, the team won two games against Sri Lanka in the qualifiers for the 2018 World Cup. The win moved them swiftly up the FIFA table to number 159. 'We kept our calm and let our football talk for us,' said Captain Karma Shedrup Tshering about the game.

3 Complete the sentences. Read the article again to check.

1 Playing football for fame and glory is an _____ motivator.
2 Thimphu is situated at a high altitude and can make people feel _____ .
3 The former king of Bhutan was the first to use the term Gross National Happiness – he _____ it.
4 _____ , Bhutan's national sport, involves firing arrows towards a target to score points.
5 The game against Kuwait has become _____ – well-known for being so bad.

4 🎧 **2 15** Listen and circle the correct answers.

1 The bottom *eight / twelve* teams battle it out to qualify.
2 FIFA made *$30,000 / $300,000* available.
3 Thailand offered the use of their *football stadium / training camp.*
4 The team needed to get used to the *humidity / altitude.*
5 Tickets for the home game were *cheap / free.*
6 The winning goal was scored in the *nineteenth / ninetieth* minute.

VOCABULARY Teams and teamwork

5 Match the verbs (1–8) with the phrases (a–h).

1	to be	a	as a group
2	to do your	b	a team player
3	to go	c	part of things
4	to pull	d	a sense of belonging
5	to bond	e	the extra mile
6	to feel a	f	your weight
7	to have	g	the load
8	to share	h	fair share

6 Complete the sentences with the correct form of the expressions from Exercise 5.

1 To _____ you have to be good at working with others and work towards the same goals.
2 If any new players join, it's important to _____ as early as possible, and build good relationships both on and off the pitch.
3 Once new players have settled in and have _____ , the real training can begin.
4 Each member has to _____ but they also have to understand that players' roles may require that they contribute differently to the team effort.
5 To players, _____ may seem like different amounts for different people, but a skilful coach will smooth out any differences.
6 _____ means that individuals do what they can do best to reach the overall goal for the team. They contribute different skills.
7 The more the players are united and feel _____ , the better they can work together.
8 A team that is highly motivated will be willing to _____ and keep achieving greater things.

WORDBUILDING Noun formation

7 Rewrite each sentence replacing the word(s) in italics with a noun to make it sound more formal. You may have to add or change words to keep the sentence grammatical.

1 The department manager didn't *seem able* to motivate the team and needed support.
   The department manager *lacked the* **ability** *to motivate the team and needed support.*
2 The enjoyment of the game itself *motivated* the team to play well.
   The enjoyment of the game itself provided _____
3 When we *awarded* extra holiday as an incentive, it proved more effective than overtime payments.
   The _____ .
4 He *knew* a great deal about the background of the match.
   He had extensive background _____ .
5 The crowd enjoyed the *exciting* game and festive atmosphere.
   The crowd _____ .
6 Thimphu is an *inconvenient* city to travel to because of the mountains.
   The _____ .
7 The Thai team was *generous* about training, making competing possible.
   The Thai team's _____ .
8 The team was highly *committed* to winning throughout the game.
   The team's _____

WORD FOCUS *work*

8 Complete the phrasal verbs with these prepositions.

at	around	in	off	on	towards

1 The best way for me to work _____ stress is to go for a run.
2 We need to try and work _____ a holiday theme for the next newsletter as it will be coming out in December.
3 It's not easy to work _____ his absence. It's a real setback at this stage.
4 I've worked _____ my French over the years but I still sound like a British man speaking schoolboy French.
5 At the moment the team is working _____ cutting costs in the department to present at the next management meeting.
6 We should both start working _____ an early retirement by saving more of our salaries each month.

9 Match the meanings a–f with the phrasal verbs (1–6) from Exercise 8.

a	include	☐	d accommodate	☐
b	practise	☐	e prepare for	☐
c	find ways to	☐	f get rid of	☐

8.4 If you'll just let me finish …

TAKING PART IN A MEETING

1 Put the words in the correct order to make phrases and decide if they are interrupting (I) or stopping interruption (S).

1 I / just / here / something / can / say? ☐ ☐
_____

2 just / saying / finish / what / could / I / I / was? ☐ ☐
_____

3 finish / me / if / 'll / let / you / … ☐ ☐
_____

4 interrupt, / hate / but / I / to / … ☐ ☐
_____

5 jump / dying / I / you're / know / to / but / in, / … ☐ ☐
_____

6 but / sorry / interrupting, / for / … ☐ ☐
_____

7 just / you / say / before / can / continue, / I / … ☐ ☐
_____

8 if / finish / you'll / me / allow / to / … ☐ ☐
_____

2 🎧 2 16 Listen to a meeting about a job rotation programme. Tick (✓) the phrases in Exercise 1 that you hear.

3 🎧 2 16 Listen again and write the phrase used to open the discussion and the one used to invite participation.

1 Opening a discussion _____
2 Inviting participation _____

4 🎧 2 17 Complete the sentences for wrapping up a meeting and inviting participation. Use these words. Then listen and check your answers.

finish	thoughts	everything	take	continue

1 What's your _____ on the benefits of changing departments?
2 Any _____ on the expanded programme?
3 Before you _____ , can I just say thank you for all your help with this?
4 I think that's nearly _____ .
5 I think we can _____ there for today.

PRONUNCIATION Emphasizing the main focus in the sentence

5 🎧 2 18 Underline the main stress in each sentence depending on the meaning in brackets. Then listen and check your answers.

1 I'd like to start the discussion by asking if everyone's read the information sent around. (This is how we'll begin the meeting.)
2 It'll probably make a difference to the discussion. (There will be more to talk about if people have done the preparation.)
3 There will be a chance for everyone to have their say. (No one will be left out)
4 You mean with hindsight it was more useful than when you were actually doing it? (After the event it took on more meaning.)
5 It could be a great retention tool, as well as promoting innovation. (A way to keep employees in the company.)
6 I would like us all to suggest one or two employees to put forward and answer the questions. (It's something I think is important.)

WRITING Debriefing questionnaire

6 Put the topics for a debriefing questionnaire in the correct order.

- **a** The biggest challenge ☐
- **b** Suggested changes for next project ☐
- **c** Project summary ☐
- **d** Successes and reasons for these ☐
- **e** The biggest learning outcome ☐

7 Read the linking devices. Tick (✓) the ones that are used to express result.

- **1** as a result of ☐
- **2** also ☐
- **3** however ☐
- **4** overall ☐
- **5** because ☐
- **6** as a consequence ☐
- **7** thanks to ☐

8 Complete the debriefing questionnaire with the linking devices from Exercise 7. More than one option is sometimes possible.

Briefly summarize your rotation assignment.

I went to the London office for four weeks from Madrid, for a project and to improve links between the two offices. I was able to contribute to processes and write documents in Spanish and in English. I was 1_____ able to improve my English.

What contributed to the assignment's success?

2_____ the fact that the organization was so good, I didn't have to spend time finding accommodation or finding my feet. This was partly 3_____ the 'buddy scheme' that was set up beforehand – I had contact with my buddy before I arrived and was looked after by them during my visit.

What was the biggest challenge?

Certainly the cultural differences were the biggest challenge. 4_____, they made the assignment very interesting.

What was most valuable for your own development and why?

I had thought that, apart from language, European countries were very similar. I actually found there were a lot of differences in the way our two countries approach things. 5_____ of these differences, I'll probably take a different approach in future. 6_____, I'm going to pass on what I've learned to my colleagues.

What could be improved about the programme and why?

7_____, I'm grateful to have taken part in the programme. I would say that more employees should be encouraged to participate; it shouldn't just be for young people like myself.

---

9 Complete the debriefing questionnaire using the model from Exercise 8, the notes below and suitable linking devices.

1 **Briefly summarize your rotation assignment.**
   a I went to Berlin for six weeks / only colleague available
   I went to Berlin for six weeks because I was the only colleague available.
   b short notice / urgent IT project
   _____
   _____
   c not well prepared / fix the problem
   _____
   _____

2 **What contributed to the assignment's success?**
   a IT systems identical / 'speak' common language
   _____
   _____
   b built good relationships
   _____
   _____

3 **What was the biggest challenge?**
   a counterparts not speak good English / I not speak good German
   _____
   _____
   b understanding German / confusing experiences
   _____
   _____
   c improved / understanding European colleagues
   _____

4 **What was most valuable for your own development and why?**
   a learning / simplify message / avoid misunderstandings
   _____
   _____

5 **What could be improved about the programme and why?**
   a recommend / basic language course
   _____
   _____

The informal email you will read in Exercise 2 is in answer to the following exam question.

From: roman@crgs.com

To: marta@mailbox.cz

Subject: Your conference

Hi Marta,

It was great to hear from you.

How did the conference go in the end? I know you were really looking forward to it. Do you feel like you learned anything new? Was it worth it?

Let me know how it went,

Roman

Write your informal email in **220–260 words** in an appropriate style.

IDEAS

1 Tick (✓) the things you would expect to see in the informal email.

- **a** advice for how to organize a conference ☐
- **b** an informal greeting ☐
- **c** information about Marta's job ☐
- **d** a reference to Roman's previous email ☐
- **e** a sign-off message, encouraging the reader to reply ☐
- **f** a general statement about how the conference went ☐
- **g** descriptions of specific events from the conference ☐

MODEL

2 Read the informal email. Match the five sections with a description (a–g) from Exercise 1.

1 ☐   2 ☐   3 ☐   4 ☐   5 ☐

3 Read the email again. Are these statements true (T) or false (F)?

1 The conference lived up to Marta's expectations. ☐

2 The first part of the day taught Marta a lot about the other conference attendees. ☐

3 The person organizing the conference didn't realize when things weren't going to plan. ☐

4 Marta felt her presentation went smoothly. ☐

5 Marta and the other attendees didn't feel comfortable doing the final activity. ☐

TO: roman@crgs.com   **FROM:** marta@mailbox.cz

SUBJECT: Conference

¹Hi Roman,

²Thanks for your message.

³The conference was a total disaster from start to finish. My colleagues and I figured it would be a great break from the day to day of the office, as it had been in previous years, but we ended up being disappointed.

⁴It started off with a 'getting to know you' activity, but we've been going to these one-day conferences for five years already and the same people are there every time! The new facilitator, the woman who was running the whole thing this time round, didn't notice that we already knew each other – she was very unobservant.

Another thing I had to do was present one of the projects we've been working on in our office. It was meant to be inspiring and motivating, but it was just before lunch and everyone clearly wanted to have a break. I was feeling nervous too, so I tried to finish as fast as possible. I couldn't wait to get it over with!

To finish the day off, we had to reflect on everything we'd learned from the conference and comment on the best and worst sessions we'd seen during the day. Nobody wanted to say anything bad about the sessions, because we all know each other. It turned out to be a complete waste of time.

All in all, I'd say we'd have been better off just staying in the office!

⁵I'd be interested to hear if you've ever been to a conference this bad. I hope they're not that common!

Marta

USEFUL LANGUAGE

4 Replace part of each sentence from the negative email with one of these positive phrases, so that it means the opposite.

| do it all again | ~~a huge success~~ | pleasantly surprised |
| it was worth every penny | the best way we could have spent our day | |

1 It was *a total disaster* from start to finish. *a huge success*

2 We ended up being really disappointed. _____

3 We couldn't wait to get it over with. _____

4 It turned out to be a complete waste of time. _____

5 All in all, I'd say we'd have been better off saving our money. _____

5 Match the phrases (a–o) with the categories (1–5).

1 Referring to the reader
2 Summarizing the experience
3 Describing how the experience started
4 Describing later parts of the experience
5 Encouraging the reader to reply

a a very memorable experience ☐
b First up, ☐
c How's everything with you? ☐
d I'd love to hear from you. ☐
e It was great to get your message! ☐
f It was very interesting at first ☐
g Let me know what you think. ☐
h Looking forward to hearing from you soon. ☐
i one of the worst days of my life ☐
j so it was a pleasant surprise when ☐
k The first thing I want to tell you about is ☐
l the holiday of a lifetime ☐
m Then it was on to ☐
n We ended up ☐
o What's up with you? ☐

6 Rewrite the more formal phrases from an email with ones from Exercise 5.

1 I'm very grateful that you sent me an email to tell me your news.
_____

2 I've just had a particularly good holiday in Thailand.
_____

3 I would like to begin by describing the hotels we stayed in.
_____

4 We were satisfied when we found out that all our food and drink was included in the price – great value for money!
_____

5 Afterwards we went to Bangkok for a week.
_____

6 I'd love to take you to Thailand one day. Could you tell me if that would interest you?
_____

7 Complete the collocations (1–6) with these adjectives. Are they positive (P) or negative (N) descriptions?

breathtaking (the) ideal	dreadful (a) rewarding	(with) disastrous welcoming

1 _____ views ☐   4 _____ results ☐
2 _____ people ☐   5 _____ weather ☐
3 _____ place ☐   6 _____ experience ☐

PLANNING

You will answer the following question.

TO:		FROM:
SUBJECT:	Great photos!	

Hi there,

I've just seen your photos. Have you been away? Where did you go? What did you do? Did you have a good time? Tell me all about it!

Sally

8 Plan your informal email. Write notes to answer these questions. Don't write full sentences yet.

1 Where will you write about? What adjectives/adverbs can you use to describe it?
2 What specific event(s) will you describe? What adjectives/adverbs can you use to describe it/them?
3 How will you summarize the experience?

WRITING

9 Write an informal email to reply to the message in Exercise 8. In your email you should:

• open and close the email in a friendly way
• summarize the experience briefly so the reader knows what to expect
• write more specifically about the place you went to and the things you did
• use vivid, descriptive language to make it clear whether you enjoyed it or not

Write **220–260 words** in an appropriate style.

ANALYSIS

10 Check your informal email. Answer the questions.

• **Content:** Does the informal email describe the place you went to and the things you did? Is it 220 to 260 words long?
• **Communicative achievement:** Is it written in an informal, friendly style? Is the text sufficiently descriptive? Is it clear to the reader whether you enjoyed the experience or not?
• **Organization:** Is the email logically organized? Are the ideas connected?
• **Language:** Does it use correct grammar and vocabulary? Is a good range of structures used?

9 Stress and relaxation

9.1 All it takes is 10 mindful minutes

TEDTALKS

ANDY PUDDICOMBE was born in 1972, raised in Bristol, England, and first discovered meditation and what it could do for his mind aged eleven. Later, he lost several close friends in a freak accident and the stress related to this led him to leave university and embrace meditation full time. From 1994 to 2004, he travelled to retreats and monasteries in Asia, Russia and Australia, studying first as a lay person, and later, after he was ordained, as a Tibetan Buddhist monk. He was a dedicated teacher and, once he'd mastered techniques himself – through up to eighteen hours of meditation a day over ten years — he worked 'to demystify meditation for a secular audience'.

After he decided to leave monastic life in 2004, he used his interest in juggling to study for a degree in circus arts in London. He also became a mindfulness consultant and set up a meditation practice. One of the people he introduced to meditation later became his business partner. This was Rich Pierson, a marketing and brand expert with whom he created and launched *Headspace* in 2010. 'We both thought, how could we present meditation in a way that our friends would genuinely give it a try?' says Puddicombe. The mission is to help create a happier, healthier world through mindfulness by teaching the skills of meditation. The *Headspace* book was published in 2011 and the app in 2012. Puddicombe has also written for and appeared in the media. Today the *Headspace* business is worth an estimated £25 million and has one million registered users. Every paid subscription triggers a donation so, rather like karma, when you get some headspace yourself, you also give some to someone else in need of headspace.

Andy Puddicombe

CAREER PATHWAYS

1 Read the text. Answer the questions.

1 Why did Andy Puddicombe drop out of university?
2 What qualifications has he gained in life?
3 What skills from each partner contribute to the business success of *Headspace*?
4 What key question helped the pair develop the concept of the business?
5 What do they aim to achieve with *Headspace*?

TED PLAYLIST

2 Other TED speakers are interested in topics similar to Andy Puddicombe's TED Talk. Read the descriptions of four TED Talks at the top of page 125. In your opinion, which is the best title for this playlist, a, b or c?

a Finding happiness through seeking pleasure
b Finding happiness through increasing mindfulness
c Finding happiness through confidence building

3 Complete the six-word summary (1–4) that corresponds to each talk in the TED playlist. Use these words.

curing	happy	living	valuable

1 From hectic _____ to finding peace.
2 Every moment is a _____ opportunity.
3 _____ crime's distorted mind with meditation.
4 Wandering minds don't make us _____.

4 Match the verbs (1–5) with their collocates (a–e). Check your answers in the playlist descriptions.

1 to gain   a advantage of
2 to take   b on the present
3 to transform   c one of the toughest prisons
4 to track   d people's state of mind
5 to focus   e incredible insights and pleasure

5 Which talk would you most like to see? Why? Watch the talk at TED.com.

▶ **Pico Iyer: The art of stillness**

Pico Iyer is a prolific traveller and travel writer. In his calm and lyrical talk he goes on a more inward journey away from the hustle and bustle of everyday life. He tells us with quiet confidence of the incredible insights and pleasure we can gain from being still and how this emptiness enables us to escape the demands of the modern world and process our thoughts.

▶ **David Steindl-Rast: Want to be happy? Be grateful**

Brother David Steindl-Rast, a monk and interfaith scholar, has a recipe for being happy which involves stopping, appreciating and being grateful. In this way, he counsels, we can ensure we fully contemplate and take advantage of the chances we're presented with in life, before they pass us by. In his contemplative talk he also reminds us that while we all seek happiness outside ourselves, it is we who ultimately create it through our own gratitude.

▶ **Kiran Bedi: A police chief with a difference**

Kiran Bedi is a trailblazer who became India's first and highest-ranking female police officer. Before that she ran and transformed one of the country's toughest prisons into a centre for learning and meditation. In her straight-talking and down-to-earth presentation, she shares her philosophy of '90:10' with us: 90 per cent of what happens to us is our own creation and it's only the remaining ten per cent that is down to fate or nature.

▶ **Matt Killingsworth: Want to be happier? Stay in the moment**

Matt Killingsworth is a researcher who gathers data on when we are happy or unhappy, using an app he built to track people's state of mind. In his talk full of data revelations, he shows us that we are happiest when we are focused on the present – but that our minds stray off topic nearly half of all our waking hours.

AUTHENTIC LISTENING SKILLS
Understanding mid-sentence changes in direction

6 🎧 2 19 You are going to hear a podcast in which a member of the *Keynote* team talks about Matt Killingsworth's TED Talk, *Want to be happier? Stay in the moment*. Listen and complete the sentences.

1 This talk was of interest to – _____ _____ because I try to practise mindfulness in my daily life.
2 His main subject is happiness, _____ _____ .
3 That is the paradox of happiness, what looked like it should bring – _____ – doesn't always.

LISTENING

7 🎧 2 20 Listen to the full podcast. Answer the questions.

1 Why was Helen drawn to the talk by Matt Killingsworth?
2 According to the podcaster, what does Killingsworth mean by the paradox of happiness?
3 What was Helen's specific question?
4 Which data might help Helen answer her question?

8 🎧 2 20 Listen again. Are these statements true (T) or false (F)?

1 Matt Killingsworth collected the data using an app. ☐
2 He analyzed 15,000 reports from 650 people. ☐
3 Mind wandering during unpopular tasks improves happiness levels. ☐
4 The podcaster finds driving makes her prone to mind wandering. ☐
5 Helen feels that her happiness can't impact on other people. ☐

VOCABULARY IN CONTEXT

9 Read the extracts from the podcast. Choose the correct meaning of the words in bold.

1 His presentation style and way of talking **emanated** a distinct scientific feel …
   a gave ☐
   b tried to contain ☐
   c hid ☐
2 What interested me particularly about the talk was what he said about staying in the moment and **wandering** minds.
   a uninteresting ☐
   b unfocused ☐
   c walking ☐
3 His research with the tracking app 'Trackyourhappiness.org' has revealed that mind wandering is **ubiquitous**.
   a rare ☐
   b dangerous ☐
   c widespread ☐
4 Matt Killingsworth analyzed data from 650,000 real-time reports from 15,000 people **hailing from** 80 countries …
   a working in ☐
   b coming from ☐
   c describing ☐
5 Driving is an activity where I am most **distracted**, so I'm going to be very conscious of staying present.
   a unable to concentrate ☐
   b busy ☐
   c focused ☐

125

GRAMMAR Intensifying adverbs

1 Choose the correct options to complete the text.

The Black-hole Château

The château is [1]*utterly / exquisitely / totally* located in [2] *beautifully / fully / totally* kept gardens and extensive wooded grounds. The spacious rooms are [3] *well / magnificently / extremely* comfortable, [4] *tastefully / absolutely / utterly* furnished and most [5] *fully / importantly / well* are [6] *tastefully / completely / well* quiet. The entire complex is [7] *extremely / fully / exquisitely* accessible for wheelchair users and all staff speak French, German and English.

At the Black-hole Château we believe that holiday breaks are to be savoured and should be [8] *completely / beautifully / tastefully* stress free. Your holiday is [9] *well / beautifully / utterly* earned and we aim to allow you every opportunity to unwind and recharge your batteries. Black-hole Château is [10] *totally / beautifully / importantly* cut off from the outside world. There are no televisions, computers or other screens on the premises and our slogan is 'slow food, slow stay and slow down'.

2 Answer the questions. Use the prompts and at least two adverbs in each answer.

| absolutely (x2) | beautifully (x2) | completely |
| exquisitely | totally (x2) | |

1 What's the hotel's unique selling point (USP)? (device free / peaceful)

_____

2 What activities can be enjoyed at the château? (walking or riding in traffic free / quiet surroundings)

_____

3 Where else can guests relax? (modern spa and pool complex / comfortable sofas and seats inside and outside)

_____

4 How should holidays be according to the brochure? (relaxing / perfect)

_____

3 Complete the sentences about the hotel with the correct adverb.

1 Our stay was *extremely / such* relaxing in every way.
2 We felt *completely / beautifully* rejuvenated when we returned.
3 Throughout our stay we *barely / always* saw or spoke to any of the other guests.
4 Every meal was *freshly / incredibly* cooked to order.
5 A substantial amount of produce is *locally / so* sourced.
6 *Utterly, / Amazingly,* I didn't miss the technology I thought I couldn't live without.
7 *Intelligently / Expertly* trained riding and golfing coaches made learning fun.
8 All amenities were also *completely / very* wheelchair accessible, I was happy to find.

4 Match the adverbs (1–5) with the adjectives (a–e) to make common combinations.

1 absolutely   **a** sociable
2 blissfully   **b** growing
3 naturally   **c** busy
4 rapidly   **d** clear
5 horribly   **e** happy

5 Use the adverb-adjective combinations from Exercise 4 to complete the sentences.

1 After a wonderful week we reluctantly said goodbye and returned to our _____ lives.
2 We don't want any more misunderstandings. Is that _____?
3 Being _____ makes her the perfect choice to work with customers.
4 Our _____ international reputation is down to word-of-mouth.
5 We notice how people arrive very stressed and leave _____.

PRONUNCIATION Stress with intensifying adverbs

6 🎧 2 21 Underline the words you think will be stressed. Then listen and check your answers.

1 Although he was nervous, he delivered the presentation incredibly calmly.
2 After the sales team had used it for a year, it was utterly ruined.
3 He learned the skills fantastically quickly.
4 The spare parts are readily available in most electronics stores.
5 We discovered this place accidentally on the way back last year.

GRAMMAR EXTRA! Time expressions

7 Complete the sentences with these time expressions. Use the context to help.

| already | finally | just | last | now |
| recently | tomorrow | yesterday | when | while |

1 I've only _____ met him.
2 I saw him _____ I was waiting for the train.
3 I haven't spoken to him _____. The last time was nearly three weeks ago.
4 I phoned him _____ but he wasn't at home.
5 I'm meeting him for coffee _____.
6 I'm looking at him _____. He's sitting in the corner.
7 _____ I see him, I'll tell him you're looking for him.
8 I _____ saw him a month ago.
9 After spending nearly an hour looking for him, I _____ found him waiting at reception.
10 I've _____ seen him twice today.

DICTATION

8 🎧 2 22 Listen and complete the paragraph.

_____ – both medical doctors – who travel every year to a different destination. _____, but take a busman's holiday where they offer their medical expertise in remote places to people in need. Before leaving _____ remove any evidence of wealth and privilege. They travel with an organization and, _____ the victims of natural disasters. _____ and arrive back eager to explain how much they have gained from the whole experience and the kindness of strangers.

READING

1 Look at the title of the article. Then complete these phrases about humour with the correct preposition/particle.

1 It's important to be able to laugh _____ yourself.
2 At the time it wasn't funny, but afterwards we had a good laugh _____ it.
3 Often I chat and joke _____ colleagues about our work.
4 It's such a funny book. It made me laugh _____ loud.

2 Read the article and answer the questions.

1 Who is the advice in the article aimed at?
2 Is there a solid scientific basis for the advice?
3 What does the writer suggest we should joke about?

3 Read the article again. Would the author definitely (D), probably (P) or almost certainly not (N) agree with these statements?

1 Laughing is a suitable response to any kind of stress.
2 Laughing is a natural way to relieve stress.
3 Stress makes us pessimistic.
4 Laughing makes people feel good about themselves.
5 Employers don't mean work to be fun.
6 Looking at non-work related websites at work is OK.
7 Never take yourself too seriously.
8 Don't worry about offending others when you make a joke.

Laugh in the **face of stress**

Now, don't get the wrong idea from the title of this article. I don't want to belittle your problems or to suggest there are times when stress isn't justified: times of financial worries or health concerns, times of loss or heartache. I just want to offer help with the type of stress that most of us live with daily, and which, joking aside, is the cause of more heart-related conditions in the USA than anything else: and that's work-related stress. Because most work is just organized stress. Deadlines, targets and critical meetings weigh heavily on us, increasing the pressure until it becomes overwhelming. Yet we all possess an in-built coping mechanism, a valve that allows us to release that pressure and rebalance ourselves. It's called the ability to laugh and if you're not exercising it, you're missing an important trick.

The physiological benefits of laughter are well-documented. The muscles stop tensing, blood pressure drops, the blood gets more oxygen, and the brain releases endorphins, the body's natural pain killers. Psychologically, our mood improves and we break out of the cycle of negative thoughts. We start to think more positively about things, including ourselves – several studies have shown that laughter boosts self-esteem. They have also shown that after a good laugh, people begin to think more clearly and more open-mindedly. So how do you build humour into your working day?

Look for the ridiculous in seemingly difficult situations. Of course you're going to take your work seriously, but don't take it too seriously. At a board meeting our chairman announced that it was nothing to get too worried about, but some big cuts were going to have to be made in the company. Everyone looked at each other, all thinking the same thing – 'Is it going to be my department?'. Then one colleague broke the tension by pointing to a sign on the fire exit door that said 'This door is alarmed' and said, 'I don't know about the rest of you, but the door's certainly worried'.

Allow yourself light-hearted breaks from work in the day to chat and joke with colleagues. Take time out to read a funny article or watch a YouTube clip. Something that just makes you smile is as good as something that makes you laugh out loud.

Laugh at yourself at least as often as you make jokes about anything else. Someone I work with, who is often criticized for changing his mind, used this Groucho Marx quote when someone disagreed with him 'Well, those are my principles and if you don't like them ... I've got others'.

Try to defuse tense situations for others. For example, when a colleague says, 'I'm going to lose my job if I don't make my targets this month', ask them if you can have their desk by the window when they're gone.

Too many of us wait, weeks or months at times, for stress to pass before we allow ourselves to look back at a situation with humour. But that doesn't actually cure the stress. You need to lighten up now. Try it – it will do wonders for your blood pressure.

4 Read the words and phrases (1–8). Find a phrase in the article that means the same.

1 Don't misunderstand me (para 1)
   Don't get the wrong idea
2 seriously (para 1) _____
3 you're not taking advantage of a useful solution (para 1)
   _____
4 written about a lot (para 2) _____
5 stop doing the same thing again and again (para 2)
   _____
6 don't worry about it too much (para 3) _____
7 Have a break and … (para 4) _____
8 don't be so serious (para 7) _____

VOCABULARY Idioms related to the body

5 Match the body idioms (1–8) with the meanings (a–h).

1 to be up to your eyeballs
2 to keep your chin up
3 to make your blood boil
4 to get cold feet
5 to let your hair down
6 to get something off your chest
7 to be a pain in the neck
8 to be a weight off your shoulders

a to anger you
b to enjoy yourself without inhibitions
c to tell someone how you feel
d to have a lot to do
e to be an annoyance
f to be a relief
g to stay positive
h to lose courage at the last moment

6 Use the correct form of the body idioms (1–8) from Exercise 5 to complete the sentences.

1 He had prepared the talk very well, but on the day of the presentation he _____ .
2 When I think about how hard you've worked and how badly they've treated you it _____ .
3 Sorry I can't help you this week. I'm _____ with work.
4 I'm trying to _____ , but that's the fourth rejection I've had in a row.
5 I'm sorry you have to rewrite the article or at least cut it down. It _____ , I know, but the magazine insists that it can't be over 300 words.
6 Sorry to bore you about my troubles at work. I just had to _____ .
7 At the end of a long year's training and participating in competitions, she can now finally go out and _____ .
8 Paying the final instalment on the car last week _____ . I'll actually have a bit of spare cash now.

WORDBUILDING -ing adjectives

7 Look at the examples of -ing adjectives then match the -ing adjectives (1–7) with the effects (a–g).

1 empowering ☐
2 thrilling ☐
3 devastating ☐
4 reassuring ☐
5 off-putting ☐
7 puzzling ☐
8 touching ☐

a makes you feel very excited
b helps you to feel everything is OK
c makes you feel sad or sentimental
d makes you feel everything is ruined and hopeless
e makes you feel confused
f makes you feel you can succeed at something by yourself
g stops you wanting to do something

8 Choose the correct intensifying adverb to go with each adjective.

1 The government's decision to go ahead with the building of the dam was *very / quite* devastating for the local community.
2 I find it *utterly / very* puzzling that they should want to move house when they have everything they want here.
3 Watching him eat the whole crab with his hands was *awkwardly / acutely* off-putting.
4 Having an experienced guide in the mountains was *extremely / exceptionally* reassuring.
5 I cried almost all the way through the film. It was *deeply / relatively* moving.
6 It's a(n) *very / overly* empowering training course. I'd strongly recommend it.
7 The amount of work I have to do at the moment is *totally / carefully* overwhelming.
8 The zip-wire ride is *absolutely / nicely* thrilling. You reach speeds of up to 100 kph.

WORD FOCUS *live*

9 Look at the phrasal verb with *live* in the article (para 1). Then match the phrasal verbs with *live* (1–6) with the phrases (a–f) that they collocate with.

1 to live on
2 to live through
3 to live for
4 to live with
5 to live down
6 to live up to

a everyone's expectations
b the shame of coming last
c just a few dollars a day
d difficult times
e the weekend
f my decision

10 Complete the sentences with the phrasal verbs (1–6) from Exercise 9. Use the correct form.

1 In the war they _____ a great deal of hardship.
2 I don't think I will ever _____ the embarrassment of having to sing in front of 200 people.
3 She feels a lot of pressure to _____ the achievements of her elder sister.
4 She _____ her work. It's the thing that she enjoys above everything else.
5 We weren't good enough and we're just going to have to _____ that fact.
6 After we've paid all the bills, we have hardly anything left to _____ .

9.4 Have you got a minute?

DEALING WITH AWKWARD SITUATIONS

1 🎧 2 23 Complete the conversation. Then listen and check your answers.

Y: Hedvig. Have [1]_____?

H: Yes, OK, let me just finish this sentence … Yep. What can [2]_____?

Y: There's something [3]_____.

H: OK. What is it, Yassin?

Y: Well, [4]_____, I think I've opened an email with a virus or something. I'm not sure what to do.

H: Oh, dear. That's a [5]_____. Well, we'll have to alert IT straightaway.

Y: You [6]_____ contact them for me, could you? I feel so stupid.

H: I [7]_____, but I'm afraid I can't. You'll have to deal with it as they'll have questions about the email, etc. I'll put you through …

2 🎧 2 24 Complete the conversation with phrases a–g so that it means the same as the conversation in Exercise 1. Then listen and check your answers.

a Unfortunately

b Could I have a word

c I've got a confession to make

d I don't suppose

e What's on your mind

f there's a slight problem with

g That's a bit of a pain

Y: Hedvig [1]_____?

H: Yes, OK, let me just finish this sentence … Yep. [2]_____?

Y: [3]_____.

H: OK. What is it, Yassin?

Y: Well, [4]_____ an email I've opened with a virus or something. I'm not sure what to do.

H: Oh, dear. [5]_____. We'll have to alert IT.

Y: [6]_____ you could contact them for me, could you? I feel so stupid.

H: [7]_____, I can't. You'll have to deal with it as they'll have questions about the email, etc. I'll put you through …

3 Complete the phrases or questions for each function (1–4). Use the prompts to help you.

1 Starting a conversation:

a (sorry / if / have / moment)

_____

2 Raising an awkward topic:

a (have / apologize)

_____

3 Asking a favour:

a (there / any)

_____

b (have / favour / ask)

_____

4 Responses:

a (shame / understand)

_____

b (worry / matter)

_____

130

PRONUNCIATION Polite and assertive intonation

4 🎧 2 25 Listen to two versions of each sentence. Decide which version (a or b) is polite (P) and which is assertive (A).

		a	b
1	Could I have a word?	☐	☐
2	What's on your mind?	☐	☐
3	I have a favour to ask.	☐	☐
4	Is there any way … ?	☐	☐
5	Actually, that's a bit awkward.	☐	☐
6	Don't worry. It's not important.	☐	☐

WRITING SKILL Reporting verbs

5 Match the reporting verbs (1–8) with a more informal equivalent (a–h).

1	admitted	**a**	accepted
2	denied	**b**	encouraged
3	acknowledged	**c**	said … wasn't true
4	proposed	**d**	claimed
5	urged	**e**	said no to
6	alleged	**f**	said yes to
7	agreed to	**g**	agreed … was true
8	refused	**h**	suggested

6 Correct one mistake in each sentence of the report.

1 This report details the oversight the store claiming to be the reason for not executing policy.

_____

2 It was allegedly that the purchasing department hadn't ordered sufficient tablets.

_____

3 But the purchasing department denied make a mistake.

_____

4 The error was admitted for the store manager and traced to a mistake in an email that had been hastily written.

_____

5 He acknowledged that the mistake and apologized.

_____

6 It has since been propose that tablets will be bought locally.

_____

7 The board has agreed of the higher costs.

_____

8 All managers urge to check substantial orders carefully.

_____

7 Choose the correct reporting verbs to complete the minutes of the meeting.

Present: James (C), Angie, Mia, Xavier
Apologies: Betty and Alastair

A meeting regarding recent problems with a key client was called. The team [1]*acknowledged / claimed* the need to discuss sensitive issues openly to avoid repeating any mistakes in the future. Xavier [2]*accepted / admitted* to having forgotten to add an update to the existing order prior to his holiday. Angie [3]*accused / urged* Xavier of being careless and reminded him of a similar situation the previous year. Xavier [4]*denied / insisted* being careless but apologized for causing problems and [5]*suggested / alleged* using checklists in future to increase the accuracy of information being gathered. Mia [6]*refused / insisted* that there were enough steps in the process without adding more and concluded that working closer together was the only solution. James collected concrete ideas as to how this was to be done and [7]*agreed / urged* to book a training session to improve communication.

8 Complete the minutes of a meeting about how email is used in an office. Use the prompts.

1 The team (acknowledge / not / always / answer emails / quickly enough)

_____

2 They (discuss / briefly / acceptable / agree / reply customers / within twenty-four hours)

_____

3 It (claim / emails / more time / information gathering)

_____

4 It (propose / short email / update / contact concerned)

_____

5 Two members (allege / see / no system / who to copy in)

_____

6 They (urge / look / today's emails / as examples)

_____

7 Several members (admit / copying in / too many)

_____

8 All (ask / monitor / reduce recipients / if possible)

_____

YOUR IDEA

1 Read the paragraphs about developing skills in different ways. Match the paragraphs with the summaries (a, b, c).

1 Since I started working here, I've learned a lot of things. I've had to work out how to use specialist software, like image-editing programs and presentation packages. I've had the chance to develop my public-speaking skills through delivering staff training sessions. I work in quite a large department, so it's common for us to be grouped into teams for particular projects. That means having to work as part of a team, negotiating your role within the group, organizing tasks as necessary – dealing with different personalities can be a hard thing to do. It's quite a skill to have to be able to get on with people in a work setting, if you ask me. ☐

2 Lots of people don't realize the skills they use every day. I mean, for example, you might think that you don't know very much or there isn't very much you can do. I'd get people to think about what they do every week or even every day. Do you do the shopping? That means you have to know how to manage money and you might be good at budgeting. Do you ever cook from a recipe book? That means you can follow simple instructions and know how to measure quantity and time. There are lots of skills we can develop all the time, if we only recognize them. ☐

3 Joining a football team is one of the most challenging things I have ever done. I've had to manage my time to make sure I don't miss training sessions. There is quite a lot of kit and equipment that I need, so I have to make sure it's all ready for each game. It's quite a challenge to be organized enough, but I manage to do it. Team games like football also require you to work as part of a team – you have to be able to communicate otherwise there's no way you'll be successful. ☐

a Skills I've learned from my hobbies.
b Skills I've learned from my job.
c Skills you can learn from your home life.

2 Write notes about things that you have done and the skills you might have developed. Think about your work, studies, home life and any hobbies you have.

_____

_____

_____

3 Look at your notes and identify the different skills you have developed. Place them into categories like these.

Organizational skills _____

_____

Interpersonal skills _____

_____

Financial management skills _____

_____

Time management skills _____

_____

4 Practise talking about your skills out loud. Try to consider your audience:

- What do they already know about the topic?
- What might get them excited and interested in the talk?

ORGANIZING YOUR PRESENTATION

5 Match the four steps of a presentation with two examples of useful language (a–h).

1 Starting the presentation ☐ ☐
2 Introducing the area of your life you're going to talk about ☐ ☐
3 Explaining what skills you have developed ☐ ☐
4 Finishing the talk ☐ ☐

a This relates to my day job and the tasks I have to complete in this role.
b That's the end of my talk. Do you have any questions for me?
c Through doing this I have been able to …
d Today, I'd like to talk about how I have developed some important skills.
e You might wonder what I gained from this. Actually, I …
f So, that's all about what I've managed to do. Do we have any questions from the audience?
g In this talk I'm going to tell you about how I developed some useful skills from different areas of my life.
h I've gained a lot of experience and learned how to do things just from my home life.

YOUR PRESENTATION

6 Read the useful language on the left and make notes for your presentation.

1 Start the presentation Today, I'd like to talk about … This talk is going to be about … Today, I'd like to explain …	
2 Introduce the area of your life you're going to talk about This relates to … I've learned this from … From … I've managed to develop some skills.	
3 Explain what skills you have been able to develop Through doing this I have … From this I've been able to … What I have learned is …	
4 Finish the talk and encourage the audience to recognize their own skills That's it about my skills. Have you got any … ?	

7 Film yourself giving your presentation or practise in front of a mirror.
Give yourself marks out of ten for …

- considering the audience   ☐ /10
- following the four steps in Exercise 6.   ☐ /10
- using correct grammar.   ☐ /10

10 Risk

10.1 Protecting Twitter users (sometimes from themselves)

TEDTALKS

DEL HARVEY's TED profile describes her as a security *maven* – meaning expert or connoisseur. She's worked for Twitter since 2008 and, according to her LinkedIn profile, rose steadily and impressively from being the only member of the safety department to becoming Vice President of Trust and Safety in September 2014. This promotion reflects her success in keeping people safe and encouraging others to report abuse. She and her team work closely with every department at Twitter so the 288 million active users per month can be protected from abuse and remain as spam- and troll*-free as possible. Harvey passionately believes in making the Internet a safer place.

Del Harvey is her professional name – on- and off-line – not her real name, presumably to allow her to have a private as well as a public life. She uses her Twitter handle @delbius to respond to pleas for help from users and as a PR tool for events and groups she supports in her very public position. Before working for Twitter she worked for PJFI – a group fighting child exploitation. Working there and bringing criminals to justice must have made her particularly mindful of the need for identity protection and also informed her current job. Despite the unpleasantness she is probably privy to, she's optimistic enough to have had the heart emoticon symbolizing hope tattooed on her wrist.

troll (n) someone who posts deliberately controversial, offensive or abusive comments on the Internet

Del Harvey

CAREER PATHWAYS

1 Read the text. Answer the questions.

1 How has Del Harvey been promoted?
2 Why might she give herself a different name to her legal one?
3 What previous experience taught her the importance of protecting identities?
4 What example is given of her optimistic attitude?

TED PLAYLIST

2 Other TED speakers are interested in topics similar to Del Harvey's TED Talk. Read the descriptions of four TED Talks at the top of page 135. In your opinion, which is the best title for this playlist, a, b or c?

a Connectedness in a fast-changing modern world
b The slowdown of progress in technology
c Privacy and control in the modern world

3 Complete the six-word summary (1–4) that corresponds to each talk in the TED playlist. Use these words.

need	others	preferences	risks

1 _____ reveal more than we think.
2 The effect of connecting with _____ .
3 The _____ of posting information online.
4 The _____ for a Plan B.

4 Match the verbs (1–5) with their collocates (a–e). Check them in the playlist descriptions.

1 to educate   a privacy
2 to spread   b users
3 to reveal   c information
4 to preserve   d people of the need
5 to warn   e through social networks

5 Which talk would you most like to see? Why? Watch the talk at TED.com.

▶ **Jennifer Golbeck: The curly fry conundrum: Why social media 'likes' say more than you might think**

Jennifer Golbeck is a computer scientist with our best interests at heart. She studies how people use social media and thinks about ways users can be aware of their interactions. In her eye-opening talk she tells us about what can be accurately deduced from social media 'likes' because of the sheer volume of data involved. With half the planet using Facebook she thinks it's time to educate and inform users on being more cautious with and taking control of the data they share.

▶ **Nicholas Christakis: The hidden influence of social networks**

Nicholas Christakis is a physician and social scientist. He explores how social networks influence our lives and how characteristics like obesity, altruism, political preferences, emotions and more can be spread through them. In his talk, he uses animated statistics to explain how social networks change and grow almost like living things. He's now investigating the genetic and evolutionary beginnings for the social networks that humans form. What, according to Christakis is at the root of them? Goodness.

▶ **Alessandro Acquisti: What will a future without secrets look like?**

Alessandro Acquisti studies the behavioural economics of privacy in social media networks. His talk is both thought-provoking and chilling as he describes how easily we reveal information about ourselves, our preferences and our identities. His research focuses on how, by not preserving our privacy, we potentially put ourselves at risk and enable others to access this information.

▶ **Danny Hillis: The Internet could crash. We need a Plan B**

Internet pioneer Danny Hillis is an inventor, scientist and engineer. In his TED Talk, he describes the world when the Internet had just begun and only a handful of people had email addresses. Nowadays, it's hard to imagine a life without the Internet – something that we use for almost everything. He urges us to remember that the Internet was never expected to become so big and warns us of the need for a back-up plan in the event of the Internet breaking down.

AUTHENTIC LISTENING SKILLS Avoiding frustration

6 🎧 **2 26** You are going to hear a podcast in which a member of the *Keynote* team talks about Nicholas Christakis's TED Talk *The hidden influence of social networks*. Listen to the introduction to the podcast and complete the sentences to convey the main information.

1 The podcaster's name is _____ .
2 He is the senior consultant for _____ .
3 He has _____ around the world.
4 Before he was a rep he was a _____ .
5 Every _____ means the beginning of a new network.

LISTENING

7 🎧 **2 27** Listen to the full podcast. Answer the questions.

1 What increased the podcaster's social network?
2 What does he particularly value in his network?
3 What did the talk make him think about?
4 What feels like a 'big responsibility' to him?

8 🎧 **2 27** Are the statements (T) true or (F) false? Listen again to check your answers.

1 The podcaster used to live in a small town in northern England. ☐
2 Christakis's research into obesity changed his view of the world and the course of his research. ☐
3 The risk of suffering from obesity is higher the closer your relationship is to someone else with it. ☐

4 Christakis includes the saying about 'training with lions' to remind us that we should try to be brave and strong. ☐
5 Michael recommends the talk to encourage people to appreciate the positive influence networks can have. ☐

VOCABULARY IN CONTEXT

9 Read the extracts from the podcast. Choose the correct meaning of the words in bold.

1 ... I was living in a small **quaint** town in the North of England ...
  a attractive and old-fashioned ☐
  b ugly and old-fashioned ☐
  c odd and old-fashioned ☐
2 I love the **notion** that social networks are fundamentally something related to goodness, ...
  a knowledge ☐ b idea ☐ c fact ☐
3 This talk left me **pondering** a number of things.
  a believing ☐ b suggesting ☐
  c wondering about ☐
4 After doing research into widowhood, he found that when someone is widowed, its effects aren't limited to the **spouses** ...
  a children ☐ b family ☐ c partners ☐
5 He later studied other topics like happiness and **altruism** ...
  a thinking of others ☐ b noticing others ☐
  c rewarding others ☐

10.2 Not as risky as it sounds

GRAMMAR Passive reporting verbs

1 Complete the text with the correct form of the words in brackets.

The history of insurance

Early forms of household insurance in the seventeenth century [1] _____ (mostly / consider) to be necessary for protection against fire. In the Great Fire of London 13,000 houses [2] _____ (report) to have been lost. Nowadays it [3] _____ (widely / believe) that you can buy insurance for just about everything. But why do people need insurance? Since the early twentieth century it [4] _____ (generally / consider) to be too risky for expensive items like property and cars not to have insurance cover – the potential loss [5] _____ (think) to be too high and it has become illegal not to insure our properties and vehicles. Additionally, in recent years, private individuals [6] _____ (sometimes / know) to buy insurance for very specialized items. Indeed, a pianist or surgeon insuring their hands or a ballet dancer their legs is not unusual as these are key to their profession. It [7] _____ (expect) that user connectivity will change insurance products, particularly for motoring and health. Usage based insurance (UBI) – where actual client behaviour can be monitored using tracking technology – [8] _____ (estimate) to become more widespread in the future.

2 Match the two parts of the sentences.

1 The UK insurance industry is reported ☐
2 It is thought that life insurance ☐
3 It's estimated that over 100,000 ☐
4 It's been revealed that about a third of people ☐
5 An Italian bride is understood ☐

a people work in the insurance industry in the UK.
b underestimate the value of their possessions.
c to have made a claim for her dress after it caught fire during her wedding.
d was invented in 1693 by Edmund Halley, who is more famous for his discoveries about comets.
e to be the biggest in Europe.

3 Complete the sentences with the correct form of the verb in brackets.

1 At the time, the Titanic _____ (say) to be the most luxurious ocean liner ever built.
2 It _____ (report) in the press that, despite the high claim of a million pounds, the insurers paid out the sum for the Titanic within thirty days.
3 It _____ (fear) that insurance premiums will rise as a result of climate change.
4 Since the floods it _____ (agree) that a fund to repair extensive damage in the area will be set up.
5 It _____ (decide) at a recent meeting that claims under a certain value would be paid immediately.
6 It _____ (estimate) that the damage amounts to at least €250,000.

7 After investigation it _____ (allege) that the transaction was fraudulent.

8 It _____ (not expect) that insurance company profits will report reduced revenues this year.

4 Rewrite the sentences using type 1 passive reporting verbs in brackets (subject + *be* + past participle of reporting verb + *to* infinitive). You may need to change some of the other verbs.

1 News of the sinking of the Titanic caused shock worldwide. (report)
News of the sinking of the Titanic was reported to have caused shock worldwide.

2 Captain Edward John Smith must have drowned though his body was never found. (presume)
_____
_____

3 1,500 passengers and crew didn't survive. (know)
_____
_____

4 A technical failure wasn't the cause in the surveyors' reports. (show)
_____
_____

5 The Titanic is the most famous shipwreck. (say)
_____
_____

6 The Titanic was unsinkable when it was built. (believe)
_____
_____

7 The Titanic was a low marine risk according to Lloyd's. (consider)
_____
_____

5 Rewrite the sentences from Exercise 4 with type 2 passive reporting verbs (*It* + *be* + past participle of reporting verb + (*that*) + clause). Keep the meaning the same.

1 It *was reported that the sinking of the Titanic caused shock worldwide.*

2 It _____
_____

3 It _____

4 It _____

5 It _____
_____

6 It _____

7 It _____
_____

DICTATION

6 🎧 2 28 Listen to someone talking about Lloyd's of London. Complete the paragraph.

Lloyd's of London _____
_____.

Technically, _____
_____ but a corporate body of 94 syndicates or 'Names', as they are called. It was founded in a City coffee house in 1688 where merchants bought insurance for their ships. The Lutine Bell _____
_____ , as has been done for all other ships lost or missing since 1799.
_____
_____ and in fact incurred gigantic losses due to asbestos claims flooding the market. _____
_____ , where the insurance market is much less developed than Britain.

READING

1 You are going to look at a questionnaire about attitude to risk. Decide which of these areas (a–f) you would expect to see in a questionnaire about risk.

a making financial decisions
b work
c social life
d sports or activities
e trust of others (strangers and friends)
f driving

2 Read the questionnaire. Which items don't fall into any of the categories above?

_____

_____

General attitude to risk questionnaire

Circle the answer that best describes you.

1 When undertaking a new project, you ...
A first look at all the things that could possibly go wrong.
B weigh up the pros and cons and then seek the guidance of someone experienced.
C are generally confident that if anything goes wrong, you can extricate yourself.

2 In your professional life you ...
A tend to avoid conflict and competition.
B take competition into account and look for fair ways to further your own interests.
C like to compete and win.

3 When driving a car, you ...
A always obey traffic laws and avoid dangerous situations.
B are ready to break the laws if you think you won't be caught.
C often exceed the speed limit and overtake other cars when you can.

4 If the opinion of the majority of people differs from your own ...
A you adopt it, accepting it must be a more valid view.
B it irritates you but you go along with it.
C you stick firmly to your own opinion and try to persuade others to change to it.

5 You like the company of people who ...
A are trustworthy and competent.
B are determined and energetic.
C are adventurous and courageous.

6 In social situations you ...
A don't like to be the centre of attention, but join in with what's going on.
B seek out the company of the people who interest you most.
C like to be the leader of the group and actively dictate the agenda.

7 When it comes to clothes ...
A you like to be elegant and smart, but not in a showy way.
B your main consideration is just to feel comfortable.
C you like to wear something eye-catching and different.

8 When faced with a difficult decision, you ...
A put off making it in the hope that some new evidence will come to light.
B trust to luck rather than any reasoned approach.
C trust in your own rightness and banish any thoughts of later regret.

9 If a friend offered you a chance to invest in their business you ...
A would decline the offer, not wanting to mix business and friendship.
B would see what guarantees they could give you that the investment was safe.
C would look for the quickest and most substantial return.

10 Your main concern in life is ...
A to have financial security.
B to be professionally competent and well-respected.
C to keep seeking out new challenges and experiences.

3 Choose the correct meaning for each of these phrases.

1 'extricate yourself' (question 1)
   a start the project again
   b get out of a difficult situation
2 'further your own interests' (question 2)
   a help your career progress
   b explore new areas
3 'go along with it' (question 4)
   a accept it
   b change your view
4 'dictate the agenda' (question 6)
   a decide what everyone should do
   b organize social events for everyone
5 'banish any thoughts of' (question 8)
   a postpone thinking about
   b stop thinking about
6 'the most substantial return' (question 9)
   a the easiest way to get your money back
   b the largest amount of profit

4 🎧 2 29 Listen to an expert talking about this questionnaire. Answer the questions.

1 What doesn't he like about questionnaires in general?
2 What doesn't he like about this questionnaire?
3 What does he like about this questionnaire?

VOCABULARY Risk and probability

5 Complete the sentences with the missing word. The first letter has been given.

1 I'm sorry I have to go now, I don't want to r _____ the risk of missing the flight.
2 The virus only p _____ a threat if you try to open the attachment in the email. So just delete the email.
3 Taking vitamin C and zinc tablets doesn't prevent you from getting a cold. It just r _____ the chances of your getting one.
4 What is the l _____ of it raining tomorrow? We're planning to take a boat out on the river.
5 The o _____ of being struck by lightning in your lifetime are about 12,000 to one.
6 I'd love you to come and stay, but the chances are h _____ that we'll be out of the country in July.
7 Even if there's only a one i _____ a million chance of the cable breaking, it's not a risk I want to take.

WORDBUILDING Suffix -ity

6 Complete the second sentence so that it means the same as the first, replacing the adjective with a noun ending in -ity.

1 My main concern in life is to be financially secure.
   My main concern in life is to have financial *security.*
2 Can you check if the Kingston Suite is still available?
   Can you check the _____ of the Kingston Suite?

3 The people in Tunisia were so generous, I was overwhelmed.
   I was overwhelmed by the _____ of the people in Tunisia.
4 Just so that it is clear, could you write the details down for me?
   For the sake of _____ , could you write the details down for me?
5 We respect that our clients have the right to remain anonymous.
   We respect our clients' right to _____ .
6 Thank you for being so hospitable.
   Thank you for all your _____ .
7 They sent the Picasso drawing to an art gallery to confirm it was authentic.
   They sent the Picasso drawing to an art gallery to confirm its _____ .
8 It's not necessary to reserve a seat. We still have plenty.
   There's no _____ to reserve a seat. We still have plenty.
9 I really love how simple the painting is. There's a childlike quality to it.
   I really love the _____ of the painting. There's a childlike quality to it.

WORD FOCUS face

7 Choose the correct options to complete the idiomatic phrases with face.

1 We need to **face** *facts / information* here. No one is going to spend $100 on a toothbrush.
2 To write such a horrible article about us when he was so complimentary on the phone is completely *one-faced / two-faced*.
3 I know it's disappointing to lose, but we need to **put a brave face** *in it / on it* and move on.
4 Just go and tell her that you messed up. You're going to have to **face the** *music / song* sooner or later.
5 To find out they were going on holiday without me after all the research I did for them was a real *touch / slap* in the face.
6 I don't think things are going very well for her, because when I asked her, she just **pulled a** *short / long* face.

8 Match the definitions (a–f) with the idioms 1–6 from Exercise 7.

a an insult *a slap in the face*
b show you're not affected by a setback
   _____
c be realistic
   _____
d be hypocritical
   _____
e accept punishment or criticism
   _____
f make a sad expression
   _____

139

ASSESSING RISK

1 Match the business risks (1–4) to the risk areas (a–d).

1	data security	**a**	market / environmental risks
2	fraud	**b**	theft
3	fire	**c**	industry regulations
4	burglary	**d**	financial risks

2 🎧 2 30 Listen and decide what risk from Exercise 1 is being talked about. _____

3 🎧 2 30 Choose the correct options in these phrases to discuss alternatives. Listen to the conversation again and check your answers.

1 *They were / There are* some pretty interesting options to choose from.

2 *Possibly / Probably* the most obvious one is …

3 A *drawback / hurdle* of the camera is that …

4 *Additionally / According to* the brochure, a combination lock is another option to consider.

5 On the plus side, we *wouldn't / don't* need keys any more.

6 … but the *downside / downsize* is we're only strengthening the door.

7 An alarm system protects doors and windows, which makes it a very *attractive / alternative* possibility.

8 Hmm, yes but considering the price, I'm not *secure / sure* it's the best option.

4 🎧 2 31 Listen to the continuation of the conversation and complete the sentences.

1 In _____ the increase in criminal activity in the area, I think we should invest in an alarm and a safe.

2 A _____ that might do the job is a dog.

3 Ultimately, _____ does seem to be the alarm system.

4 OK. _____ , it makes sense to go with an alarm …

5 Write the phrases from Exercises 3 and 4 under the correct heading.

Presenting options

_____

_____

_____

_____

Discussing pros and cons

_____

_____

_____

_____

Considering options

_____

_____

_____

_____

PRONUNCIATION Saying lists

6 🎧 2 32 Say the following lists as closed lists, and then as open lists. Listen and check. Use *and* only for the closed lists.

1 In the burglary they took two computers, a printer, €450 in cash (and) a mobile phone.

2 I've heard about it happening to the bookstore, the sandwich shop on the corner (and) the DIY store.

3 What did she lose from her handbag? A phone, her wallet including credit cards, her car keys (and) some jewellery.

WRITING SKILL Using qualifiers

7 Look at the examples (a–g). Then write the correct qualifier in bold next to the descriptions (1–5) below.

a It was a **pretty** easy solution in the end to install a video camera.
b It is a **fairly** straightforward procedure to follow.
c The instructions were **a bit** unclear.
d He was **quite** pleased that he'd invested in the security system.
e It was **rather** more than he had expected to pay for it.
f The cost of this one seems **a little** high in comparison.
g We would have to pay **slightly** more for that model.

1 _____ modifies adverbs and adjectives. It means 'to a limited degree'.
2 _____ modifies adverbs, adjectives, nouns and verbs to a higher degree than item 1.
3 _____ modifies adverbs and adjectives to an even higher degree (informally) than items 1 and 2. It can also mean 'more than usual'.
4 _____ , _____ and _____ soften adverbs, adjectives and verbs, making criticism less direct.
5 _____ softens adverbs, adjectives, nouns and verbs, making criticism less direct. Also used to show disappointment, criticism or surprise.

8 Read these sentences about the qualifiers in Exercise 7. Are they (T) true or (F) false?

1 All of them can soften adjectives. ☐
2 Only two of them soften nouns. ☐
3 Three of them soften adjectives, adverbs, nouns and verbs. ☐
4 Four of them can be used to make criticism less direct. ☐

9 Rewrite the sentences more diplomatically. Use the qualifiers in brackets.

1 It was a waste of money. (rather)

2 They were poorer quality than we'd expected. (slightly)

3 The XJ7 model is more complicated to install. (a bit)

4 He was impatient and unfriendly when he explained it. (quite, a little)

5 I found it uninspiring and old-fashioned. (rather, pretty)

6 The company is disorganized. (fairly)

7 That's a worrying state of affairs. (rather)

8 The model they chose was easy to use. (reasonably)

10 Choose the correct qualifiers to make three-, two- and one-star reviews.

★★★ We bought this system on a friend's recommendation. We were [1] *quite / rather* satisfied with the service and the pricing was [2] *a bit / fairly* competitive.

★★ We had a [3] *bit / rather* lengthy wait for the system modifications we'd requested. We paid [4] *quite / slightly* more for it than we were quoted.

★ The order took [5] *quite / fairly* [6] *rather / a bit* longer than we were promised. It was [7] *rather / fairly* disappointing.

11 Write a short review for a new door intercom with a camera using the notes.

- low price attractive
- product arrived promptly
- faulty
- better maintenance service than expected
- overall package
- reasonable

The letter of thanks you will read in Exercise 2 is in answer to the following exam question.

> A training company recently ran a health and safety course at your company's office. Afterwards, you received this email from your manager:
>
> Hi,
>
> Can you put together a thank you letter for HSAW for running the training day on Tuesday? It went really well in the end, despite the initial problems. Please mention the excellent job their trainer did, and how clear everything was. Feel free to offer them a 10% discount next time they need something from us. I'll sign it when you're done.
>
> Thanks,
>
> DW
>
> Write your letter of thanks in **220–260 words** in an appropriate style.

IDEAS

1 Tick (✓) the things you would expect to see in the letter of thanks.

a a formal greeting ☐
b descriptions of the products the company sells ☐
c compliments for the HSAW staff and their communication skills ☐
d advice for how to organize a health and safety course ☐
e the reason the letter has been written ☐
f details of a reward for HSAW's good service ☐
g a description of a problem ☐

MODEL

2 Read the letter of thanks. Match the five sections with a description (a–g) from Exercise 1.

1 ☐   2 ☐   3 ☐   4 ☐   5 ☐

3 Read the letter of thanks again. Are these statements true (T) or false (F)?

1 The course was originally planned for the 18th September. ☐
2 The HSAW staff dealt well with problems when they occurred. ☐
3 The staff at the company were expecting to learn a lot from the course. ☐
4 Information supplied during the course will still be used in the office at a later date. ☐
5 Della would like to work with HSAW again soon. ☐

---

[1]To whom it may concern:

[2]We are writing to thank you for the informative and useful health and safety course which Emma from HSAW ran at our office on Tuesday 18th September.

[3]We were initially worried when we had to cancel the original day set for the training due to unforeseen circumstances. [4]However, your team took it in their stride and new arrangements were made with the minimum of fuss. The whole day ran smoothly and this reflects very well on the professionalism of your staff, who organized everything thoroughly beforehand and communicated regularly with us throughout the whole process.

On behalf of our whole team, please convey our thanks to Emma for the excellent job she did at explaining health and safety requirements to a group of office workers who thought the course would all be common sense and would not challenge us. I am pleased to say that this was not true and we all came away from the course feeling as if we had learned something new.

Finally, I'd like to mention the resources given to us by HSAW which are all very clear and are now being used around the office. I am sure we will continue to refer to them for a long time to come.

[5]In token of our gratitude, we would like to offer all HSAW staff a 10% discount on any products from our catalogue. We look forward to doing business with you again in the near future.

Yours sincerely,

Della Walters

USEFUL LANGUAGE

4 Match the two parts of the sentences to make letter beginnings.

1 We are so grateful ☐
2 I wanted to let you know how much ☐
3 Thank you ☐
4 I would just like to express ☐
5 Let me take this opportunity ☐
6 We would like to thank you for ☐
7 I cannot thank you ☐
8 I would like to ☐

a my gratitude for …
b the excellent service we received at …
c enough for …
d for the assistance we received on …
e compliment you on …
f so much for your help with …
g we appreciate …
h to thank you for …

5 Complete the sentences used to pay compliments in a letter of thanks. Use these words.

dedication	knowledgeable	professionally
prompt	remarkably	wealth

1 Your staff are very _____ and polite.
2 The responses we received were always _____ .
3 The brochure contained a _____ of useful information.
4 Everyone has been _____ patient and helpful.
5 They handled any problems very _____ .
6 Their _____ to their careers is to be commended.

6 Complete the letter of thanks. Use these words and phrases.

a time	fortunate	impressed	not only
once again	regret	stood out	

Dear Miss Sanchez,

I would like to say a huge thank you for the meditation course which I attended last week at the yoga centre.

The course was a gift from my sister when she realized that I was starting to get ill from work-related stress. I was not sure if I would enjoy it as I have never been interested in yoga or meditation, but in the end I did not [1] _____ going for one moment. I can't remember [2] _____ when I have ever felt as calm as I have in the past week. [3] _____ did you help me to relax on the evening, but you also taught me useful exercises which I can use whenever I feel the stress coming on.

I would like to mention how [4] _____ the yoga centre is to have such a caring, committed instructor on their team. One thing that particularly [5] _____ was the time you spent on each of the course participants' individual needs. I was particularly [6] _____ by this, given that the group was much larger than you expected due to your colleague being absent.

[7] _____ , I would like to express my thanks and to say that I will certainly return to the centre for further courses.

Yours sincerely,

Amy Jefferson

---

7 Put the words into the correct order to create recommendations.

1 recommend / to / we / not / customers / will / hesitate / you / our / to
2 recommend / restaurant / my / I / friends / will / all / your / to
3 hotel / I / certainly / again / use / your / will
4 we / forward / to / soon / with / you / again / look / doing / business
5 continuing / look / we / forward / business / our / relationship / to
6 to / we / others / recommended / company / have / your …
7 … will / to / and / continue / so / do

PLANNING

You will answer the following question.

> You have just been on holiday where you stayed in a hotel. Write a letter of thanks. In your letter, mention the staff, the restaurant and one idea of your own.

8 Plan your letter of thanks. Write notes to answer these questions. Don't write full sentences yet.

1 Where did you go on holiday?
2 What will you write about the staff?
3 What will you mention about the restaurant?
4 What other aspect of your stay will you write about?

WRITING

9 Write a letter of thanks based on the situation in Exercise 8. In your letter you should:

- give your reason for writing
- mention the hotel staff and the restaurant
- write about one more idea of your own
- state what you will do as a result of your stay at the hotel (e.g. recommend it?)

Write your letter in **220–260 words** in an appropriate style.

ANALYSIS

10 Check your letter of thanks. Then answer the questions.

- **Content:** Does the letter mention the staff, the restaurant and one other idea? Is it 220 to 260 words long?
- **Communicative achievement:** Is it written in a neutral or formal style? Is it clear to the reader why you are thanking them?
- **Organization:** Is the letter logically organized? Are the ideas connected?
- **Language:** Does it use correct grammar and vocabulary? Is a good range of structures used?

11 Vision

11.1 How to build with clay and community

TEDTALKS

DIÉBÉDO FRANCIS KÉRÉ was born in 1965 in Gando, Burkina Faso, the eldest son of the chief of the village. His father hoped that his son would learn to read and write but Kéré learned a great deal more. First, he completed an apprenticeship in carpentry in the country's capital Ouagadougou and then he studied to become a teacher. In 1990, he won a scholarship to Berlin and moved there to finish his schooling. He went on to train to be an architect, completing his degree in 2004 at the Technical University of Berlin where he has since lectured.

In 1998, he founded the company 'Bricks for Gando School' through which he raised funds for his first building project, the construction of Gando primary school. When he came back he did so with skills, funds and a government grant to train people in the village to build with local materials in order to give them marketable skills.

He won an award with his first building, the primary school he built with others in his village. Other awards followed, six by 2015. He started his own architecture business in 2005 and has designed buildings in Africa, India, the USA and Europe. His designs have been exhibited in DAM, the Architecture museum in Frankfurt, and in MoMA in New York, and he's a fellow at both the British and American Institutes of Architects. When he left to study in Germany all those years ago, the village women gave him pennies to ensure his return. Not only did he return, but what he brought back with him has allowed him to improve and empower his community.

Diébédo Francis Kéré

CAREER PATHWAYS

1 Read the text. Answer the questions.

  1 What did his father hope for Diébédo Francis Kéré?
  2 What did Kéré study?
  3 How did he finance the first school in Gando?
  4 How much recognition has his work received?

TED PLAYLIST

2 Other TED speakers are interested in topics similar to Diébédo Francis Kéré's TED Talk. Read the descriptions of four TED Talks at the top of page 145. In your opinion, which is the best title for this playlist, a, b or c?

  a Community matters matter
  b Training communities to build
  c Sustainable housing solutions

3 Complete the six-word summary (1–4) that corresponds to each talk in the TED playlist. Use these words.

design	space	surprising	sustainable

  1 A neglected _____ becomes an attraction.
  2 Promoting _____ development for minority communities.
  3 Building clever homes in _____ places.
  4 Collaborative _____ solves local problems creatively.

4 Match the verbs (1–5) with their collocates (a–e). Check your answers in the playlist descriptions.

  1 to bring   **a** the world
  2 to suffer   **b** for equality
  3 to campaign   **c** injustice
  4 to travel   **d** with issues of scale
  5 to deal   **e** people together

5 Which talk would you most like to see? Why? Watch the talk at TED.com.

▶ **Candy Chang: Before I die I want to …**

Candy Chang is an artist, urban planner and TED Fellow. In her New Orleans neighbourhood she turned an abandoned building into a massive community chalkboard with the incomplete statement that is also the title of her TED Talk. Her moving talk describes how similar community art projects have brought people together and begun important conversations in over 1,000 cities in 70 countries.

▶ **Majora Carter: Greening the ghetto**

Majora Carter is an activist and winner of the MacArthur 'Genius' Award. She talks emotionally and with conviction about the environmental injustice suffered by the residents of high-poverty and high-minority neighbourhoods. In her own neighbourhood of the South Bronx in New York City, she successfully campaigned for more environmental equality and brought a waterfront park and additional funds for green development to the community.

▶ **Iwan Baan: Ingenious homes in unexpected places**

Iwan Baan is an urban documentary photographer who's interested in built environments, particularly makeshift ones. He travels the world, exploring and photographing communities and their individual solutions to the problem of adequate, affordable housing. His talk is a lively illustrated account of communities living in resourceful ways in unusual places in Nigeria, Venezuela, Egypt and China.

▶ **Alejandro Aravena: My architectural philosophy? Bring the community into the process**

Alejandro Aravena is an urban architect used to solving difficult problems in unusual ways. He routinely deals with issues of scale, speed and scarcity of means. In his engaging talk he takes us through the problem-solving steps he used in some of his projects, and highlights how his work was improved when he invited community members to help come up with some of the solutions.

AUTHENTIC LISTENING SKILLS Dealing with accents: different stress patterns

6 🎧 2 33 You are going to hear a podcast in which a member of the *Keynote* team talks about Iwan Baan's TED Talk, *Ingenious homes in unexpected places*. Listen to each sentence being read first by the Greek podcaster and then an English native speaker. Underline the part of the word or compound in bold which is stressed in each version.

1 **a** My job involves **extensive** travelling …
  b My job involves **extensive** travelling …
2 **a** … I've seen many 'weird-looking' homes around the world.
  b … I've seen many 'weird-looking' homes around the world.
3 **a** Originally, the title made me think that it was going to be one more of those demonstrations of funny, posh or extravagant houses some **techno-geek** or multi-millionaire has built.
  b Originally, the title made me think that it was going to be one more of those demonstrations of funny, posh or extravagant houses some **techno-geek** or multi-millionaire has built.

LISTENING

7 🎧 2 34 Listen to the full podcast. Are these statements true (T) or false (F)?

1 Baan showed photographs of homes in Greece. ☐
2 The podcaster describes refugees in Greece wanting to build somewhere to cook, to sleep and to pray. ☐
3 The speaker explains why people find themselves in these difficult situations. ☐

8 🎧 2 34 Listen again. Answer the questions.

1 What did the podcaster fear the talk would show?
2 What does he say people like to do with their homes?
3 Why did the talk resonate with the podcaster?
4 What made Baan a good TED speaker?
5 Who will Eftychis recommend the talk to?

VOCABULARY IN CONTEXT

9 Read the extracts from the podcast. Choose the correct meaning of the words in bold.

1 One of my favourite TED Talks is Iwan Baan's '**Ingenious** homes in unexpected places'.
  a strange ☐   **b** clever ☐   **c** remote ☐

2 Originally, the title made me think that it was going to be one more of those demonstrations of funny, **posh** or extravagant houses …
  a expensive-looking ☐   **b** old-fashioned ☐
  c humble ☐

3 He showed people living … in **dwellings** on and in the rubbish heaps.
  a sheds ☐   **b** homes ☐   **c** tents ☐

4 Generally people are unhappy with '**cookie-cutter**' solutions; they like to personalize their environments.
  a instant ☐   **b** childish ☐   **c** standardized ☐

5 … what cities can look like away from the **tourist spots** and off the beaten track.
  a motorways ☐   **b** top destinations ☐
  c historic sites ☐

11.2 A vision for saving the world

GRAMMAR Subordinate clauses

1 Complete the text with these words.

> although   by the time   given that   in case
> in spite of the fact   once   provided that
> when   whereas

Making banana bread, not wasting bananas!

The German business studies students Lars Peters and Tim Gudelj were travelling in Australia in 2012 [1]_____ they tried banana bread for the first time. It was love at first bite. [2]_____ it's called 'bread' as it's baked in a loaf form, it is actually like cake. [3]_____ that it's sold in fast-food chains, it's not fast food per se; it's more of a health food and has just seven basic ingredients. [4]_____ Peters and Gudelj got back to Germany, they'd made a plan. Their parents consented to lend them the seed capital for their business [5]_____ the students agreed to complete their master's degrees. They founded their company, Bebananas, in 2013, selling their bread in bakeries, local cafés and online. The entrepreneurial pair are food sharers which – [6]_____ you don't know – involves picking up food legally from shops, markets or restaurants [7]_____ it's been thrown away. Ripe bananas can't be sold in supermarkets [8]_____ they are exactly what's required for banana bread. [9]_____ their product is made of fifty per cent bananas, this provides a cheap and sustainable way to make delicious banana bread.

2 Use the prompts and the conjunctions to write sentences.

1 food fads / go / banana bread / healthy / as / made / fifty per cent / bananas (as far as)
As far as food fads go, banana bread is a healthy one, as it's made of fifty per cent bananas.

2 I / eat / banana bread / when / live / Australia (the last time)
_____
_____ .

3 I / late / save me / piece of cake (in case)
_____
_____ .

4 not waste / food / banana bread / excellent idea (as far as)
_____
_____ .

5 it / taste / very sweet / no sugar (considering)
_____
_____ .

6 he / smell / the dish / reminds / home (whenever)
_____
_____ .

7 she / not like / bananas / chose / carrot cake instead (in view of the fact that)
_____
_____ .

3 Choose the correct options to complete the sentences so that they all have a similar meaning

1 *As long as / If* they don't finish their studies, they won't receive the loan.
2 They won't receive the loan *unless / provided that* they finish their studies.
3 *Supposing / As long as* they finish their studies, they'll receive the loan from their parents.
4 *As long as / Supposing* they don't finish their studies, they will have to pay back the entire loan.
5 *Provided that / Unless* they continue studying and finish their course, they'll receive the loan.

GRAMMAR EXTRA! Other conjunctions

4 Choose the correct options to complete the recipe.

1 Take four bananas. They are ready to use *as soon as / while* they are ripe. Mash them well.
2 Cream half a cup of sugar and half a cup of butter *by the time / until* they are fluffy.
3 Mix two eggs into the butter mixture. *Until / Once* it is blended together well, add the bananas.
4 *Once / After* mixing in the dry ingredients – two cups of flour, a quarter of a teaspoon of salt and a teaspoon of baking powder – pour into a loaf tin.
5 *Until / By the time* it's been in an oven at 175 degrees C for about an hour, it will be cooked. Enjoy!

5 Put the words in the correct order to make good housekeeping and dietary advice.

1 fruit and vegetables / as / buy / far / in season / when / are / concerned, / them / as / they / are

2 recipes / new / necessary, / find / use / leftovers / if / to / up

3 doubt, / when / sell-by date / don't / past / in / food / that's / eat / its

4 eat / told / unless / your / foods / of / a / otherwise / by / different / doctor, / variety

5 learned / once / you'll / meals / you've / to / cook / fresh food, / it / prefer / processed / to

DICTATION

6 🎧 2 35 Listen to someone talking about food sharing. Complete the paragraph.

The amount of food waste increases _____
_____ .

Ninety million tons of food are thrown away each year by Europeans. Food sharing _____
_____ colossal waste. Valentin Thurn's documentary film *Taste the Waste* raised awareness and, _____
_____ .

The www.foodsharing.de website connects people who have food to give to people who need it and, _____
_____ strategic points, too. Food sharing is happening in 240 cities in Germany _____
_____ .

It's not only individuals, but also businesses that benefit from this practice, _____
_____ .

Finally, health and safety laws ensure that no one shares anything unfit for consumption.

147

READING

1 Match the four types of writing (1–4) with the definitions (a–d).

1 a feature article

2 an editorial

3 an advertisement

4 an advertorial

a a notice or display designed to sell something

b a piece that deals with a topic or person in depth

c a piece that looks like a regular article but is actually designed to sell something

d an article that expresses the opinion of the publisher

2 Read the text. Decide which of the four writing types in Exercise 1 it is.

3 Read the text again. Are these statements true (T) or false (F)?

1 The company's products are aimed at all types of businesses. ☐

2 Small business owners are generally not enthusiastic enough about what they do. ☐

3 Small businesses mainly get new customers from personal recommendations. ☐

4 Most business cards do their job adequately, but not excitingly. ☐

5 A B-Creative Cards business card is something you will be proud of owning. ☐

6 All the examples of B-Creative Cards in the article give you extra useful information beyond just someone's contact details. ☐

7 The gardener's business card is the only one not made of paper or card. ☐

8 The main benefit of the cards is that they help people to share your enthusiasm for your work. ☐

How a business **card can transform your sales**

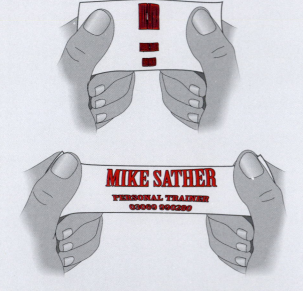

MIKE SATHER
PERSONAL TRAINER
03069 990280

This is one for all you small business owners out there – whether you be a sole-trading painter and decorator or a team of IT consultants, a yoga studio or a garage owner. You care passionately about what you do; it's what you do all day and often think about at night. But you haven't managed to transmit that passion to enough potential customers. Because you're only small, your advertising budget is limited. Yes, you've got a website and from time to time you place advertisements in the local newspaper. You hand out business cards to interested parties whenever you get the opportunity, but mainly you're just relying on word-of-mouth. You want to take your business to another level, but it just isn't happening. Well, here's an idea that could be a shortcut to more business and help transform your fortunes.

B-Creative Cards specialize in making business cards that really stand out. Let's face it – most business cards end up at the back of our wallets or collecting dust on a shelf somewhere and never get looked at again. They only fulfil one function – to have a written record of a contact – and most don't even do that very well if they get put to one side and forgotten. What B-Creative Cards do is to produce cards that become objects of desire in themselves – cards that are so fun and original that you want to show them off to other people. Here are some examples:

- a rubber card for a personal fitness trainer that you have to stretch out with both hands before the name and contact details of the trainer become visible

- a gardener's calling card that is actually a little envelope with a few free flower seeds inside

- a first aid trainer's card that opens out into a leaflet with some key first aid tips inside

- an Italian restaurant's business card in the shape of an aubergine with a recipe for Aubergine Parmigiana on the back

The clever thing about these calling cards is a) you actually want to keep them and b) they bring a smile to your face. They're also great for handing out at trade fairs or roadshows. They may cost more than a standard business card, but what you end up with is a personal calling card that truly reflects your personal calling.

4 🎧 **2 36** Listen to the owner of a yoga studio who used B-Creative Cards to make a business card. Write down the adjectives used to describe these things.

1 their advertising budget _____
2 the first B-Creative design (straw) _____
3 the cost of the straw _____
4 the second design (card) _____
5 what customers think of the card _____

5 Match the meanings a–e with the adjectives (1–5) from Exercise 4.

a impressive ☐   d tiny ☐
b fashionable ☐   e expensive ☐
c original and attractive ☐

VOCABULARY Expressions with *look* and *see*

6 Match the expressions with *look* and *see* (1–6) with the definitions (a–f).

1 to look into   a to agree (on)
2 to see eye to eye (on) b to supervise
3 to be on the lookout for c attend to / deal with
4 to see about   d to investigate
5 to look up to   e to be waiting to find/do/get
6 to oversee   f to admire

7 Use the correct form of the expressions from Exercise 6 to complete the sentences.

1 We agreed about the main points but we didn't _____ some details.
2 I felt very honoured to be put in charge of _____ the whole project.
3 We _____ experienced people, but they're not easy to find.
4 If you can sort out the publicity, I'll _____ hiring a venue.
5 I've always really _____ my older brother and listened to his advice.
6 I'll _____ how we can get tickets, but I can't promise anything.

WORDBUILDING Compound nouns

8 Look at these compound nouns from the text. What type(s) of word is each noun composed of?

website	newspaper	shortcut	roadshow

9 Complete the compound nouns 1–8 with these words.

cross	data	dead	note
self-	share	short	work

1 _____line   4 _____roads   7 _____holder
2 _____space   5 _____book   8 _____base
3 _____list   6 _____esteem

10 Match the two parts of the sentences.

1 The deadline for applications is written ☐
2 I feel I'm at a crossroads ☐
3 We drew up a shortlist ☐
4 A list of the principal shareholders is kept ☐
5 Not getting the associate director job was a blow ☐
6 I have a small workspace ☐

a of potential candidates.
b to my self-esteem.
c at home.
d in my notebook.
e on our database.
f in my life.

WORD FOCUS *time*

11 Complete the idioms using these words.

behind	dead	hard	high
kill	make	move	pushed

1 Numbers for students wanting to do psychology at university is **at an all-time** _____ .
2 Your phone doesn't have the Internet? You're a bit _____ **the times**, aren't you?
3 Sorry I can't speak now. I'm rather _____ **for time**.
4 It's very good of you to _____ **time** to see me. I know how busy you are.
5 The plane was delayed for two hours so we just had to _____ **time** at the airport.
6 You may not like using social media, but everyone else is using it. You've got to _____ **with the times**.
7 Swiss trains are incredibly reliable. They always arrive and leave _____ **on time**.
8 Please don't **give** her **a** _____ **time**. She was only doing what she thought was right.

12 Complete the sentences with the idioms from Exercise 11.

1 There's Jack now – _____ . I told you he wouldn't be late.
2 I always _____ to do some exercise during the day, because otherwise I'm just sitting down in front of my computer all day long.
3 She _____ about missing the meeting. But actually I didn't even know about it until ten minutes before.
4 Temperatures this winter were _____ . It was exceptionally mild.
5 We just _____ chatting and playing cards during the journey. We were there before we knew it!

11.4 A dream come true

TALKING ABOUT A VISION OF THE FUTURE

1 Match the skills (1–4) to the jobs (a–d).

1 Communication   **a** journalist, artist, designer, chef
2 Being creative   **b** doctor, nurse, teacher, receptionist
3 Helping people   **c** IT specialist, mechanic, consultant
4 Problem solving   **d** sales rep, manager, blogger

2 🎧 2 | 37 Match the two parts of the sentences. Listen to a coaching session to check your answers.

1 We've always fancied
2 I can envisage
3 If money were no object,
4 To be perfectly honest I'd like to
5 I could see myself cooking
6 But I can't see

a a quieter life, having a smaller B&B place somewhere nice.
b do something different.
c setting up our own business.
d myself at the front desk any more. I need a bit more of a challenge.
e I'd buy my own hotel somewhere.
f in a restaurant or café.

3 Put the words in the correct order to make phrases.

a wouldn't / great / be / it / to
b see / I / myself / can
c money / no / could / were / if / object, / we
d fancied / always / I've
e love / to / I'd
f envisage / can't / I

4 🎧 2 | 38 Complete the conversation with the phrases from Exercise 3. Listen and check.

Dan: It was interesting what we found out in the session. Turned out a little different to what I was expecting. ¹_____ exactly what we might do yet though.

Maja: Yeah, I know what you mean. I've got so many ideas going round my head now. But ²_____ combine the things we love doing with a small business?

Dan: ³_____ buy somewhere nice and have lots of bikes and rent them out to tourists, but I don't think we could afford it.

Maja: And ⁴_____ bake tasty cakes for all those hungry cyclists and serve them tea in a café … Yes, ⁵_____ doing that.

Dan: I can see it too actually. If it was a biggish place we could have a couple of rooms for B&B, but not too many. We can have a look around here and in a couple of the tourist spots down south.

Maja: ⁶_____ living somewhere pretty, by the sea or in the hills. We've always lived in cities. It's time for a change, don't you think?

PRONUNCIATION Sure and unsure tones

5 🎧 **2** **39** Listen. Decide which version (a or b) of the sentence is sure (S) and which is unsure (U).

	a	b
1 Can you envisage us buying a new place?	☐	☐
2 But wouldn't it be great to combine the things we love doing with a small business?	☐	☐
3 If money were no object, I'd buy somewhere pretty.	☐	☐
4 Yes, I can see myself doing that.	☐	☐
5 I've always fancied living somewhere by the sea or in the hills.	☐	☐

WRITING An endorsement

6 Read the comments endorsing people. Tick (✓) the two most positive adjectives / adverbs.

1 We were … with his programming skills.
   a highly impressed ☐
   b pleased ☐
   c satisfied ☐
2 She … helping us achieve our aims.
   a was good at ☐
   b excelled at ☐
   c was extremely good at ☐
3 His … communication style was an asset to the team.
   a confident ☐
   b natural ☐
   c reserved ☐
4 She has … sense of responsibility.
   a an admirable ☐
   b a strong ☐
   c quite a strong ☐
5 He was … proactive in completing the tasks set.
   a generally ☐
   b completely ☐
   c consistently ☐
6 Working with her was a real …
   a privilege ☐
   b honour ☐
   c support ☐

7 Choose the best adjectives / adverbs to complete the endorsements.

Dan worked [1]*consistently / completely* hard to integrate new members into the team seamlessly. He demonstrates [2]*a reserved / an admirable* sense of personal and professional responsibility and his sense of humour meant he was a pleasure to work for.

Maja was [3]*a pretty / an extremely* hard-working and proactive member of the team. She was often chosen to represent the staff at management meetings because of her [4]*reserved / confident* communication style and sociable nature.

Maja was [5]*not bad / a pleasure* to work with and a great example for the rest of us. She was always focused and hard-working and [6]*pleased / quick* to solve problems or ease dissatisfaction with customers proactively.

Dan was an asset to the organization, his ambition to [7]*generally / consistently* improve performance paid off with real results. He inspired others with his vision and his ability to get the [8]*best / strong* out of and support staff at the same time.

8 Match the verbs (1–8) with their collocates (a–h), then read the endorsements to check.

1 to integrate ☐
2 to demonstrate ☐
3 to represent ☐
4 to be quick ☐
5 to ease ☐
6 to improve ☐
7 to inspire ☐
8 to get the best ☐

a with the vision
b to solve problems
c customer dissatisfaction
d performance
e new members into the team
f out of staff
g staff at a meeting
h a sense of professional responsibility

9 Complete an endorsement for Carolyn, written by Dan and Maja. Use the collocations from Exercise 8 and complete the sentences. Add any additional words which will contribute to the overall positive impression.

1 Carolyn / demonstrate / strong
   Carolyn demonstrated a consistently strong sense of professional responsibility.
2 She / quick / proactively / creatively
   _____
3 The coaching / improve / decision making
   _____
4 We / inspire / help / form
   _____
5 The life coaching session / help / best / new situation
   _____

YOUR IDEA

1 Look at the three images. Match the images with the paragraphs about improvements in the local area (a, b, c).

1 ☐

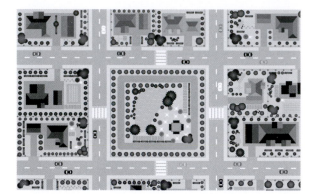

2 ☐

3 ☐

a Do you want to meet new people in the neighbourhood? Do you like to read and discuss literature? If so, this new book club may be the perfect thing for you. Come along – sessions last for two hours and are held every fortnight at the local library. It's free of charge and refreshments are provided.

b A group of young people have decided to work together to do something about the terrible state of their local park. Recently the park has become something of a dumping ground – often at the end of the day it's covered in rubbish. But these youths have decided to try to make a difference.

c The estate's new development will provide a green space between the housing blocks where residents can walk, relax and meet up together. This will be somewhere for families to come to get away from their busy home lives, making this a more peaceful place to live.

2 Write notes about an improvement you have made in your local area or one that you would like to see happen. Think about places in your local area, clubs that people could join and neighbourhood schemes that could be implemented.

_____

_____

_____

_____

3 Match the two parts of the sentences to describe the possible effects of improvements in your area.

1 This development would make ☐
2 Investment in this area would create ☐
3 Setting up a youth club would give ☐
4 A park would give ☐
5 This club would improve ☐

a young people something to do.
b job opportunities.
c people happier.
d people's lives greatly.
e people somewhere to relax.

4 Practise talking about an improvement in your area. Remember to …
- speak clearly and don't rush through your points – this will help you relax and your audience will be able to follow your talk more easily.
- use examples or short stories to illustrate your points.
- pause to emphasize the main points and essential information in your talk – but don't overdo it.

ORGANIZING YOUR PRESENTATION

5 Match the six steps of the presentation with the examples of useful language (a–f).

1 Start the presentation ☐
2 Tell a brief personal story ☐
3 Introduce the improvement to the area ☐
4 Explain how this improvement can be made ☐
5 Say what this improvement means to you ☐
6 Conclude ☐

a Growing up in my area …
b A big thank you for listening.
c It's good to see everyone. Let me get started.
d We could do this by …
e I feel this is so important because …
f What we need where I live is …

YOUR PRESENTATION

6 Read the useful language on the left and make notes for your presentation.

1 Start the presentation Hello and welcome. It's good to see everyone. Let me get started.	
2 Tell a brief personal story Where I live … Growing up in my area … I have a good friend who …	
3 Introduce the improvement to the area What we need here is … An improvement for this area is …	
4 Explain how this improvement can be made We could do this by … To do this …	
5 Say what this improvement means to you I feel this is particularly important because … If this improvement was made I …	
6 Conclude Thanks so much for … A huge thank you for … Does anyone have any questions?	

7 Film yourself giving your presentation or practise in front of a mirror.
Give yourself marks out of ten for …

- speaking clearly. ☐ /10
- using the pace of your talk for emphasis. ☐ /10
- following the six steps in Exercise 6. ☐ /10
- using correct grammar. ☐ /10

12 The future

12.1 Image recognition that triggers augmented reality

TEDTALKS

When they wowed the TED audience with their talk in 2012, **MATT MILLS** and **TAMARA ROUKAERTS** did so as a team – he was Global Head of *Aurasma* and she was Head of Marketing. *Aurasma* is the world's leading augmented-reality app and online platform which launched in 2011 and now has customers in 100 different countries. Since its launch, the app has received several awards, including the Mobile Excellence Award two years in a row. They describe augmented reality as 'the next step on from simply browsing the Internet' because it allows the 'digital content we discover, create and share' to be integrated with what we see around us.

Tamara Roukaerts and Matt Mills

Tamara Roukaerts started her career in advertising at Saatchi & Saatchi before working on Light Blue Optics – a joint venture between Cambridge University and Massachusetts Institute of Technology (MIT). She is now a founding Director of TRM&C, a company that supports high-tech companies with strategic marketing advice.

Matt Mills is a technologist. Before starting at *Aurasma*, he worked first for Autonomy, the company that developed *Aurasma*, managing European sales. Since 2013, Mills has been Commercial Director at Featurespace – a cutting-edge tech company that develops applications to manage and prevent fraud.

CAREER PATHWAYS

1 Read the text. Answer the questions.

  1 What roles did Matt Mills and Tamara Roukaerts have at *Aurasma* at the time of giving the talk?
  2 What professional background did Roukaerts bring?
  3 How has she moved on from *Aurasma*?
  4 What area did Mills start working in after 2013?

TED PLAYLIST

2 Other TED speakers are interested in topics similar to Matt Mills's and Tamara Roukaerts's TED Talk. Read the descriptions of four TED Talks at the top of page 155. In your opinion, which is the best title for the playlist, a, b or c?

  a Future ways to experience the world's wonders safely
  b Interfaces between technology, mind and matter
  c Using Google for education and new inventions

3 Complete the six-word summary (1–4) that corresponds to each talk in the TED playlist. Use these words.

eye	greater	minds	redefining

  1 _____ online maps with 3D capabilities.
  2 _____ experiences from technology in sports.
  3 Making _____ contact with the world.
  4 Using our _____ to control reality.

4 Match the verbs (1–5) with their collocates (a–e). Check your answers in the playlist descriptions.

1 to showcase	**a** the idea
2 to pitch	**b** somebody's brainwaves
3 to engage with	**c** the world
4 to read	**d** virtual and physical objects
5 to control	**e** capabilities

5 Which talk would you most like to see? Why? Watch the talk at TED.com.

Blaise Aguera y Arcas: Augmented-reality maps

Blaise Aguera y Arcas now works on machine learning at Google. Earlier in his career he was the co-creator of Photosynth, a technology that assembles digital photos into 3D environments. In his hands-on talk, he uses futuristic technology, Google Maps and his friends strategically placed at a market to showcase the capabilities of these jaw-dropping augmented-reality maps.

Chris Kluwe: How augmented reality will change sports … and build empathy

Chris Kluwe is a former professional American football player. He pitches the idea of using augmented-reality technology on the sports field in order to more accurately convey the pace and excitement the players experience. Beyond the sports arena, he also suggests that this technology could help people appreciate real global issues and ultimately become more empathetic.

Sergey Brin: Why Google Glass?

Sergey Brin is one half of the team who founded Google and leads the development of special projects like Google Glass. Brin explains the philosophy behind this amazing new technology: the desire to engage with the physical and digital worlds simultaneously head on, rather than hunched over our mobile devices.

Tan Le: A headset that reads your brainwaves

Tan Le is a technologist and founder and CEO of Emotiv, a bioinformatics company. In her talk she demonstrates an incredible innovation: a headset that reads the wearers' brainwaves and enables them to control virtual and physical objects with only their mind. As she herself says, the demonstration only scratches the surface of what we may ultimately be able to do with technology like this.

AUTHENTIC LISTENING SKILLS Listening for grammatical chunks

6 ∩2 40 You are going to hear a podcast in which a member of the *Keynote* team talks about Tan Le's TED Talk, *A headset that reads your brainwaves*. Listen to the sentences and underline the stressed words. Then listen again and circle the grammatical chunks (that are often unstressed).

1 One of my favourite TED Talks is the one from Tan Le called *A headset that reads your brainwaves*.
2 Tan Le starts her talk with her vision to expand human and computer interaction.
3 She reminds us that interpersonal communication is more complex than mere commands.
4 The headset will cost only a few hundred dollars, not thousands.

LISTENING

7 ∩2 41 Listen to the full podcast. Answer the questions.

1 According to the podcaster, in what ways is the new technology accessible?
2 What does Rosane mention enjoying about Tan Le's presentation style?
3 What real-life applications are mentioned for the headset?
4 Why will Rosane recommend the talk?

8 ∩2 41 Complete the missing words about the talk and the demonstration. Listen again and check your answers.

1 It is explained clearly in three sections: _____ , _____ and _____ .

2 For the demonstration, Evan Grant _____ on stage, _____ the headset and _____ out two tasks.
3 First he tried a simple _____ – he chose 'pull' – and second he tried the much more _____ command, 'disappear'.
4 When the second task didn't quite work he _____ a second neural signal which made the cube disappear.
5 The wheelchair user uses blinks and _____ to tell his chair which way to move.

VOCABULARY IN CONTEXT

9 Read the extracts from the podcast. Choose the correct meaning of the words in bold.

1 Tan Le starts her talk with her vision to expand human and computer **interaction** to include facial expressions and emotions …
   a science ☐   b communication ☐
   c programmes ☐

2 Tan Le manages the whole presentation in such a calm, clear and collected **fashion** that it seems effortless.
   a way ☐   b sense ☐   c mannerism ☐

3 Mr Grant was a willing **guinea pig** and performed the first task perfectly.
   a display ☐   b robot ☐   c volunteer ☐

4 If Ms Tan had called someone randomly it could have given even more **credibility** to it.
   a estimation ☐   b admiration ☐   c value ☐

5 Some people, like this young woman, are **dedicating** their time to developing systems that can help … people.
   a engaging ☐   b giving ☐   c doing ☐

GRAMMAR Future in the past

1 Choose the best options to complete the text.

The massive impact of a tiny invention

Texas Instruments made the first transistor radio in May 1954 and a few months afterwards [1]*were about to / were to* produce the first ones to sell to the mass market. At about this time the company also employed engineer Jack Kilby, who [2]*was about to / was bound to* invent the integrated circuit for which he received a Nobel Prize. The portable transistor radio [3]*would / was likely to* dramatically change people's listening habits and lifestyles. It [4]*was bound to / were bound to* be a hit with the younger generation, but it also became a hugely popular mobile communications device and billions were manufactured. However, if it hadn't been for another research group's earlier invention, the transistor component by Bell laboratories in 1947, the small size of the transistor [5]*wasn't / wouldn't have been* possible at all. When the small team of three inventors made their discovery, they didn't know how it [6]*was going to be / were going to be* used just a few years later. When they presented it at a conference it was considered [7]*likely to be / unlikely to be* useful and rather odd. Had they known then what it's used for now, it [8]*would have been / would be* a sensation. Walter Brattain, John Bardeen and William Shockley were awarded the Nobel Prize in Physics in 1956 for inventing the small component that [9]*was to be / was bound to be* essential for telecommunications, audio and video recording and aviation systems in years to come.

2 Complete the sentences with these words.

bound	going	likely	was	were	would

1 If you were _____ to listen to the radio in 1955 it was probably on a TR19 transistor.

2 The invention of the transistor _____ to have a huge impact on electronic products being produced in the fifties and sixties.

3 The pocket-sized transistor radio launched in October 1954 was _____ to attract large sales as it allowed people to listen to the radio anywhere.

4 When Brattain, Bardeen and Shockley were working on their invention they didn't know they _____ to be later awarded the Nobel Prize for physics.

5 Other companies were _____ to have been planning similar devices but Texas Instruments were the first to corner the market for transistor radios.

6 The invention of the transistor _____ transform people's listening experience for ever.

3 Match the two parts of the sentences.

1 Until he lived in France he believed the language wouldn't ☐
2 She was bound to get nervous ☐
3 They were about to close the gate ☐
4 The new recruit was unlikely to need help ☐
5 It looked likely to rain ☐
6 We were going to fly ☐

a so she put an umbrella in her bag.
b before the presentation; she always did.
c but the train was much cheaper.
d interest him.
e when he appeared and managed to board the plane.
f from anyone as he was extremely self-sufficient.

4 Choose the best expressions describing the future in the past.

1 A Spanish woman, Juliana Morrell, *was to become / was becoming* the first woman to obtain a university degree in 1608.

2 For many years women *were going to be / were about to be* in the minority in further education.

3 It was *bound to be / unlikely to be* straightforward for women to get the same educational rights as men.

4 Women *would not teach / were to teach* at university until Laura Bassi, an Italian, became the first to teach at a European university in 1732.

5 In 1850 Lucy Sessions *will / would* earn a degree in the USA, becoming the first black woman to do so.

6 The Edinburgh Seven, a group of female students who began studies in medicine in 1869, could not finish their studies but *were / would* to gain publicity for the rights of women to study at university.

7 Legislation was going *to pass / to be passed* in 1877 to allow women to attend university.

GRAMMAR EXTRA! Tentative use of the past when talking about the future

5 🎧 **2** **42** Listen to the conversation. When do they make an appointment for?

6 🎧 **2** **42** Try to complete the conversation with the correct form of the verb in brackets. Then listen and check. Which verb isn't a tentative use of the past to talk about the future?

I: Hi, Frank. How's it going? Actually, I
   ¹ _____ (wonder) if we could squeeze in a meeting before I go away.

F: OK. Let's see. When ² _____ (have) in mind?

I: Well, I was going to go to Frankfurt for two days, but that's been cancelled. So I ³ _____ (think) of Wednesday the twelfth or Thursday the thirteenth.

F: Well, I ⁴ _____ (be) down to be in a teleconference on Wednesday afternoon ….

I: It's just that I ⁵ _____ (hope) to hand over the project before I go away. How about Thursday morning?

F: OK. What time ⁶ _____ (want) to meet? Any time after ten is fine with me.

I: Let's say ten-thirty then. Thank you. That's great. It wouldn't have been possible if the Frankfurt trip
   ⁷ _____ (cancel).

PRONUNCIATION Sentence stress in explaining outcomes

7 🎧 **2** **43** Underline the word(s) that will be stressed in order to convey the meaning expressed in brackets. Then listen and check your answers.

1 The project team was going to meet again before my holiday. (not after)
2 They were going to cancel the launch meeting. (not rearrange)
3 I was thinking of Thursday morning. (not Tuesday)
4 I thought Ricardo was going to call. (not you)

DICTATION

8 🎧 **2** **44** Listen to someone talking about a fair. Complete the paragraph.

In 1964, _____
of the future than we have today? Ryan Ritchey thinks so and explores the topic in his documentary, *After the Fair*, about the World's Fair in 1964 in New York. This fair
_____
and other technological and cultural trends face to face for the first time. It _____
made it in the two six-month seasons it was open. It was a vision of the future, _____
_____ colonies on the moon and cities underwater. On the other hand, many visitors _____
_____ and getting an answer, something many of us do regularly now. There were also picture phones that _____
because outward appearances were less important then than they are nowadays.

157

READING

1 🎧 2 45 Match the generations (1–5) with the dates (a–e). Then listen and check.

1	Generation Y / Millennials ☐	3	Baby Boomers ☐
2	Generation Z ☐	4	Mature Silents ☐
		5	Generation X ☐

a 1927–1945 **d** 1981–2000
b 1946–1964 **e** 2001 onwards
c 1965–1980

2 Complete the article (a–e) with the generation headings from Exercise 1 (1–5).

What about the future?

I've been thinking about the future: do generations see it differently? I contacted people I know belonging to each demographic and asked: 'What changes do you think the next five years will bring?'

a _____ is the most ethnically diverse and it's the 'Kids Growing Older Younger' generation or KGOY. This generation aren't children for long and are making their own choices earlier than any previous generation. They embrace computers, digital content and learning and say:

'People will spend more time using their mobile phones but actually communicate less.' Lily

'Cities will be even more crowded, there will be more plastic waste. I think more people will be vegetarians.' Mia

b _____ is the 'latchkey' generation where both parents worked and whose world view is based on change. Most had computers at high school and are comfortable with technology. They are entrepreneurial with little commitment to one career or company. They say:

'The biggest changes will come from quantum leaps in technology as the Internet of things finally arrives.' Nick

'I hope 2020 brings scientific developments in medical advancement to reduce suffering due to disease.' Dy

c _____ is a disciplined and cautious generation. It was the first to have television and rock and roll. Men tended to be the breadwinners and were loyal to one company while women stayed at home to look after the children. They say:

'I just want my grandchildren to inherit a clean and safe world.' Sonia

'The drive to automate jobs; for example: self-service check-outs, driverless vehicles, online services, means there is a real threat, perhaps even more than global warming. There's a real risk that many people will have no work.' Mike

d _____ are concerned with both family and friends and the world beyond their own neighbourhoods – the local and global community. The first digital natives, they are very comfortable with the latest technologies. They don't expect a job for life and prefer more relaxed work environments. They say:

'Consumerism will increase but the education system will improve. It will be easier for kids with special needs to attend the same school as their peers.' Adrian
'I think that in five years' time, it will be even more important for people to speak up and start working actively towards change.' Janis

e _____ have two subsets: the 'hippies' concerned with harmony and happiness, and 'yuppies' who climbed the career ladder and earn and live very well. Women started to work and children became independent quickly. They were the first physically fit and wealthy generation and have grown up with television but are digital immigrants. They say:

'I guess, unfortunately, that the social gap between people doing well and those doing less well will increase significantly.' Tina

'Mainstream consumer goods like music, clothes and digital content will cost almost nothing once you are a member of an accepted social community. But anything special will cost much more.' Sam

Overall, interestingly, the comments showed more similarity than difference in their hopes for a better world.

3 Read the article. Are these statements true (T) or false (F)?

1 The youngest generation is the most ethnically diverse. ☐
2 The opinions in the final section (e) include those of both yuppies and hippies. ☐
3 The oldest generation are the most comfortable with change. ☐
4 Baby Boomers expected to have a lifetime career with the same company. ☐
5 At least two generations are described as being good at making their own way in the world. ☐
6 Generation X is the first generation to live with fewer diseases. ☐

4 🎧 2 46 Listen and choose the correct options to complete the notes about predictions for the next five years.

1 Generation Z: *more / less* laziness; *more / less* understanding
2 Generation Y: *everything / some things* worse; hope for *less / more* support for each other
3 Generation X: *very little / a great deal of* change; *fewer / more* phones
4 Baby Boomers: should be *more / less* concerned with technological changes; should *appreciate / try to improve* what we have
5 Mature Silents: should *return to / move away from* old family traditions; this is *likely / unlikely* to happen

VOCABULARY Optimism and pessimism

5 Complete the sentences. Use these words and phrases.

| bad things | bright side | cloud | dark cloud |
| half empty | half full | hope | tunnel |

1 She's ever the optimist isn't she? She always finds a way to look on the _____ .
2 It's time we faced up to it. There really is no _____ in sight for our team. They'll certainly go down a division next season.
3 The way I see it is that he's a glass _____ type of person; he tends to think that the outlook is bleak.
4 The project is nearly finished; we can finally see a light at the end of the _____ .
5 'If _____ can happen, they certainly will' is almost a self-fulfilling prophecy. I prefer positive thinking; then good things are more likely to happen.
6 Our colleagues from Marketing are paid to see the glass as _____ . They say we can focus our efforts on maximizing the strengths of the brand.
7 I can't help seeing a _____ on the horizon; the last meeting made it clear they don't want to work with us on this. I think we are back to square one.
8 He wasn't selected for promotion but then he found a better job at another company. Every _____ has a silver lining.

WORDBUILDING Compound adjectives

6 Compound adjectives are made up of two adjectives or an adverb + adjective combination. Match the opposites (1–6) with the adjectives they collocate with (a–f) to make compound adjectives.

1 open- / narrow-   a populated
2 highly / poorly   b witted
3 quick- / slow-   c minded
4 densely / sparsely   d willed
5 well- / poorly-   e skilled
6 strong- / weak-   f educated

7 Complete the sentences with the correct compound adjectives from Exercise 6.

1 Along with Mongolia and Namibia, Australia is one of the most _____ countries in the world with just three people or fewer per square kilometre.
2 He's very _____ ; he's kept to the strict diet the doctor put him on for the last six months.
3 The company philosophy is an _____ one, embracing all forms of diversity.
4 Massive Open Online Courses (MOOCs), widely available since 2012, allow less _____ people with access to the Internet to get a university-level education.
5 She's such a _____ young woman. She comes up with great ideas and she picks things up very quickly.
6 Rather than exploit _____ people in areas of high unemployment, companies could offer training to improve their skills.

WORD FOCUS Partitive expressions

8 Partitive expressions are used to describe a part of or an example of something. Match the partitives (1–6) with the nouns they are used with (a–f).

1 a glimmer   a of luck
2 a drop   b of inspiration
3 a bundle   c of information
4 a flash   d of hope
5 a stroke   e of rain
6 a mine   f of laughs

9 Complete the sentences with the partitive expressions from Exercise 8.

1 She was lost for ideas but suddenly had a _____ for her presentation opening and used a short film clip.
2 The weekend meeting wasn't a _____ as you can imagine. Think yourself lucky you didn't have to go.
3 When I was an intern, my colleagues were such a _____ . I learned so much from them.
4 Thanks to a worldwide campaign there is now a _____ for this endangered species.
5 Despite what the weather forecast predicted there wasn't a _____ at the wedding.
6 That was a _____ ! I was late but my train was even later.

159

MAKING ARRANGEMENTS

1 Match the verbs (1–6) with the correct words (a–f).

1 to arrange to	**a** work
2 to make the	**b** something in
3 to make something	**c** someone
4 to organize / cancel	**d** meeting
5 to pencil	**e** a meeting
6 to confirm with	**f** meet

2 [🎧 2 47] Listen to a conversation. What is the meeting about? Tick (✓) the expressions from Exercise 1 as you hear them.

1 I want to arrange to meet about ☐
2 you could make the meeting ☐
3 like to cancel our meeting ☐
4 make something work ☐
5 Let's pencil it in ☐
6 can confirm with everyone else ☐

3 [🎧 2 47] Complete the phrases for making arrangements under each heading. Then listen again and check your answers.

Asking about availability
1 _____ if you could make the meeting next week.
2 _____ Tuesday morning?
3 _____ that work for you?

Saying yes
4 _____ be good.
5 If I can participate by phone _____ .

Saying no
6 It's not ideal timewise, _____ .
7 Wednesday and Thursday are _____ , I'm afraid.
8 Tuesday morning? I'm _____ .

Agreeing
9 _____ pencil it in.
10 _____ great.

4 Complete the emails. Use these words.

any good	can reschedule	confirmed then
postpone to	supposed to	was meant

a

> Thanks Sam. Yes. I can make it by phone. My train's ¹ _____ leave at 18.15 so I can join the meeting then. Hope Bert and Liz can make it. Looking forward to it. Felix.

b

> Hi all,
> I ² _____ to be in Bert's team meeting on Tuesday as well, so I can make it.
> Have a good day.
> Liz

c

> Hi all,
> Thanks everyone. That's ³ _____ . Tuesday at six thirty. The board is forwarding us some information about what they'd like so we can think things over beforehand.
> Best wishes
> Sam

d

> Hi all,
> Hope you had a good holiday, Felix. Anyway, yes, the meeting. I was going to have a team meeting at that time, but I ⁴ _____ it easily. So, yeah, I'm around. Any time after six is fine.
> Bert

e

> Hi all,
> About meeting next week to discuss our 25-year anniversary event: is Tuesday after six ⁵ _____ for you? Please accept or decline as soon as possible.
> Best wishes, Sam

f

> Hi all,
> Good you can all make it. I'm supposed to be in another meeting until half past but I can attend, if we ⁶ _____ six thirty.
> Or if everyone's ready early, start without me.
> All the best, Norma

5 Put the emails to and from the team (a–f) in the order in which they were likely to have been sent (1–6).

1 ☐ 2 ☐ 3 ☐ 4 ☐ 5 ☐ 6 ☐

PRONUNCIATION Sentence stress in making arrangements

6 🎧 2 48 Listen to the conversation. Underline the words that are most strongly stressed in each question or statement.

1 a Is Thursday afternoon any good for you?
  b Any time after two is fine.
2 a Would Friday at nine work for you?
  b I'm supposed to be meeting Jake but I may be able to postpone it.
3 a It's not ideal, to be honest, but if we make it ten instead of nine I can manage it.
  b Sure, yeah, I'm around.
4 a How about Monday morning?
  b Monday's out for me but Tuesday would work.

WRITING SKILL Impersonal language

7 Complete the email from the management team to the planning committee about the event. Use these phrases.

another suggestion	been planned	one proposal
the objection	various suggestions	was agreed
was discussed	was suggested	

Dear Sam and the rest of the team,

We met last week to discuss plans for our anniversary event. ¹_____ were made about the form it should take. ²_____ was to invite retired employees to attend as well as staff and their families and our customers. It ³_____ that this would be a good idea.

An overall theme for the event ⁴_____ , but not everyone could agree on it. ⁵_____ for activities was to have a light-hearted quiz with prizes but ⁶_____ to this was that it's difficult to hold 200 people's attention. Catering ⁷_____ and we agreed on a budget. We also decided to use a local catering firm so that our canteen staff can attend the event. A short programme of speeches, announcements and a short film has ⁸_____ . We would like you to suggest two other activities, an overall theme and a final highlight.

We look forward to hearing your ideas.

Best regards

Mary, Ben & Donald, The management board

8 Complete the notes recording what has been agreed so far.

1 Participants _____
2 Overall theme _____
3 Activity 1 _____
4 Activity 2 _____
5 Food and drinks _____
6 Official programme _____
7 Highlight _____

9 Rewrite the ideas from the meeting in impersonal language.

1 Bert proposed a local catering company who have vintage BBQ carts and cater for summer parties.
(food and drink) One proposal was to use a local catering company, who cater for summer parties with vintage BBQ carts.
2 Felix suggested a Western theme – inspired by our latest product range.
The suggestion _____.
3 Sam suggested fireworks as a highlight, but Norma didn't think it was a good idea.
Not everyone _____.
4 Sam, Norma, Bert, Felix and Liz said a barn dance would match the theme and be fun.
It _____.
5 Liz suggested a rodeo bull-riding machine as an activity that's fun to do and watch.
The suggestion _____.

10 Complete the email to the board with the suggestions from the meeting. Use impersonal language and the information from Exercise 9 and the notes below.

Dear Mary, Ben and Donald,
1 **Opening:** We / pleased / present ideas / anniversary event / from / recent meeting
_____
2 **Overall theme:** / most appropriate
_____
3 **Food and drinks:** / fits theme
_____
4 **Activity 1:** / after discussion
_____
5 **Activity 2:** / unusual
_____
6 **Highlight:** / in the end / activities are enough
_____

Best regards

The planning committee

Writing 6 | AN ESSAY

The essay you will read in Exercise 2 is in answer to the following exam question.

> You have recently attended a seminar about how tourism can be made more environmentally friendly. You made the following notes while at the seminar:
>
> **Ways to make tourism more environmentally friendly**
>
>   Supporting conservation projects
>   Limiting the number of visitors to some sites
>   Using vehicles run on renewable energy
>
> Some opinions expressed in the discussion:
>   'That's a great way to learn about the place you're visiting.'
>   'I'd hate to arrive somewhere and find I couldn't get in!'
>   'Who is going to pay for the new vehicles?'
>
> Write an **essay** discussing **two** of the ways tourism could be made more environmentally friendly. You should **explain which you think will be more effective, giving reasons** to support your opinion.
> You may, if you wish, make use of the opinions expressed in the discussion, but you should use your own words as far as possible.
> Write your essay in **220–260 words** in an appropriate style.

IDEAS

1 Tick (✓) the things you would expect to see in the essay.

  a one or two sentences summarizing the aim of the essay ☐
  b a conclusion, summarizing the writer's opinion ☐
  c a description of one way tourism could be made more environmentally friendly ☐
  d a second way tourism could be improved, with reasons ☐
  e a third paragraph describing another way tourism could be made more sustainable ☐
  f a description of an ideal tourist destination ☐

3 Read the essay again. Are these statements true (T) or false (F)?

  1 The impact travel has on the environment has increased. ☐
  2 Discovering the local culture may encourage tourists to change their habits. ☐
  3 You can visit Machu Picchu at any time. ☐
  4 Limiting visitor numbers means important sites will be accessible in the future. ☐
  5 The writer believes that there should be restrictions on visitor numbers to important sites. ☐

MODEL

2 Read the essay. Match the four paragraphs with a description (a–f) from Exercise 1.

  1 ☐   **2** ☐   **3** ☐   **4** ☐

---

[1]Human society is having an increasing effect on our environment, particularly through our desire to travel to other places. It is important to consider the consequences of this, and how to reduce the negative effects tourism can have.

[2]A good way of encouraging tourists to find out about the culture of the places they're visiting would be to help them participate in local conservation projects.

If they understand the impact their actions have on the environment, visitors may be more likely to look after it, for example, by recycling more or not leaving rubbish behind. Tourists may also reduce their carbon footprint by choosing to holiday closer to home or travelling by bus or train rather than by plane.

[3]One area where tourism has a particularly big impact is the amount of people who visit sensitive sites like Machu Picchu in Peru. The authorities introduced a licence system to limit the number of people walking the Inca Trail each day and give the area time to recover. Although it can be disappointing for tourists who have not planned ahead, it is an important method of controlling our impact on these important places and preserving them for future generations. It may also encourage tourists to find out more about their destination before they travel.

[4]Taking all of these points into consideration, I feel the best way to make tourism more sustainable, and reduce our impact, would be to limit the number of visitors who can go to each place. This will show them that we cannot travel without considering the consequences.

USEFUL LANGUAGE

4 Match the two parts of the introductory sentences.

1 The question of whether volunteers or paid workers are better ☐
2 The way a charity's money should be divided is often ☐
3 More and more companies ☐
4 Over the past twenty years or so, ☐
5 With the large number of charities that now exist, ☐
6 Undoubtedly, it is important to volunteer, ☐

a the number of charities has increased considerably.
b are giving their employees time to volunteer.
c always causes debate.
d how can you decide which one to volunteer for?
e a contentious issue.
f but the question is how can we encourage people to do it.

5 Find and correct the mistake in each sentence. It may be a grammar, vocabulary or punctuation mistake.

1 To begin, by visiting a nature park people can experience the natural world first hand.
2 It would be therefore easier for them to watch programmes on their own television.
3 Besides companies are much more likely to listen to the government than their customers.
4 It is well-known fact that travelling on the underground is faster than using buses.
5 On the other side, a rapid bus system would be much cheaper to develop than a new underground system.
6 Instead of create a large area of solar panels, we could put them on individual buildings.

6 Complete the summarizing sentences. Use these words.

balance	bearing	compared	favour
former	outweigh	rather	sum

1 On _____, while both visits to nature parks and programmes about the natural world are important, I am in _____ of the latter as the best way to teach people about the environment.
2 _____ all that in mind, I believe that the government should focus on reducing the amount of plastic used in packaging _____ than on trying to make us recycle it.
3 To _____ up, while both types of public transport have their advantages and disadvantages, in my opinion, the benefits of a rapid bus system _____ those of a new underground system.
4 In conclusion, if the advantages of solar power are _____ to those of building new wind turbines, the _____ is clearly more useful to the community.

PLANNING

You will answer the following question.

> Your company has recently been discussing whether they should start a volunteering scheme. As part of the discussion, the following notes were made about possible ways to organize it:
>
> **Structuring the volunteer scheme**
> Each employee chooses their own project
> One project per team
> A company-wide project
>
> Some opinions expressed in the discussion:
> 'We can all choose something that speaks to us.'
> 'We'll work together so much better after that.'
> 'What if you're not interested in the chosen project?'
>
> Write an **essay** discussing **two** of the ways the scheme could be organized. You should **explain which you think will be more effective, giving reasons** to support your opinion.
>
> If you use some of the opinions expressed in the discussion, use your own words as far as possible.

7 Plan your essay. Write notes to answer these questions. Don't write full sentences yet.

1 Which two structures will you write about?
2 Which do you think is more effective?
3 What reasons will you give to support your choice?

WRITING

8 Write an essay to answer the question in Exercise 7. In your essay you should:

- introduce the topic so the reader knows what to expect
- discuss two of the possible structures for the volunteer scheme, saying which you think will be more effective
- give reasons to support your opinion
- write a conclusion which summarizes the essay

Write **220–260 words**.

ANALYSIS

9 Check your essay. Then answer the questions.

- **Content:** Does the essay cover two of the possible structures for the scheme? Does it give supporting reasons? Is it 220 to 260 words long?
- **Communicative achievement:** Is it written in a neutral or formal style? Is it clear?
- **Organization:** Is the essay logically organized? Are the ideas connected?
- **Language:** Does it use correct grammar and a good range of structures and all your own words?

Workbook
answer key

Units 7–12

Answer key

UNIT 7

7.1 Taking imagination seriously

1

1 She imagines her goals as a reality, then works backwards.
2 It is a 745-foot net sculpture which is partly powered by the public
3 She studied art and counselling psychology at university.
4 She tries to pay attention to her inner voice, she draws and writes using her less dominant hand.

2

c Stories and art that stretch the imagination

3

1 carpet   2 Pushing   3 everywhere
4 between

4

1 e   2 d   3 b   4 c   5 a

6

1 relevance   2 living   3 attention   4 belief
5 director

7

1 F – His narrative is so exciting that he doesn't need visuals to bring it to life – surprisingly for a film director, his presentation included no slides or film clips.
2 T
3 T
4 F – His dream was to see the Titanic wreck at the bottom of the ocean with his own eyes.

8

1 He was particularly interested in oceans and space.
2 He convinced the Hollywood studio it was necessary to film the ship's wreckage, the studio then funded the expedition, his movie became a success, delivering profit to the studio and entertainment to audiences.
3 CG animation, because he'd noticed that audiences were mesmerized by the magic of it.
4 That our ideal job will build from our personal interests and passions and that we shouldn't be afraid of exploring these for the benefit of both our work and personal life.

9

1 c   2 c   3 b   4 b   5 a

7.2 The power of daydreaming

1

1 B   2 C   3 A   4 E   5 D

2

1 were doing
2 controls
3 may not have known
4 will be doing

5 were working on
6 requires
7 are constantly changing
8 had never considered

3

1 Were you daydreaming
2 was thinking
3 Are you being
4 wasn't implying
5 was just wondering
6 've been daydreaming
7 was always getting caught
8 've been reading
9 'll probably be daydreaming

4

1 'd been working
2 're coming / 'll be coming / 're going to come
3 've been going
4 was working / 'd been working
5 hadn't been listening / wasn't listening
6 'll be exhibiting / 's going to be exhibiting / 's exhibiting
7 was dreaming / 'd been dreaming
8 's hoping

5

1 for the summer
2 last week
3 before last year
4 but there's a strike
5 she's moving this week
6 when they heard the news
7 before the end of the year
8 ever since I can remember

6

1 b   2 a   3 b   4 c   5 a

7

1 probably   2 definitely   3 probably
4 undoubtedly   5 certainly   6 definitely
7 most probably   8 surely

8

1 long, renting   2 staying   3 using   4 living
5 long, renting

9

Well, they say that daydreaming makes you more creative. I remember one time I had been trying to work out the details of a presentation. I'd got stuck trying to connect two distinct parts in the final section and needed a way of bringing them together. I'd been racking my brains for about a week and nothing had worked. Then I was travelling home by train and had started reading the paper but actually was just staring out of the window, daydreaming and sort of allowing my mind to freewheel. Suddenly there it was, the answer I had been looking for. It just popped into my head from nowhere. The perfect solution.

7.3 In my mind's eye

1

1 c   2 e   3 a   4 b   5 f   6 d

2

1 global cuisine
2 tailor-made service
3 Vermont Fresh Network
4 bold imagination
5 impeccable service

3

1 T
2 T
3 F – The chef and catering team tease out some details that are personal. When a clear idea has been established, Susanna starts to add her own ideas.
4 F – Mostly sourced locally.
5 T
6 F – Staff learn about the food to pass on relevant information to guests.

4

1 c   2 f   3 h   4 a   5 g   6 e   7 d   8 b

5

1 put my mind to it
2 bear in mind
3 in two minds
4 blow your mind
5 keep an open mind
6 ease my mind
7 see (the finish line) in your mind's eye
8 gave him peace of mind

6

1 hang   hanged b   hung a
2 go   been a   gone b
3 cost   costed a   cost b
4 lie   laid a   lied b
5 shine   shined b   shone a

7

1 laid   2 shined   3 gone   4 lied   5 costed
6 been   7 cost   8 hanged   9 hung
10 shone

8

1 f   2 d   3 a   4 b   5 c   6 e

9

1 keep an eye on
2 is / was, eye-catching
3 see, with the naked eye
4 up to their eyes in
5 do, with his eyes shut
6 opened my eyes to

7.4 That doesn't seem possible

1

1 I expect she's on holiday. ✓
2 I imagine she's on a training course.
3 She must be ill.
4 One of her children might be ill.
5 She's probably stuck in traffic. ✓
6 She may have overslept.✓

2

1 Perhaps she's gone to the doctor.
2 Maybe there's been an accident that's delayed her.

3

1 she can't have had her phone with her
2 everyone must have left the building in time.
3 it's likely to have been a serious fire.
4 I guess she'll need a day off.
5 the children will probably be tired.
6 The firemen are bound to have found the cause of the fire by now.

4

1 've   2 've   3 've   4 've, 've   5 have   6 've

5

1 That can't be right.
2 I think you're onto something there.
3 I'm not entirely convinced.
4 It certainly looks that way.
5 That doesn't seem at all likely to me.
6 That seems a likely explanation.

6

1 reportedly   2 believe   3 claim
4 Apparently   5 said to   6 allegedly
7 speculation   8 by all accounts

7

1 Speculation   2 reportedly   3 is believed
4 by all accounts   5 said to   6 allegedly
7 claim   8 apparently

8

1 by ~~each~~ all accounts   2 claim~~ing~~ed
3 allegedly   4 ~~belief~~ believed   5 ~~say~~ said
6 ~~speculate~~ speculation

9   (Possible answers)

2 Allegedly, when employees are physically fitter it has a positive effect on the business too.
3 Top management is quoted as saying this is the reason they started the annual relay race five years ago.
4 By all accounts the race strengthens the company's corporate identity, provides year-long entertainment for staff and is fun.
5 Speculation about tactics builds throughout the year while departments bond through training regularly outside working hours.
6 It's said to be almost certain that the R&D department (will) win every time, as indeed they did this year too. But as ever there were some surprises in innovative tactics and the other positions.
7 Apparently a total of 250 employees, friends and family attended the race this year. The summer party was held afterwards in glorious weather with drinks and snacks provided by the company.
8 It's believed by many to be a highlight in the corporate year.

PRESENTATION 4

1

1 b   2 c   3 a

3   (Example answers)

1 When I was a child, I'd often go to the woods and pretend to be a courageous explorer.

2 I used to go there with my brother – we'd pretend to discover new imaginary lands together.
3 I remember that we felt so free when we were out in the woods – like nothing else mattered.

5

1 a, e   2 b, d   3 c, g   4 f, h

6   (Example answers)

1 Hello and thanks for joining me today. My name's (name).
2 I loved stories when I was younger. I would always be reading some fantasy or science fiction novel. I wouldn't just read, but I'd also write my own stories. Even though I don't think they were really that good, I think it helped me develop different ways of thinking.
3 It's so important for your day-to-day life really. If you can use your imagination, you can think of different solutions to problems and find unusual answers. Without imagination and creativity it's quite easy to become stuck.
4 Thank you so much for listening today.

UNIT 8

8.1   Build a tower, build a team

1

1 Because he's a visual thinker and communicator.
2 Although he now works in the fields of design and visual thinking, he originally studied Astronomy and Psychology at the University of Toronto.
3 Work at the museum designing interactive exhibits.
4 He attended his first TED conference in 1994. In addition to giving seven TED Talks, he's also been a visual artist and host at TED conferences, and he lists TED among his clients.
5 He's a fellow at Autodesk and is writing his fifth book.

2

b Collaboration drives innovation

3

1 origin   2 create   3 collaboration   4 complex

4

1 e   2 a   3 b   4 c   5 d

6

1 Gawande is able to take a step back from the detailed work of his job as a practising doctor to look at medicine as a whole.
2 He sets out to provide clarity to problems that show bewildering complexity.
3 … in 1970 the average hospital visit required care from two full-time clinicians. By the end of the twentieth century the number had risen to fifteen.
4 Gawande's message is an important one: medicine is broken but there are answers to its problems so it can be fixed.

7

1 Gawande steps back from his job and looks at the bigger picture of medicine as a whole.
2 The complexity comes from the increase in the number of people, procedures and drugs used in the health industry.
3 High-risk ones like aviation and high-rise construction.
4 His personal interest is his daughter's rare illness and the respect he's gained for the medical profession.

8

1 4,000, 6,000   2 40 per cent of, 60 per cent of, two million people   3 finding the failures, devising solutions, implementing the ideas
4 checklists   5 reduced complications, 47 per cent

9

1 a   2 c   3 a   4 b   5 a

8.2   Having an off day?

1

1 b   2 c   3 a

2

1 A recent audit resulted in the revelation that our small team of six don't work together as well as we could.
2 Taking part in a facilitated workshop was the consequence of the audit recommendations.
3 The boss's observations led to some proposals for change in some key areas.
4 Despite our initial scepticism, the workshop fostered rapport.
5 The feedback session contributed to us tightening our processes.
6 The workshop will bring about closer communication between us.

3

1 brought about
2 caused
3 gave rise to
4 stemmed from
5 resulted from
6 contributes to
7 fostered
8 resulted in

4

2 a The flights are so cheap that …
  b There are such cheap flights that …
3 a The order is so large that …
  b It is such a large order that …
4 a The presentation was so good that …
  b It was such a good presentation that …
5 a The workshop was so successful that …
  b The workshop was such a success that …
6 a Travelling in the rush hour was so time consuming that …
  b Travelling in the rush hour was such a time-consuming activity that …
7 a The setback caused by IT problems was so serious that …
  b There was such a serious setback caused by IT problems that …

8 a There were so many complaints that …
  b There were such a lot of complaints that …
9 a The product was so popular that …
  b It was such a popular product that …

5

1 workshop **2** shut **3** lack/lag **4** work

6

1 bad **2** Please **3** come **4** I.D.

7

When I have to achieve big goals, and <u>when this results in me having lots to deal with, I try to follow the</u> 'eating an elephant model'. Creighton Abrams, a US army general, came up with it and, <u>due to its bizarre nature, it's a memorable idea.</u> The fact that the originator was in the army <u>contributes to the notion of discipline and task completion.</u> Given the elephant's large size, the idea is that <u>breaking it down into smaller parts results in it being easier to deal with.</u> Otherwise, reaching a big goal might seem unobtainable <u>and kill motivation and jeopardize the work itself.</u> Last year, before moving premises, we agreed to throw away any unwanted papers and files. <u>The only way to achieve this</u> enormous task successfully was to deal with it bit by bit. <u>As a result, we threw away almost a ton of paper</u> and cleared the way for the move. As Abrams said: 'When eating an elephant, take one bite at a time'.

8.3 How *not* to motivate people

1

1 F – in 2000 (20-0 the most goals against)
2 T
3 T
4 F – archery is the national sport

2

1 Extrinsic motivation comes from something outside of the person being motivated, like money, and intrinsic from something within, like desire to do the task well.
2 Being relatively new to football, losing dramatically and being in position 209 of 209 in FIFA's ranking.
3 They didn't feel pressure being bottom as the only way was up!
4 Television and the Internet were allowed into the country in 1999, tourism is limited to package tours.
5 GNH is measured to help people strike a balance between material and spiritual concerns.
6 There were no new players to replace the ones retiring and funds were needed elsewhere for health and education.

3

1 extrinsic **2** giddy **3** coined **4** Archery
5 infamous

4

1 twelve **2** $300,000 **3** training camp
4 humidity **5** free **6** ninetieth

5

1 b **2** h **3** e **4** f **5** a **6** c **7** d **8** g

6

1 be a team player
2 bond as a group
3 a sense of belonging
4 pull their weight
5 doing your fair share
6 Sharing the load
7 a part of things
8 go the extra mile

7

2 The enjoyment of the game itself provided the *motivation* for the team to play well.
3 The *awarding* of extra holiday as an incentive proved more effective than overtime payments.
4 He had extensive background *knowledge* of the match.
5 The crowd enjoyed the *excitement* of the game and festive atmosphere.
6 The *inconvenience* of travelling to Thimphu is because of the mountains.
7 The Thai team's *generosity* about training made competing possible.
8 The team's *commitment* to winning was high throughout the game.

8

1 off **2** in **3** around **4** at **5** on **6** towards

9

a 2 **b** 4 **c** 5 **d** 3 **e** 6 **f** 1

8.4 If you'll just let me finish …

1

1 Can I just say something here? I
2 Could I just finish what I was saying? S
3 If you'll let me finish … S
4 I hate to interrupt …. I
5 I know you're dying to jump in, but … S
6 Sorry for interrupting, but … I
7 Before you continue, can I just say … I
8 If you'll allow me to finish … S

2

2, 4, 5, 6, 8

3

1 I'd like to start the discussion by ...
2 I'd also be interested in hearing your views on ...

4

1 take **2** thoughts **3** continue
4 everything **5** finish

5

1 I'd like to <u>start</u> the discussion by asking if everyone's read the information sent around?
2 It'll probably make a difference to the <u>discussion</u>.
3 There will be a chance for <u>everyone</u> to have their say.
4 You mean with <u>hindsight</u> it was more useful than when you were actually doing it?

5

5 It could be a great <u>retention tool</u>, as well as promoting innovation.
6 I <u>would</u> like us all to suggest one or two employees to put forward and answer the questions.

6

a 3 **b** 5 **c** 1 **d** 2 **e** 4

7

1, 6, 7

8

1 also
2 Thanks to / As a result of
3 as a result of / thanks to
4 However
5 As a consequence / Because
6 As a consequence
7 Overall

9

(Example answers)

1
b I left at relatively short notice <u>because</u> the IT project was urgent.
c <u>As a result</u> I wasn't well prepared to fix the problem.

2
a <u>Because</u> the IT systems were identical we could 'speak' a common language.
b <u>As a result</u> we built good relationships.
3
a My counterparts didn't speak very good English and <u>also</u> I don't speak good German / <u>neither/nor</u> do I speak good German.
b My biggest challenge was not understanding German. <u>As a consequence</u> I had many confusing experiences.
c <u>However</u>, this experience improved my understanding of my European colleagues.
4
a <u>As a result of</u> learning to simplify my message I can avoid misunderstandings.
5
a <u>Overall</u>, I would recommend a basic language course before the programme.

WRITING 4

1

b, d, e, f, g

2

1 b **2** d **3** f **4** g **5** e

3

1 F **2** F **3** T **4** F **5** T

4

1 It was **a huge success** from start to finish.
2 We ended up being **pleasantly surprised**.
3 We couldn't wait to **do it all again**.
4 It turned out to be **the best way we could have spent our day**.
5 All in all, I'd say **it was worth every penny**.

5

a 2   b 3   c 1   d 5   e 1   f 3   g 5   h 5
i 2   j 4   k 3   l 2   m 4   n 4   o 1 & 5

6

1 It was great to get your message!
2 I've just had **the holiday of a lifetime** in Thailand.
3 **The first thing I want to tell you about is** the hotels we stayed in.
4 **It was a pleasant surprise when** we found out that all our food and drink was included in the price – great value for money!
5 **Then it was on to** Bangkok for a week.
6 I'd love to take you to Thailand one day. **Let me know what you think**.

7

1 breathtaking views P
2 welcoming people P
3 (the) ideal place P
4 (with) disastrous results N
5 dreadful weather N
6 (a) rewarding experience P

9 (Example answer)

Hi Sally,

Thanks for your message. How's everything with you?

I've just got back from the adventure of a lifetime! I left work on Friday and got the train from San Diego to Los Angeles, my first experience of the American railroad – their trains are so much bigger than the ones we have in Europe! In LA, I changed onto the train that travels across to Chicago. Can you believe it takes over two days to get there? Luckily, I was only on it for about 12 hours, getting off in Flagstaff.

I went for breakfast in a proper American diner, full of friendly people. At 9am, I was collected by a small tour bus which already had six other people on it, and the most enthusiastic guide I've ever met. Two hours later we arrived at what had been the goal all along: the Grand Canyon National Park. The guide made us get out of the van and walk along looking at his feet. He walked backwards and we weren't allowed to look up until he told us to. When we did, the view was truly breathtaking. The whole Grand Canyon was spread out in front of us, stretching away to the horizon. It was the perfect weather for taking photos, and through the day we stopped in loads of places to get different views of this true wonder of nature.

We've all seen photos, but that's nothing compared to the real thing. If you ever get a chance to go there, you definitely should! I hope you do!

Write soon,

Adam

UNIT 9

9.1 All it takes is 10 mindful minutes

1

1 He dropped out because he lost several friends in an accident and the stress led him to embrace full-time meditation.
2 He has a circus arts degree and is a mindfulness consultant, he has learned to meditate while being a monk and learned to teach it to others.
3 Andy Puddicombe contributes the meditation expertise and Rich Pierson the marketing and brand knowledge.
4 The question of how to present meditation in such a way that friends would give it a try.
5 To create a happier and healthier world by teaching the skills of meditation and mindfulness.

2

b Finding happiness through increasing mindfulness

3

1 living   2 valuable   3 Curing   4 happy

4

1 e   2 a   3 c   4 d   5 b

6

1 it really resonated with me
2 actually, rather the causes of happiness
3 or was likely to make us happy

7

1 Because she practises mindfulness activities most days and is interested in being present.
2 That although we live longer and are richer we aren't measurably happier.
3 Is it just as good to think about the past or the future when doing something, or is it better to stay focused on the present?
4 His finding that it's better to stay focused on the present.

8

1 T
2 F – He analyzed 650,000 real-time reports from 15,000 people.
3 F – When doing unpopular tasks, staying focused improved the happiness rating.
4 T
5 F – She is aware that the people she sees every day would be happier too.

9

1 a   2 b   3 c   4 b   5 a

9.2 Even holidays are stressful

1

1 exquisitely   2 beautifully   3 extremely
4 tastefully   5 importantly   6 completely
7 fully   8 completely   9 well   10 totally

2

(Suggested answers)

1 It's absolutely device free and completely peaceful.
2 Walking or riding in totally traffic free and beautifully quiet surroundings.
3 In the exquisitely modern spa and pool complex and the beautifully comfortable sofas and seats inside and outside.
4 Holidays should be totally relaxing and absolutely perfect.

3

1 extremely   2 completely   3 barely
4 freshly   5 locally   6 Amazingly
7 Expertly   8 completely

4

1 d   2 e   3 a   4 b   5 c

5

1 horribly busy   2 absolutely clear
3 naturally sociable   4 rapidly growing
5 blissfully happy

6

1 Although he was nervous, he delivered the presentation incredibly <u>calmly</u>
2 After the sales team had used it for a year, it was <u>utterly</u> ruined.
3 He learned the skills <u>fantastically</u> quickly.
4 The spare parts are <u>readily</u> available in most electronics stores.
5 We discovered this place <u>accidentally</u> on the way back last year.

7

1 just   2 while   3 recently   4 yesterday
5 tomorrow   6 now   7 When   8 last
9 finally   10 already

8

<u>I recently became acquainted with a couple</u> – both medical doctors – who travel every year to a different destination. <u>Unusually, they don't relax on the beach</u>, but take a busman's holiday where they offer their medical expertise in remote places to people in need. Before leaving <u>for somewhere completely different and utterly remote, they totally</u> remove any evidence of wealth and privilege. They travel with an organization and, <u>once thoroughly briefed, they work tirelessly to</u> <u>assist</u> the victims of natural disasters. <u>They are unreservedly enthusiastic about these trips</u> and arrive back eager to explain how much they have gained from the whole experience and the kindness of strangers.

9.3 Alert and alive

1

1 at   2 about   3 with   4 out

2

1 Everyone who works.
2 Yes (well-documented; several studies).

3 The ridiculous in difficult situations, tense situations, yourself, jokes we come across on a break from work.

3

1 N **2** D **3** D **4** D **5** P **6** P **7** D **8** N

4

2 joking aside **3** you're missing an important trick **4** well-documented **5** break out of the cycle **6** don't take it too seriously **7** Take time out **8** lighten up

5

1 d **2** g **3** a **4** h **5** b **6** c **7** e **8** f

6

1 got cold feet **2** makes my blood boil
3 up to my eyeballs **4** keep my chin up
5 is a pain in the neck **6** get it off my chest
7 let her hair down **8** was a weight off my shoulders

7

1 f **2** a **3** d **4** b **5** g **6** c **7** e

8

1 quite **2** very **3** acutely **4** extremely
5 deeply **6** very **7** totally **8** absolutely

9

1 c **2** d **3** e **4** f **5** b **6** a

10

1 lived through **2** live down **3** live up to
4 lives for **5** live with **6** live on

9.4 Have you got a minute?

1

1 you got a minute
2 I do for you
3 I wanted to talk to you about
4 the thing is
5 nuisance
6 couldn't
7 'm sorry

2

1 b **2** e **3** c **4** f **5** g **6** d **7** a

3

1 a Sorry, but if you have a moment …
2 a I have to apologize.
3 a Is there any way … ? b I have a favour to ask.
4 a That's a shame, but I understand. b Don't worry. It doesn't matter.

4

1 a P b A **2** a A b P **3** a A b P
4 a P b A **5** a P b A **6** a A b P

5

1 g **2** c **3** a **4** h **5** b **6** d **7** f **8** e

6

1 claimed **2** allegedly **3** making **4** admitted by **5** acknowledged that **6** proposed **7** agreed of to **8** are urged / are being urged

7

1 acknowledged **2** admitted **3** accused
4 denied **5** suggested **6** insisted
7 agreed

8

(Suggested answers)

1 The team acknowledged that they don't always answer emails quickly enough.
2 They discussed briefly what was acceptable and agreed to reply to customers within twenty-four hours.
3 It was claimed that some emails need more time to reply to due to information gathering.
4 It was proposed that a short email be sent to update the contact concerned.
5 Two members alleged that they could see no system in who to copy into emails.
6 They urged us to look at today's emails as examples.
7 Several members admitted to copying in too many people.
8 All were asked to monitor things and reduce the number of recipients if possible.

PRESENTATION 5

1

1 b **2** c **3** a

3 (Example answers)

Organizational skills
managing groups of people, planning trips, making lists
Interpersonal skills
communicating with others, understanding others, organizing tasks
Financial management skills
managing a budget, making savings
Time management skills
maintaining a schedule, meeting deadlines

5

1 d, g **2** a, h **3** c, e **4** b, f

6 (Example answers)

1 Today, we're going to look at an aspect of daily life and the skills that you can develop. I'm going to talk about how I've managed to gain some skills.
2 This relates to one of my hobbies – running. People don't realize how many different skills you can develop doing an activity like this.
3 I'm actually part of a running club, so I've been able to develop my communicative skills by interacting with the other members. Running is also a very demanding physical activity, especially when you're training for a race. I've proven to myself that I have been able to plan my time, been dedicated and committed to my training schedule, and taken care when planning my meals.

4 So, that's all about my skills. I hope you found my talk interesting. Have you got any questions for me?

UNIT 10

10.1 Protecting Twitter users (sometimes from themselves)

1

1 From the only member of the department to the Vice President of Trust and Safety in 2014.
2 To enable her to have a private as well as a public life.
3 Her work for PJFI, fighting child exploitation and bringing criminals to justice.
4 She has a tattoo on her wrist that symbolizes hope.

2

c Privacy and control in the modern world

3

1 Preferences **2** others **3** risks **4** need

4

1 b **2** e **3** c **4** a **5** d

6

1 Michael (Cummings)
2 National Geographic Learning
3 friends and colleagues
4 teacher
5 classroom

7

1 Working abroad.
2 The diversity and the notion that they are fundamentally something good.
3 It made him think about what a relationship is, what social networking is and how he might be influencing the lives of people he doesn't even know.
4 That he has the ability to spread happiness or even obesity via his social networks.

8

1 T
2 F – It was his discoveries about widowhood.
3 T
4 F – The motto is to encourage people to make connections with people who share the same goals.
5 T

9

1 a **2** b **3** c **4** c **5** a

10.2 Not as risky as it sounds

1 were mostly considered
2 were reported
3 is widely believed
4 has generally been considered
5 is thought
6 have sometimes been known
7 is expected
8 is estimated

2

1 e 2 d 3 a 4 b 5 c

3

1 was said
2 was reported
3 is feared
4 has been agreed
5 was decided
6 is estimated / has been estimated
7 was alleged
8 isn't expected

4

2 Captain Edward John Smith is/was presumed to have drowned.
3 1,500 passengers and crew are known to have died.
4 A technical failure wasn't shown to be the cause in the surveyors' reports.
5 The Titanic is said to be the most famous shipwreck.
6 The Titanic was believed to be unsinkable when it was built.
7 The Titanic was considered to be a low marine risk by Lloyd's.

5

2 It is presumed that Captain Edward John Smith drowned.
3 It's known that 1,500 passengers and crew died.
4 It wasn't shown that a technical failure was the cause in the surveyors' reports.
5 It is said that the Titanic is the most famous shipwreck.
6 It was believed that the Titanic was unsinkable when it was built.
7 It was considered by Lloyd's that the Titanic was a low marine risk.

6

Lloyd's of London is known to be the oldest insurance market in the world. Technically, it's not considered to be a company but a corporate body of 94 syndicates or 'Names', as they are called. It was founded in a City coffee house in 1688 where merchants bought insurance for their ships. The Lutine Bell was reported to have been rung when the Titanic sank in 1912, as has been done for all other ships lost or missing since 1799. In the eighties and nineties Lloyd's was shown to be at risk itself and in fact incurred gigantic losses due to asbestos claims flooding the market. It was announced recently that Lloyd's has opened offices in China and Dubai where the insurance market is much less developed than Britain.

10.3 Follow your gut instinct

1 Students' own answers.

2 7 and 10

3

1 b 2 a 3 a 4 a 5 b 6 b

4

1 They don't always get honest answers as people tend to see themselves in an overly favourable way.
2 All the answers follow the same pattern so you can tell which kind of approach to risk each answer represents.
3 Some of the answers are not so obvious so people would be more likely to have to think about them. Also there's a good mix of situations.

5

1 run 2 poses 3 reduces 4 likelihood
5 odds 6 high 7 in

6

2 availability 3 generosity 4 clarity
5 anonymity 6 hospitality 7 authenticity
8 necessity 9 simplicity

7

1 facts 2 two-faced 3 on it 4 music
5 slap 6 long

8

a a slap in the face
b put a brave face on it
c face facts
d be two-faced
e face the music
f pull a long face

10.4 All things considered …

1

1 c 2 d 3 a 4 b

2

burglary

3

1 There are
2 Possibly
3 drawback
4 According to
5 wouldn't
6 downside
7 attractive
8 sure

4

1 the light of
2 third alternative
3 the best choice
4 All things considered

5

Presenting options
There are some pretty interesting options to choose from
Possibly the most obvious one is
Additionally X is another option to consider
A (third) alternative that might do the job is
Discussing pros and cons
A drawback of X is
On the plus side
The downside is

X makes it a very attractive possibility
Considering options
I'm not sure it's the best option
In the light of
Ultimately, the best choice does seem to be
All things considered

7

1 fairly 2 quite 3 pretty 4 a little, a bit, slightly 5 rather

8

1 T
2 T (rather and quite)
3 F – only one (rather)
4 T (slightly, a bit, a little and rather)

9

1 It was rather a waste of money.
2 They were slightly poorer quality than we'd expected.
3 The XJ7 model is a bit more complicated to install.
4 He was quite impatient and a little unfriendly when he explained it.
5 I found it rather uninspiring and pretty old-fashioned.
6 The company is fairly disorganized.
7 That's rather a worrying / a rather worrying state of affairs.
8 The model they chose was reasonably easy to use.

10

1 quite 2 fairly 3 rather 4 slightly 5 quite
6 a bit 7 rather

11 (Example answer)

The system's low price made it fairly attractive and it arrived pretty promptly. Unfortunately, it was a little faulty but we were given a slightly better maintenance service than I had expected. So overall the package was quite reasonable.

WRITING 5

1

a, c, e, f, g

2

1 a 2 e 3 g 4 c 5 f

3

1 F 2 T 3 F 4 T 5 T

4

1 d 2 g 3 f 4 a 5 h 6 b 7 c 8 e

5

1 knowledgeable 2 prompt 3 wealth
4 remarkably 5 professionally 6 dedication

6

1 regret 2 a time 3 Not only 4 fortunate
5 stood out 6 impressed 7 Once again

7

1 We will not hesitate to recommend you to our customers.
2 I will recommend your restaurant to all my friends.
3 I will certainly use your hotel again.
4 We look forward to doing business with you again soon.
5 We look forward to continuing our business relationship.
6 We have recommended your company to others ...
7 ... and will continue to do so

9 (Example answer)

Dear Sir or Madam,

I would like to express my gratitude for the wonderful experience we had at your hotel at the end of last month.

We landed at the airport late at night, very tired as our flight had been delayed. We were very relieved when we were met by one of your excellent members of staff, Maja – we had forgotten that the transfer was included. She came prepared with water and snacks to help us wake up for long enough to get to the hotel. It was the little touches like this which made our stay particularly memorable.

On arrival at the hotel, we were upgraded to a better room with a breathtaking view of the mountains as Maja had discovered it was our wedding anniversary during our trip and had passed this on to the reception staff without our knowledge. This was a pleasant surprise, and even better were the roses and champagne that appeared in our room on the day itself. Altogether, it was probably our most enjoyable anniversary since we got married eighteen years ago!

I would like to finish by complimenting you on your restaurant. However busy it was, the staff were always calm and professional. The service they provided was prompt and they were able to accommodate my wife's food allergies.

All in all, it was a very pleasant holiday and we will not hesitate to recommend your hotel to our friends. I hope that we can stay there again at some point in the future.

Thank you very much,

Yours faithfully

Len Holder

UNIT 11

11.1 How to build with clay and community

1

1 That he would learn to read and write.
2 He trained in carpentry, teaching and architecture.
3 He raised funds through the company he set up 'Bricks for Gando School'.
4 He'd won seven awards by 2015, he has been exhibited in Frankfurt and New York museums and is a fellow at both the British and American Institutes of Architects.

2

a Community matters matter

3

1 space   2 sustainable   3 surprising
4 design

4

1 e   2 c   3 b   4 a   5 d

6

1 a extensive   b ex<u>te</u>nsive
2 a weird-<u>look</u>ing   b <u>weird</u>-looking
3 a techno-<u>geek</u>   b <u>tech</u>no-geek

7

1 F – Baan showed homes in China, Nigeria and Egypt. Eftychis talked about his great grandfather in Greece.
2 T
3 F – Eftychis would like to learn more about it.

8

1 Funny, posh or extravagant houses some techno-geek or multi-millionaire has built.
2 They like to personalize their living environments and they are highly creative.
3 He feels his people also had to improvise and make homes in unusual situations, his grandfather for example.
4 He gave very interesting information and didn't make it seem as if this situation only happened in certain areas or to certain people.
5 Particularly to people who don't travel very much so they see what life looks like in other places (away from the tourist spots).

9

1 b   2 a   3 b   4 c   5 b

11.2 A vision for saving the world

1

1 when   2 Although   3 In spite of the fact
4 By the time   5 provided that   6 in case
7 once   8 whereas   9 Given that

2

2 The last time I ate banana bread was when I was living in Australia.
3 In case I'm late, save me a piece of cake.
4 As far as not wasting food is concerned, banana bread is an excellent idea.
5 It tastes very sweet, considering there's no sugar in it.
6 Whenever he smells the dish it reminds him of home.
7 In view of the fact that she didn't (or doesn't) like bananas, she chose carrot cake instead.

3

1 If   2 unless   3 As long as   4 Supposing
5 Provided that

4

1 as soon as   2 until   3 Once   4 After
5 By the time

5

1 As far as fruit and vegetables are concerned, buy them when they are in season.
2 If necessary, find new recipes to use up leftovers.
3 When in doubt, don't eat food that's past its sell-by date.
4 Unless told otherwise by your doctor, eat a variety of different foods.
5 Once you've learned to cook fresh food, you'll prefer it to processed meals.

6

The amount of food waste increases <u>as the world's economies develop.</u> Ninety million tons of food are thrown away each year by Europeans. Food sharing <u>started in the light of this to counteract the</u> colossal waste. Valentin Thurn's documentary film *Taste the waste* raised awareness and, <u>after crowdfunding 11,000 euros, a non-profit company was born.</u> The www.foodsharing.de website connects people who have food to give to people who need it and, <u>given not everyone is connected, there's a low-tech solution</u> at strategic points, too. Food sharing is happening in 240 cities in Germany <u>and, according to the website, it is growing rapidly.</u> It's not only individuals, but also businesses that benefit from this practice, <u>given that they can save waste collection fees by donating goods to the organization.</u> Finally, health and safety laws ensure that no one shares anything unfit for consumption.

11.3 A personal calling

1

1 b   2 d   3 a   4 c

2

An advertorial

3

1 F – Mainly small businesses.
2 F – The problem is communicating it to enough potential customers.
3 T
4 T
5 T
6 F – Sometimes it's a free gift or just an extra bit of fun.
7 F – The personal trainer's card is rubber.
8 F – It's the fact that people like them as objects and therefore they keep them and show them to other people.

4

1 non-existent   2 innovative
3 pricey   4 striking   5 cool

5

a 4 (striking)
b 5 (cool)
c 2 (innovative)
d 1 (almost non-existent)
e 3 (pricey)

6

1 d   2 a   3 e   4 c   5 f   6 b

7

1 see eye to eye on
2 overseeing
3 are on the lookout for
4 see about
5 looked up to
6 look into

8

Two other nouns.

9

1 deadline 2 workspace 3 shortlist
4 crossroads 5 notebook 6 self-esteem
7 shareholder 8 database

10

1 d 2 f 3 a 4 e 5 b 6 c

11

1 high 2 behind 3 pushed 4 make
5 kill 6 move 7 dead 8 hard

12

1 dead on time
2 make time
3 gave me a hard time
4 at an all-time high
5 killed time

11.4 A dream come true

1

1 d 2 a 3 b 4 c

2

1 c 2 a 3 e 4 b 5 f 6 d

3

a Wouldn't it be great to
b I can see myself
c If money were no object, we could
d I've always fancied
e I'd love to
f I can't envisage

4

1 f I can't envisage
2 a wouldn't it be great to
3 c If money were no object we could
4 e I'd love to
5 b I can see myself
6 d I've always fancied

5

1 a S b U 2 a S b U 3 a U b S
4 a S b U 5 a U b S

6

1 highly impressed, pleased
2 excelled at, was extremely good at
3 confident, natural
4 an admirable, a strong
5 completely, consistently
6 privilege, honour

7

1 consistently 2 an admirable 3 an extremely
4 confident 5 a pleasure 6 quick
7 consistently 8 best

8

1 e 2 h 3 g 4 b 5 c 6 d 7 a 8 f

9

(Example answers)

2 She was incredibly quick to solve problems proactively and creatively.
3 The coaching considerably improved our performance in decision making.
4 We were greatly inspired by the vision she helped us form.
5 The life coaching session helped us hugely to get the best from our new situation.

PRESENTATION 6

1

1 b 2 c 3 a

3

1 c 2 b 3 a 4 e 5 d

5

1 c 2 a 3 f 4 d 5 e 6 b

6 (Example answers)

1 Hello and welcome. Let's get started.
2 Where I live there aren't many things for people to do for fun. As a result, people don't seem very happy.
3 What we need is some kind of club to give people something to do. I would like to set up a film club so people can get together to watch films and discuss them.
4 We could do this by installing a big TV screen in a communal space. They're not all that expensive these days if you go for an older model. If we get a DVD player we can get people to donate their old films for everyone to watch.
5 I feel this is important because people need to spend time together. By making a space where people can relax and watch films, neighbours in the area would be able to get to know each other and friendships could develop.
6 Thanks so much for listening to me talk about this improvement that could be made. Does anyone have any questions?

UNIT 12

12.1 Image recognition that triggers augmented reality

1

1 He was Global Head of *Aurasma* and she was Head of Marketing.
2 She brought an advertising background.
3 She's now a founding Director of TRM&C.

4 He started working at Featurespace, working against fraud with high-tech solutions.

2

b Interfaces between technology, mind and matter

3

1 Redefining 2 Greater 3 eye 4 minds

4

1 e 2 a 3 c 4 b 5 d

6

Stressed content words **in bold**, grammatical chunks underlined.
1 One of my **favourite TED talks** is the one from Tan Le called 'A **headset** that reads your **brainwaves**'.
2 Tan Le starts her talk with her **vision** to expand **human** and **computer interaction**.
3 She reminds us that **interpersonal communication** is more **complex** than mere **commands**.
4 The **headset** will cost only a few **hundred** dollars, not **thousands**.

7

1 She's able to present it live on stage and the price isn't too high.
2 She thinks it's well explained, calm and seems effortless. Also she likes that Tan Le invited Evan Grant onto the stage to demonstrate the headset.
3 Opening and closing curtains, turning lights off and on and controlling a wheelchair through facial expressions.
4 To spread the message that technology can be used in our favour and for good causes, not only for fun and for entertainment.

8

1 background, demonstration, applications
2 comes, wears, carries
3 command, difficult
4 submitted
5 smiles

9

1 b 2 a 3 c 4 c 5 b

12.2 They saw it coming

1

1 were to
2 was about to
3 would
4 was bound to
5 wouldn't have been
6 was going to be
7 unlikely to be
8 would have been
9 was to be

2

1 going 2 was 3 bound 4 were 5 likely
6 would

3

1 d 2 b 3 e 4 t 5 a 6 c

4

1 was to become
2 were going to be
3 unlikely to be
4 would not teach
5 would
6 were
7 to be passed

5

Thursday 13th at 10.30.

6

1 was wondering
2 did you have
3 was thinking
4 was
5 was hoping
6 did you want
7 hadn't been cancelled

No 7 isn't a tentative use of the past.

7

1 The project team was going to meet again before my holiday.
2 They were going to cancel the launch meeting.
3 I was thinking of Thursday morning.
4 I thought Ricardo was going to call.

8

In 1964, were we more likely to have exciting predictions of the future than we have today? Ryan Ritchey thinks so and explores the topic in his documentary, *After the Fair,* about the World's Fair in 1964 in New York. This fair was going to enable people to encounter computers and other technological and cultural trends face to face for the first time. It was to have had 70 million visitors but in fact only 51 million made it in the two six-month seasons it was open. It was a vision of the future, so not everything would come to pass that was on show, for example colonies on the moon and cities underwater. On the other hand, many visitors were to have the experience of asking a computer a question and getting an answer, something many of us do regularly now. There were also picture phones that were unlikely to appeal to visitors then because outward appearances were less important then than they are nowadays.

12.3 Half full or half empty?

1

1 d 2 e 3 b 4 a 5 c

2

a Generation Z   b Generation X   c Mature Silents   d Generation Y   e Baby Boomers

3

1 T
2 T

3 F – Generation X is probably most comfortable with change.
4 F – It's the Mature Silents.
5 T Baby Boomers are independent / able to find their own ways and Generation X.
6 F – The Baby Boomers were the first relatively fit generation but those following have been too.

4

1 more, more
2 some things, more
3 a great deal of, fewer
4 less, appreciate
5 return to, unlikely

5

1 bright side
2 hope
3 half empty
4 tunnel
5 bad things
6 half full
7 dark cloud
8 cloud

6

1 c 2 e 3 b 4 a 5 f 6 d

7

1 sparsely populated   2 strong-willed
3 open-minded   4 well-educated
5 quick-witted   6 poorly-skilled

8

1 d 2 e 3 f 4 b 5 a 6 c

9

1 flash of inspiration
2 bundle of laughs
3 mine of information
4 glimmer of hope
5 drop of rain
6 stroke of luck

12.4 Is Friday good for you?

1

1 f 2 d 3 a 4 e 5 b 6 c

2

It's about brainstorming ideas for the company's twenty-five year celebration.
1 I want to arrange to meet about
2 you could make the meeting
4 make something work
5 Let's pencil it in
6 can confirm with everyone else

3

1 I was wondering
2 How about
3 Would
4 That would
5 I can manage it
6 to be honest
7 out for me
8 afraid not

9 Let's
10 Sounds

4

1 supposed to
2 was meant
3 confirmed then
4 can reschedule
5 any good
6 postpone to

5

1 e (the kick off email)
2 a (mentions Bert and Liz so they haven't replied yet)
3 d
4 b (must come after d as she is due to be in the meeting that is rescheduled)
5 f (mentions the other replies)
6 c (confirms the meeting)

6

1 a Is Thursday afternoon any good for you?
  b Any time after two is fine.
2 a Would Friday at nine work for you?
  b I'm supposed to be meeting Jake but I may be able to postpone it.
3 a It's not ideal, to be honest, but if we make it ten instead of nine I can manage it.
  b Sure, yeah, I'm around.
4 a How about Monday morning?
  b Monday's out for me but Tuesday would work.

7

1 Various suggestions
2 One proposal
3 was agreed
4 was suggested
5 Another suggestion
6 the objection
7 was discussed
8 been planned

8

1 two hundred: current and retired staff and families, catering staff and customers.
2 not agreed on
3 open
4 open
5 budget decided, local catering company to be used – which to be decided
6 speeches, announcements and a short film
7 open

9

2 (Overall theme) The suggestion was a Western theme – inspired by our latest product range.
3 (Highlight) Not everyone agreed on fireworks as the highlight.
4 (Activity 1) It was agreed a barn dance would match the theme and be fun.
5 (Activity 2) The suggestion was a rodeo bull-riding machine (as it's fun to do and watch).

10

1 We are pleased to present our ideas for the anniversary event, from our recent meeting.

2 For the overall theme the most appropriate suggestion was a Western theme – inspired by our latest product range.

3 One proposal for food and drinks was to use a local catering company with vintage BBQ carts, which fits well with this theme.

4 After some discussion, it was agreed a barn dance would match the theme and be fun.

5 The unusual suggestion for the second activity was a rodeo bull-riding machine that's fun to do and watch.

6 In the end not everyone agreed on fireworks as the highlight and it was decided that perhaps the activities are highlights enough.

WRITING 6

1

a, b, c, d

2

1 a **2** c **3** d **4** b

3

1 T **2** T **3** F **4** T **5** T

4

1 c **2** e **3** b **4** a **5** d **6** f

5

1 To begin **with**, by visiting a nature park people can experience the natural world first hand.

2 It would **therefore be** easier for them to watch programmes on their own television.

3 **Besides,** companies are much more likely to listen to the government than their customers.

4 It is **a** well-known fact that travelling on the underground is faster than using buses.

5 On the other **hand**, a rapid bus system would be much cheaper to develop than a new underground system.

6 Instead of **creating** a large area of solar panels, we could put them on individual buildings.

6

1 On <u>balance</u>, while both visits to nature parks and programmes about the natural world are important, I am in <u>favour</u> of the latter as the best way to teach people about the environment.

2 <u>Bearing</u> all that in mind, I believe that the government should focus on reducing the amount of plastic used in packaging <u>rather</u> than on trying to make us recycle it.

3 To <u>sum</u> up, while both types of public transport have their advantages and disadvantages, in my opinion, the benefits of a rapid bus system <u>outweigh</u> those of a new underground system.

4 In conclusion, if the advantages of solar power are <u>compared</u> to those of building new wind turbines, the <u>former</u> is clearly more useful to the community.

8 (Example answer)

Volunteering has many possible benefits for companies and their employees, but it is important that any scheme is set up in a way that allows both to make the most of it. In this essay, I will examine two possible structures for a volunteer scheme and say which I believe is the most effective.

The first structure to look at is where each person is given a certain number of hours to volunteer anywhere they would like to. This way they can find a project which appeals to them, increasing the positive feelings they get from it. If they are not forced to work on something which they have no interest in, employees are more likely to want to volunteer their time and will feel more motivated. The downside is that it may prove difficult for employees to choose where they would like to spend their time.

An alternative way of organizing such a scheme would be for each team to choose a project to contribute to. This will have all of the benefits of an individual scheme, as well as encouraging teamwork and collaboration. The skills each team develops will help the company as well, as they will be able to carry over their increased sense of team spirit to their day-to-day work. Fewer decisions would need to be made as one person can suggest a project and others can join in with it.

In conclusion, I believe that team projects are more effective since they promote collaboration within the company in addition to the other benefits of volunteering.

Workbook
audioscripts

Units 7–12

Audioscript

TRACK 2

My name's Doruk Denkel and I'm the General Manager of the Abu Dhabi branch of National Geographic Learning.

This talk has personal relevance for me and not only me but for any professional. Everyone has some degree of motivation for choosing what they do for a living and in this talk James Cameron revealed some personal reasons why he made particular film choices.

James Cameron has an easy confident way of talking, without relying on emotional outbursts and high-pitched statements for his audience's attention. This confidence may come in part from Cameron's phenomenal business success, but I think it's also based on his belief in what he does. This belief is impersonal and fact based, in other words, he disconnects his ego from his work when he talks about it and he isn't the block-buster director but a man doing a job and living a life.

I found that Cameron's way of talking was especially compelling because of his lack of ego about his work.

In his talk, Cameron explains that, from an early age, he was driven by his insatiable curiosity and was always amazed by how boundless nature's imagination is. His narrative is so exciting that he doesn't need visuals to bring it to life – surprisingly for a film director, his presentation included no slides or film clips. He describes how he was always outside as a child, making discoveries by exploring the neighbourhood woods and looking at things under the microscope. He was also an avid reader of science fiction and read for at least two hours a day. Television, when he was growing up, was about going beyond the known world – man was exploring the oceans and space – two areas he was fascinated by. He would spend time drawing – as a creative outlet. He drew strange creatures and worlds. Being desperate to experience some of these worlds, he learned how to scuba dive but it wasn't until he moved to California that he was able to properly use this skill, and it wasn't until the film *Titanic* that he had a chance to make a personal dream come true. He wanted to see the Titanic wreck at the bottom of the ocean with his own eyes and making a film about it was the perfect vehicle to do this.

Cameron wanted to use computer-generated animation (CG) in the film *Titanic*. He'd already worked extensively on CG animation in a less successful film *The Abyss* and even founded a company to explore it further. He'd noticed that audiences were mesmerized by the magic of CG and he rightly saw this as a big opportunity.

This was the part that particularly grabbed me: how Cameron realized his dream in a way that also created value for others. He convinced the Hollywood studio it was necessary to film the ship's wreckage, the studio then funded the expedition, his movie became a success, delivering profit to the studio and entertainment to audiences. If he hadn't been driven by the passion of his own personal motivation, the film may not have been such a success.

I would recommend this talk to others and feel its message is important. Your ideal job will build from your personal interests and passions. Don't be afraid of exploring these for the benefit of both your work and personal life. In James Cameron's case, he'd imagined a reality where he could dive to the wreck of the Titanic and one day he found himself doing just that. As he said in the talk: 'Imagination is a force that can actually manifest a reality.' It has done that for me too.

TRACK 6

J = Jon, D = Danny, S = Simone

J: Has anyone seen or heard from Nicky this morning?

D: I expect she's on holiday. She was talking about a holiday last week.

J: Yes, but that's next month, not today. She was going to be doing a training course but it was cancelled at the last minute on Friday.

S: She's probably just stuck in traffic. I called her just now and got her voicemail.

D: Have you called her landline? She may've overslept.

S: That seems highly improbable with three children! I hope nothing's happened. It seems likely that she's stuck in traffic, but then she'd call in or something.

J: She might've forgotten her phone.

S: But she never forgets her phone. That doesn't seem likely at all. Perhaps she's gone to the doctor but normally she'd have mentioned it before.

D: Maybe there's been an accident that's delayed her. I don't mean she's been in one but that the road's maybe blocked.

J: That seems a likely explanation, something unavoidable for sure. But it's still strange she hasn't phoned.

TRACK 7

N = Nicky, J = Jon

N: Hi. Is that Jon?

J: Yes. Oh, hi, Nicky. Is everything all right?

N: Yes, we're all alright…

J: We've been wondering what happened and thought there's bound to be a sensible explanation.

N: … but there's been a fire in the building next to ours.

J: Oh, how awful! What happened?

N: We don't know exactly yet, but we've been out in the street most of the night and we're all suffering from shock so I'm afraid I won't be in today; we're really tired. But don't worry, there are no casualties and everyone's all right. It seems likely the firemen'll find the cause soon – I can't really talk, it's not my phone. I'll call again later.

J: OK, bye, take care. Thanks for letting us know.

TRACK 9

W: That can't be right that there's a light on across the road.

M: Oh, you mean because they're away? I think you're onto something there.

W: I'm not entirely convinced that everything is OK.

M: It certainly looks that way, or do you think they've come back early?

W: That doesn't seem at all likely to me. I didn't see their car on the street. Maybe they've got those automatic lights that go on and off even when you're away.

M: Yes! That seems a likely explanation but let's call them anyway. You never know.

TRACK 11

My name's Daniel Barber. I'm the writer of one of the Teacher's Books for the Keynote course. One of my favourite TED Talks is by a doctor, Atul Gawande, and it's called 'How do we heal medicine?'

I've heard Atul Gawande speak before about doctors, hospitals and the health system and he always impresses me as a speaker. He has a wonderfully calm voice, speaking slowly and thinking carefully about every word. I like to see the bigger picture on issues, and Gawande is able to take a step back from the detailed work of his job as a practising doctor to look at medicine as a whole. He sets out to provide clarity to problems that show bewildering complexity.

He explains this complexity by means of some facts and figures. Medical progress has meant that there are now 4,000 medical procedures and a doctor can prescribe any of the 6,000 drugs available. He says that's too much knowledge for anyone to 'know' and people need to be cared for by systems, not individuals any more. There was a study that compared the number of clinicians required now and in the past – in 1970 the average hospital visit required care from two full-time clinicians. By the end of the twentieth century the number had risen to fifteen. According to Gawande, another problem is the enormous cost of the technology and the human resources needed to make people better in the twenty-first century.

Despite our best efforts, these complex and expensive systems can fail: for example, 40 per cent of heart patient admissions don't get appropriate care, and 60 per cent of asthma or stroke patients don't either. Shockingly, there are two million people who pick up an infection, in the very hospital that should cure them, from staff not following basic hygiene practices.

Gawande's message is an important one: medicine is broken but there are answers to its problems so it can be fixed. He shows that there are surprisingly cheap and simple solutions.

In the next part of the talk, he outlines the methodology to find these solutions using three skills: find the failures, devise solutions and implement the ideas. His particular interest was reducing the number of deaths in surgery and Gawande decided to look at other high-risk industries to see how they tackled complex systems. He looked at aviation and high-rise construction. He was startled by what he found: checklists. Something as straightforward as a checklist could actually help make experts better. He implemented the checklists in eight hospitals worldwide and complication rates fell in every single one. Death rates fell by a staggering 47 per cent. That point deserved the standing ovation it got.

My interest in medicine has grown ever since my daughter, who's eleven, was diagnosed with a rare genetic condition called cystic fibrosis. People with this disease used to live just a few years but, thanks to the sorts of technological advances in medicine that Gawande talks about, there is every chance my daughter will live a long and healthy life. I am reminded every day of the enormous cost to the local health authorities for her treatment and I am so very grateful that it is there for my family and the millions of people who benefit from the work of doctors and nurses.

We all operate in complex systems ourselves and we will all need the expertise of a doctor at some point in our lives, which is why I'd recommend this TED Talk to everyone.

TRACK 15

F: Did you read about Bhutan winning?
M: Yes, I saw some tweets coming in yesterday. It was quite exciting.
F: I didn't know they started at the bottom like that.
M: Yes, the bottom dozen play two matches against each other to qualify in the next World Cup.
F: I read that they nearly didn't take part at all because of the costs involved.
M: That's right, then FIFA made $300,000 available to support the teams and the Thai team let them have a training ground for a month to get used to the humidity.
F: That's right. They're used to playing at altitude but aren't used to humidity. That was pretty good of the Thais!
M: Their story is pretty amazing really – it's like going back in time. They've only had TV and Internet since 1999.
F: I read that when they played at home no-one had to pay to attend the match and civil servants had the day off work. It's quite a big deal, isn't it?
M: The coach reckons the players all play much better than he did thanks to television; they have access to games and interviews with other coaches. Even the captain said he wouldn't play like he does without television. He can't remember a time without it.
F: It's nice to hear something positive about TV.
M: They scored the winning goal in the ninetieth minute and said they heard the dragon roar. What a great story!

TRACK 16

D – Bela, K – Ken, A – Ali, J – Jordan
A: Can we start?
J: Yes. I'd like to start the discussion by asking if everyone's read the information sent around before the meeting …
J: OK. That sounds good. Anyone have any personal experience of a rotation programme before we continue?
A: Yes, actually I …
K: Sorry for interrupting, but could we just clarify what it is first?
A: … could I just finish what I was saying? I was going to say I've had experience. It was before I came here and I wanted to know the same thing as Ken – in case you understand something different here.
K: Sorry. I just didn't want to waste time.
J: Well, here we define it as a programme involving working in different departments that's good for gaining experience and good for professional development. Exactly Ken, we don't want to waste time. That's partly why I sent you the proposed concept so you'd have time to think about it. Currently, as you know, we use rotation on the trainee programme and with interns, but as we've been looking into better collaboration and …
B: I hate to interrupt, but …
J: I know you're dying to jump in, Bela and we'll come to you. If you'll allow me to finish …
B: Yes, you're right.
K: There'll be a chance for everyone to have their say.
J: Thank you. OK. As I was saying, we've noticed that innovation opportunities are in fact forged by making new connections and mixing teams up. OK. This is where Bela comes in as he was a trainee and he can tell us what he learned. In a couple of minutes, I'd also be interested in hearing your views on expanding the scope of the programme. But first, I'd like to return to the first question and …

TRACK 17

J: So Bela, what's your take on the benefits of changing departments?
B: Well, if you ask me, I can only praise any system that means you can learn about different parts of the organization, in a structured way. When I was on the trainee programme itself I didn't really see how valuable it was until I made use of the connections I made afterwards. Sorry, I didn't explain that very well.
J: Thanks. That's helpful – you mean with hindsight it was more useful than you realized when you were actually doing it?
B: Yeah, that's right.
J: OK. Any thoughts on the expanded programme? And before you continue – Ken, can I just say thank you for all your help with this?
K: Well, I think the crucial thing about talented employees is that if you don't help them find positions that they'll be effective in quickly, they'll end up leaving for somewhere else. The programme

could be a great retention tool, as well as promoting innovation. It could be really exciting.
J: All right, I think that's nearly everything but I would like us all to suggest one or two employees to put forward and answer the questions I've prepared here. If you complete the information and get it back to me by Friday then I think we can finish there for today …

TRACK 20

I'm Helen Smedley and I'm the National Geographic Learning sales representative for the south of the UK and Malta. I watched Matt Killingsworth's TEDxCambridge talk 'Want to be happier? Stay in the moment'. This talk was of interest to – it really resonated with me because I try to practise mindfulness in my daily life.

Matt Killingsworth has a PhD in Psychology from Harvard University. His main subject is happiness, actually rather the causes of happiness.

His presentation style and way of talking emanated a distinct scientific feel although, as the topic is a universally relatable one, the talk was easily understandable. He conveys passion and enthusiasm for his topic that quickly builds rapport and interest with the audience. He begins by describing how we all seek happiness and that, despite being richer and living longer than we did 50 years ago, we don't necessarily lead happier lives. We aren't measurably happier. That is the paradox of happiness, what looked like it should bring – or was likely to make us happy – doesn't always.

What interested me particularly about the talk was what he said about staying in the moment and wandering minds. This was a main focus of the talk. His research with the tracking app 'Trackyourhappiness. org' has revealed that mind wandering is ubiquitous. Matt Killingsworth analyzed data from 650,000 real-time reports from 15,000 people hailing from 80 countries and from 86 occupational categories, and he discovered that on average our minds wander 47 per cent of the time. I attend yoga classes three times a week and meditate for 10 minutes a day to music, and try to stay mindful when doing household tasks, but I had a question at the back of my mind which was 'I sometimes think happy thoughts about pleasant past memories and have positive thoughts about future events – is this just as good for my mind as staying on the present?'

Matt Killingsworth addresses precisely this question in his talk and found in his research that mind wandering causes unhappiness because when we are not focused on the present, most of us inevitably think unhappy thoughts as well as happy ones. This made me realize that when I think happy thoughts about memories or future plans, I can sometimes drift and think about unhappier ones too, so it certainly isn't a good thing to focus too much on the past or the future!

When research respondents stayed present in a task, they reported a high happiness factor even when they were doing something that most people strongly disliked, like commuting. We are decidedly less happy when our minds wander. Killingsworth seemed surprised by these decisive results, as if he couldn't have predicted that it would have such an impact.

As a result of watching this talk, I'm going to take on board his advice and train myself to be more mindful in my daily activities – in fact I'm going to try this tomorrow when I have a three-hour drive. Driving is an activity where I am most distracted, so I'm going to be very conscious of staying present. If I'm happier, then the people I see every day will be happier too. In fact, the world could become a better place if everyone listened to this advice and appreciated the moment more and practised mindfulness every day!

TRACK 26

Hello, my name is Michael Cummings and I am the senior consultant for National Geographic Learning in the UK, Eire and Morocco. One of my favourite TED Talks is 'The hidden influence of social networks' by Nicholas Christakis. This talk struck a chord with me, having travelled and amassed many friends and colleagues across the globe as first an English language teacher and now a rep for NGL.

Indeed, as a teacher, I noticed that every classroom featured the beginning of a new social network and one that may eventually extend beyond the goal of language learning.

TRACK 27

Hello, my name is Michael Cummings and I am the senior consultant for National Geographic Learning in the UK, Eire and Morocco. One of my favourite TED Talks is 'The hidden influence of social networks' by Nicholas Christakis. This talk struck a chord with me, having travelled and amassed many friends and colleagues across the globe as first an English language teacher and now a rep for NGL.

Indeed, as a teacher, I noticed that every classroom featured the beginning of a new social network and one that may eventually extend beyond the goal of language learning. So my own social network grew beyond all recognition from when I was living in a small quaint town in the North of England to my various posts across the globe. Christakis made me realize that we are interconnected to hundreds or even thousands of people. I love the notion that social networks are fundamentally something related to goodness, as I value greatly the diversity within mine and I believe my social circle provides me with a huge amount of insight, perspective and opportunity. When my social network grew it fundamentally changed how I perceived the world.

This talk left me pondering a number of things: what is a relationship, what is social networking and how am I influencing the lives of people I may not even know? His message was clear, concise and extremely relatable. After doing research into widowhood, he found that when someone is widowed its effects aren't limited to the spouses but extend to friends, neighbours and a wider community. He said that this knowledge changed the way he sees the world and it also changed the course of his research. He became obsessed with the influence of social networks themselves and studied obesity networks. He showed the results of a 30-year study about obesity with the use of coloured interconnected dots depicting their interconnectivity. Surprisingly, you have a 57 per cent higher risk of obesity if your friend is obese – the closer the relationship the higher the risk. He later studied other topics like happiness and altruism and how they relate to our social networks.

I had not previously considered the different ways in which my social network might affect those within it or those on the fringes of it. My ability to spread happiness or indeed obesity seems like quite a big responsibility!

It also made me want to examine how my own position in my personal network might impact my life in ways I don't even know.

Finally, this presentation reminded me of one other thing that I was told as a sports-mad young man: 'If you want to be a lion then you must train with lions!' It is important that those within your network share your goals and can help you reach your potential.

This talk made me more conscious of how I can positively influence those around me, in turn making the world a better place in my own miniscule way. I would recommend this talk to everyone in the hope that it goes some way to making them realize that our social network is a living thing that surrounds us, shapes us and binds us together.

TRACK 29

The problem with Attitude to Risk questionnaires – and in fact questionnaires that ask people to evaluate themselves in general – is that they don't always get honest answers. That's not because people are intentionally dishonest, but it's just human nature to see yourself in a favourable light. So in this case I think most people would like to see themselves as more adventurous risk-taking types. So they are more often going to answer B or C than A. And that's another problem with this. All the answers follow the same pattern: A for the least adventurous, B for the middle ground and C for the biggest risk takers. It would be much better if the answers were mixed up. Having said that, I like the fact that not *all* the answers are obvious – like in items 8 and 9. I think people would probably answer those honestly or at least have to think hard about the answer. There's also a good mix of situations – social, work, life in general.

TRACK 30

S – Sonya, B – Bert, L – Lewis

S: Well, as you've seen in the press there's been a spate of these recently and I think we should do something about it. We've invested a great deal and we don't want to put the business at undue risk.

B: There are some pretty interesting options to choose from, with different degrees of security and varying price tags, naturally.

S: Possibly the most obvious one is a camera.

L: A drawback of the camera is that the footage has to be monitored somehow, doesn't it?

S: Doesn't the security company do that?

B: According to the brochure, a combination lock is another option to consider. What about that?

S: Mmm … on the plus side we wouldn't need keys any more but the downside is we're only strengthening the door.

L: Oh, good point. Well then, is an alarm system worth thinking about? It protects doors and windows, which makes it a very attractive possibility.

B: Hmm, yes but considering the price, I'm not sure it's the best option.

TRACK 31

S: In the light of the increase in criminal activity in the area, I think we should invest in an alarm and a safe.

B: A third alternative that might do the job is a dog.

L: I thought you were allergic to dogs!

B: No, I'm just joking. Ultimately, the best choice does seem to be the alarm system.

S: Now you've got me thinking about a dog. Maybe we can have both.

B: No, come on, think how expensive and complicated that'd be. OK. All things considered, it makes sense to go with an alarm – now we just have to choose which one.

TRACK 34

My name's Eftychis Kantarakis and I'm the NGL Teacher Trainer and Sales team co-ordinator for Greece. One of my favourite TED Talks is Iwan Baan's 'Ingenious homes in unexpected places'.

My job involves extensive travelling, and this is one of the things I really enjoy about it. The topic of this talk really appealed to me as I've seen many 'weird-looking' homes around the world. Originally, the title made me think that it was going to be one more of those demonstrations of funny, posh or extravagant houses some techno-geek or multi-millionaire has built. You see pictures of those all the time in social media nowadays. The TED Talk had little if anything to do with all these, which turned out to be a very positive aspect of it, as it talks about everyday people and their lives.

What I liked the most about this talk was how it showcased the ingenious ways in which people, with nowhere else to live, found solutions to their problems! How they turned places like a slum tower awaiting the hammer into a living city for those who couldn't afford a 'real' home. He showed people living underground in China and on water in Nigeria, and the Zabaleen in Egypt, people who live in dwellings on and in the rubbish heaps. He has admiration and respect for the people because what they build is so ingenious and so varied. Generally people are unhappy with 'cookie-cutter' solutions; they like to personalize their environments. Even if they are disadvantaged, they are highly creative about shaping and designing the appearance and comfort of their homes.

It resonated with me because people in my country, too, have to find such solutions all the time. Albeit not always to such an extent. People in Greece have had to improvise solutions for their accommodation for many centuries.

My great grandfather had to live in similar settings when he brought his family to Greece as refugees in the 1920s along with thousands of others. I've heard stories about how they had to convert old wooden huts into brick ones, building the walls from the inside. Back then the first priorities were to build a kitchen, a bedroom and a place to pray.

I think Iwan Baan came across like a true TED speaker; he gave us very interesting information but also made us feel that this is not some isolated issue that happens only in certain parts of the world, and it is not necessarily something to be avoided or looked down upon. Diversity is key to human life as well as to the ecosystems we live in.

Nevertheless, I would really like to learn more about the reasons why people had to choose solutions like the ones shown here. Iwan Baan deals more with the results than the causes of the problem. Having watched this, I would recommend it to friends and colleagues, especially to ones who don't travel much. I think this talk would help them get a better idea of what cities can look like away from the tourist spots and off the beaten track.

TRACK 36

Our experience with B-Creative Cards was very positive. We have a small yoga studio which was only nine months old when we first contacted them. Our advertising budget was almost non-existent, so cost was a big consideration. The first idea they came up with was really innovative. It wasn't a card at all: it was a bendy drinking straw with a person doing a yoga pose on the part of the straw that bent. They were going to print our contact details on it too, but it was going to be too pricey. So instead they transferred the idea to a more standard business card. The design is very striking still and there's still a person in a yoga pose that flexes when you bend the card. Has it worked? Well, actually, loads of first-time visitors tell me they came along because they thought the card was so cool.

TRACK 37

C = Carolyn, D = Dan, M – Maja

C: So, the focus today is to clarify the direction you'd like your new business to go in.

D: Yes, that's right. We've always fancied setting up our own business but until now we haven't had the opportunity, but last year I was left some money by an aunt who passed away.

M: Until now we've worked in the service sector in hotels – helping people – but we're not sure if we'd like to carry on doing it as the hours can be tough for family life. On the other hand, I can envisage a quieter life, having a smaller B&B place somewhere nice.

C: Mmm. I see. You were on reception, weren't you, Maja?

M: Yes, and Dan was the manager. He's good at communicating with everyone.

C: Is that what you like doing, Dan?

D: Well, I always thought if money were no object, I'd buy my own hotel somewhere. But to be perfectly honest I'd like to do something different.

M: I know what you mean.

C: OK. So, apart from communicating, what else are you good at?

D: I like fixing things and making things work. I actually wanted to be a mechanic but I got a job in a hotel and I liked that too. I fiddle with cars and bikes in my free time.

C: OK. Thanks. How about you, Maja? Are you creative?

M: Yes, in some ways I am quite creative. I could see myself cooking in a restaurant or a café or doing events like weddings. I like doing things like that. But I can't see myself at the front desk any more. I need a bit more of a challenge. I'd love to work on special events and design the cakes and everything. I love doing that.

D: That's true, you always do the events really well. You're a good organizer – lots of people comment on it.

C: OK. Interesting. We've got quite a bit to work on …

TRACK 41

My name's Rosane Di Genova and I'm an English learning solutions manager in Brazil. One of my favourite TED Talks is the one from Tan Le called 'A headset that reads your brainwaves'.

Tan Le starts her talk with her vision to expand human and computer interaction to include facial expressions and emotions as well as verbal and mechanical commands. She reminds us that interpersonal communication is more complex than mere commands – taking non-verbal communication into account too. What follows is not the kind of new technology that you saw on a sci-fi movie that you watched ten years ago and thought: 'No way … it will never happen'. It is new technology so accessible that she demonstrates it live on stage – successfully. The headset will cost only a few hundred dollars, not thousands – making us think about how many people would benefit from that! More about that later on.

Although it's quite technical, it is well explained in three clear areas: background, demonstration and applications. Tan Le manages the whole presentation in such a calm, clear and collected fashion that it seems effortless. I liked the fact that she invited another TED fellow, Evan Grant, to come on the stage, wear the headset and help her demonstrate the system. He carried out two simple tasks that involved moving an image of a cube on a screen using just his thoughts – no verbal commands or use of his hands. First he tried a simple command – he chose 'pull' – and second he tried the much more difficult command "disappear". Mr Grant was a willing guinea pig and performed the first task perfectly. When the task to make the cube 'disappear' didn't quite work he submitted a second neural signal which then made the cube disappear perfectly too. Apparently, with repetition the signal becomes stronger.

It was an impressive demonstration, however, if Ms Tan had called someone randomly it could have given even more credibility to it, I feel. For example, she could have asked him to think about a task for the cube, without telling her what and then when the cube suddenly disappeared, the audience would've believed he was doing it completely unaided.

In addition, I think that she would've made more impact if she'd expanded the examples of how to use this technology in 'real life' in the applications part. For example, turning lights off and on, opening and closing curtains, which could be extremely useful for someone who has a physical disability. For me this is much more relevant than the tests with a person who can move a cube. She did show some footage of a wheelchair user using facial expressions to move left and right or straight on, using blinks and smiles – the potential of this clever technology is huge and very exciting.

It is inspiring to see that some people, like this young woman, are dedicating their time to developing systems that can help so many people. I would definitely recommend this talk to my friends to help to spread this message: that technology can be used in our favour and for good causes, not only for fun and for entertainment!

TRACK 42

I = Isabel, F = Frank

I: Hi, Frank. How's it going? Actually, I was wondering if we could squeeze in a meeting before I go away.

F: OK. Let's see. When did you have in mind?

I: Well, I was going to go to Frankfurt for two days, but that's been cancelled. So I was thinking of Wednesday the twelfth or Thursday the thirteenth.

F: Well, I was down to be in a teleconference on Wednesday afternoon …

I: It's just that I was hoping to hand over the project before I go away. How about Thursday morning?

F: OK. What time did you want to meet? Any time after ten is fine with me.

I: Let's say ten-thirty then. Thank you. That's great. It wouldn't have been possible if the Frankfurt trip hadn't been cancelled.

TRACK 45

The generation that you belong to is determined by the ten to twenty years in which you were born. Here are five terms to describe five demographics represented by the different generations alive today. The oldest generation, born in the late 20s until the mid-40s, are sometimes known as the Mature Silents or the Silent Generation; Baby Boomers are next and one of the largest populations in the USA and Europe – they were born between 1946 and 1964. Generation X follows and spans the second half of the 60s and the 70s. Generation Y, or the Millennials, are children of the 1980s and 1990s. Finally, Generation Z refers to those born after the year 2001.

TRACK 46

1 I reckon there will be more laziness as we use more automated things. But as the world gets more integrated and diversity grows we should understand each other better and find more productive ways of saving fuel and the planet.

2 I think in five years some situations will have improved and other issues will have worsened but I hope we help each other more locally and globally.

3 In five years, many things will seem the same but will have changed dramatically. Change is constant. In technology we'll connect to the Internet via our watches or glasses and make cashless payments. Smart phones are yesterday's news. Landline telephones will become more and more obsolete.

4 We're very lucky, we have longevity, we're healthy. In a way we should be less concerned with technological changes and more concerned with changes to quality of life. To live in peace and be satisfied with what we do have without always wanting more.

5 It's very hard to predict changes for the future. Everything changes so fast. I hope for something amazing that will ease the tension around the world. I know it won't happen but it would be nice to return to old family traditions and good social values and that we become less materialistic.

TRACK 47

S = Sam, F = Felix

S: Hey, Felix. Everything OK?

F: Yes, fine. How about you?

S: Pretty good, thanks. I'm glad I've bumped into you …

F: Sounds ominous.

S: (Laughing) No, no! Not at all. I promise you it's something good. I want to arrange to meet about the celebrations. I've been asking the others too. I was wondering if you could make the meeting next week, midweekish?

F: Oh. Sounds interesting. It's not ideal timewise, to be honest. Wednesday and Thursday are out for me, I'm afraid. But if we can do another day I'll certainly try and make it.

S: That would be good.

F: Are you planning the company's 25-year anniversary party?

S: Yes, and I'd like to organize a first meeting to brainstorm ideas and you're so good at that! Can we make something work? How about Tuesday morning?

F: Tuesday morning? I'm afraid not. I'm at a meeting. But Tuesday evening may just work. I'm supposed to be coming back by train from Amsterdam then. If I can participate by phone I can manage it. Would that work for you?

S: Sounds great.

F: Let's pencil it in, but I need to check train times to check I'm actually on the train then. About six should work.

S: Thank you. I hope Tuesday is good for the others. When you've checked, let me know and we can confirm with everyone else.

F: OK. Good. It sounds great. Really interesting.

Keynote Advanced

Student's Book

Lewis Lansford

Workbook

Paula Mulanovic with Mike Harrison and Sandy Millin

Publisher: Gavin McLean

Publishing Consultant: Karen Spiller

Project Manager: Karen White

Development Editors: Stephanie Parker, Ruth Goodman

Editorial Managers: Alison Burt, Scott Newport

Head of Strategic Marketing ELT: Charlotte Ellis

Senior Content Project Manager: Nick Ventullo

Manufacturing Manager: Eyvett Davis

Cover design: Brenda Carmichael

Text design: Keith Shaw, MPS North America LLC

Compositor: MPS North America LLC

National Geographic Liaison: Leila Hishmeh

Audio and DVD: Tom Dick and Debbie Productions Ltd

Cover Photo Caption: Beatrice Coron speaking at TED2011: The Rediscovery of Wonder, February 28 – March 4, 2011, Long Beach, CA. Photo: © James Duncan Davidson/TED.

Student's Book and Workbook Split B ISBN: 978-1-337-56133-4

National Geographic Learning
Cheriton House, North Way, Andover, Hampshire, SP10 5BE
United Kingdom

Cengage Learning is a leading provider of customized learning solutions with employees residing in nearly 40 different countries and sales in more than 125 countries around the world. Find your local representative at **www.cengage.com**.

Cengage Learning products are represented in Canada by Nelson Education Ltd.

Visit National Geographic Learning online at **ngl.cengage.com**

Visit our corporate website at **www.cengage.com**

CREDITS

The publishers would like to thank TED Staff for their insightful feedback and expert guidance, allowing us to achieve our dual aims of maintaining the integrity of these inspirational TED Talks, while maximizing their potential for teaching English.

Although every effort has been made to contact copyright holders before publication, this has not always been possible. If contacted, the publisher will undertake to rectify any errors or omissions at the earliest opportunity.

The publishers would like to thank the following for permission to use copyright material:

Cover: © James Duncan Davidson/TED

Student's Book Photos: 6 (tl, tr, ml, br) © James Duncan Davidson/TED; 6 (mr) © Ryan Lash/TED; 6 (bl) © TED Conferences, LLC; 7 (tl, tr, mr, br) © James Duncan Davidson/TED; 7 (ml) © Dafydd Jones/TED; 7 (bl) © Ryan Lash/TED; 8–9 © age fotostock/Alamy; 8 © James Duncan Davidson/TED; 10 © James Duncan Davidson/TED; 13 © Keystone-France/Gamma-Keystone/Getty Images; 15 © Digital Vision/Getty Images; 16 (l) © Exclusivepix Media; 16 (r) © Universal History Archive/Getty Images; 18–19 © Mitchell Kanashkevich/Getty Images; 18 © James Duncan Davidson/TED; 20 © James Duncan Davidson/TED; 23 (tl) © Alvaro Leiva/Getty Images; 23 (tr) © Ariel Skelley/Getty Images; 23 (ml) © Leren Lu/Getty Images; 23 (mr) © john finney photography/Getty Images; 23 (bl) © Chris Ryan/Getty Images; 23 (br) © Paul Bradbury/Getty Images; 25 © Cultura Creative (RF)/Alamy; 26 © Ffooter/Shutterstock.com; 28 © Hipcycle.com; 30 © Lebedev Artur/ITAR-TASS Photo/Corbis; 31 © Dafydd Jones/TED; 32 © Dafydd Jones/TED; 37 © Digital Vision/Getty Images; 38 © PathDoc/Shutterstock.com; 40 © Susana Gonzalez/Bloomberg/Getty Images; 41 © James Duncan Davidson/TED; 42 © James Duncan Davidson/TED; 47 © Colin Anderson/Getty Images; 48 © Stephen Simpson/Getty Images; 50 © Sijmen Hendriks/Hollandse Hoogte/Redux; 52 © SIHASAKPRACHUM/Shutterstock.com; 53 © Ryan Lash/TED; 54 © Ryan Lash/TED; 57 © steve estvanik/Shutterstock.com; 59 (t) © Romolo Tavani/Shutterstock.com; 59 (ml) Photograph by © Alfred Manner - Courtesy Friends of Peace Pilgrim; 59 (mr) © Marco di Lauro/Reportage by Getty Images for CNN/Turner Broadcasting System; 59 (bl) © Everett Kennedy Brown/epa/Corbis; 59 (br) © Ramin Talaie/Corbis; 60 © Raul Arboleda/AFP/Getty Images; 61 (t) © Leland Bobbe/Getty Images; 61 (b) © ARENA Creative/Shutterstock.com; 62–63 © Julien Vidal; 62 (l) © James Duncan Davidson/TED; 62 (r) © James Duncan Davidson/TED; 64 © James Duncan Davidson/TED; 69 (l) © Mateo_Pearson/Shutterstock.com; 69 (r) © Sharon Day/Shutterstock.com; 70 © Ruskin Photos/Alamy; 72 © Mellowcabs PTY Ltd.

Workbook Photos: 104 © James Duncan Davidson/TED; 106 © Oliver Rossi/Getty Images; 108 © Susanna's Catering; 110 © Yavuz Arslan/ullstein bild/Getty Images; 112 (t) © Hero Images/Getty Images; 112 (m) © Marc Romanelli/Getty Images; 112 (b) © Inti St Clair/Getty Images; 114 © James Duncan Davidson/TED; 116 © Hero Images/Getty Images; 118 © Kamal Kishore/Reuters; 120 © Hero Images/Getty Images; 121 © Orla/Getty Images; 124 © Dafydd Jones/TED; 126 © Vincent Jary/Getty Images; 128 © Yagi Studio/Getty Images; 130 © Alex Brylov/Shutterstock.com; 132 © Siri Berting/Getty Images; 134 © James Duncan Davidson/TED; 136 © 19th era/Alamy Stock Photo; 137 © Bob Thomas/Popperfoto/Getty Images; 138 © Muslianshah Masrie/Shutterstock.com;

Printed in China by RR Donnelley
Print Number: 01   Print Year: 2017

Student's Book Illustrations & Infographics: 12, 22, 34, 44, 56, 66 emc design; 48 MPS North America LLC.

Student's Book Infographics: 12 Sources: sciencedaily.com, english.chosun.com; 22 Source: cipd.co.uk/binaries; 34 Sources: http://en.wikipedia.org/wiki/Holmes_and_Rahe_stress_scale; 44 Sources: totalprosports.com, advancedphysicalmedicine.org, thebmc.co.uk; 56 Source: huffingtonpost.com; 66 Sources: bbc.co.uk/news, saturdayeveningpost.com, farm8.staticflickr.com.

Workbook Illustrations: MPS North America LLC